Grace

A Daily Journey to Grow in Faith and Experience God's Presence

Lorenzo A. Daughtry-Chambers

ISBN: 9798305516142

DEDICATION

To Sarah, Lauren, Alexander, & my ministry family. Thank you.

CONTENTS

ACKNOWLEDGMENTS

To my amazing family—Sarah, Lauren, Alexander, Sharon (and all others)—your love, encouragement, and prayers have been my foundation throughout this journey. Thank you for giving me the space and support to follow God's call in creating this book.

To my ministry partners, LDC Ministries, your collaboration and faithfulness inspire me daily. Thank you for your prayers, insight, and dedication to advancing God's kingdom alongside me.

To the readers of this devotional, thank you for allowing me to be part of your spiritual journey. It is my prayer that these words lead you closer to God and remind you of His unfailing grace.

Finally, to my Lord and Savior, Jesus Christ—thank You for the gift of Your Spirit, for Your guidance, and for the endless streams of grace You pour into my life. May this work glorify You.

JANUARY A NEW BEGINNING

The start of a new year is a powerful reminder of God's ability to make all things new. No matter what lies behind, His grace invites you to step into a fresh chapter with hope, purpose, and trust in His promises. January's devotionals will focus on leaving the past behind, embracing new beginnings, and setting a firm foundation in Christ. As you embark on this journey, remember that you are a new creation in Him, equipped to walk confidently into the plans He has for you.

Day	Title	Scripture
Jan 1	New Mercies Every Morning	Lamentations 3:22-23
Jan 2	A New Heart and Spirit	Ezekiel 36:26
Jan 3	Forgetting What Lies Behind	Philippians 3:13-14
Jan 4	The God of New Things	Isaiah 43:18-19
Jan 5	Walking in Newness of Life	Romans 6:4
Jan 6	Daily Renewal	2 Corinthians 4:16
Jan 7	Strength for a New Journey	Joshua 1:9

Jan 8	Be Transformed	Romans 12:2
Jan 9	New Beginnings Through Grace	Titus 2:11-12
Jan 10	He Makes All Things New	Revelation 21:5
Jan 11	Trusting God's Plan	Jeremiah 29:11
Jan 12	Start Small, Stay Faithful	Zechariah 4:10
Jan 13	The Lord's Timing	Ecclesiastes 3:11
Jan 14	Renewing Your Mind	Ephesians 4:23-24
Jan 15	A Firm Foundation	Psalm 40:2-3
Jan 16	The Power of Today	Matthew 6:34
Jan 17	A Fresh Start Through Forgiveness	1 John 1:9
Jan 18	God's Word as a Lamp	Psalm 119:105
Jan 19	Trust in the Lord	Proverbs 3:5-6
Jan 20	Born Again to a Living Hope	1 Peter 1:3
Jan 21	God's Plans Are Good	Psalm 33:11
Jan 22	Seek First His Kingdom	Matthew 6:33
Jan 23	Faith in the New Season	Hebrews 11:1
Jan 24	A New Song	Psalm 96:1

Jan 25	God's Grace Is Sufficient	2 Corinthians 12:9
Jan 26	New Strength for the Weary	Isaiah 40:31
Jan 27	Peace in the New Year	John 14:27
Jan 28	Restoring What's Broken	Joel 2:25
Jan 29	The Good Work in You	Philippians 1:6
Jan 30	God's Mercies Endure Forever	Psalm 136:1
Jan 31	The Lord Will Finish It	Hebrews 12:2

January 1st 2025: New Mercies Every Morning

Scripture:
"*The steadfast love of the Lord never ceases; His mercies never come to an end; they are new every morning; great is your faithfulness.*" (Lamentations 3:22-23, ESV)

Reflection:
Every morning offers a chance to reset. God's mercies are not leftovers from yesterday; they are fresh and abundant today. It's easy to carry the weight of our failures or frustrations into a new day, but God invites us to release them.

Imagine waking up to a beautifully wrapped gift on your doorstep each morning. That's what God's mercy is like—an undeserved, perfectly timed gift that equips you for whatever lies ahead. His steadfast love is your anchor, no matter how stormy life gets. His faithfulness never runs dry, and His grace meets you exactly where you are.

So today, instead of starting with worry or self-criticism, start with this truth: God is faithful, and His mercies are yours for the taking. Walk boldly into the day knowing you're loved and equipped to handle whatever comes your way.

Affirmation:
I am walking in God's new mercies today. His love surrounds me, and His faithfulness sustains me.

Action Step:
Identify one burden or mistake you're holding onto. Pray and release it to God, thanking Him for His new mercies.

Prayer:
Lord, thank You for new mercies today. Help me release yesterday's mistakes and walk confidently in Your love and faithfulness. Amen.

January 2nd 2025: A New Heart and Spirit

Scripture:
"I will give you a new heart and put a new spirit in you; I will remove from you your heart of stone and give you a heart of flesh." (Ezekiel 36:26, NIV)

Reflection:
Change doesn't begin with our behavior; it begins in our hearts. A hardened heart is resistant, bitter, or fearful—unwilling to trust or obey God fully. But God promises to transform us from within. He takes the hard, immovable places in our hearts and replaces them with softness, love, and sensitivity to His Spirit.

When God gives you a new heart, you'll notice the difference. You'll find it easier to forgive, quicker to love, and more open to His direction. This transformation is not something you do on your own; it's the work of His Spirit.

Today, let God search your heart. Are there areas that feel cold or unyielding? Trust Him to renew those spaces with His grace and breathe fresh life into you.

Affirmation:
I have a new heart and a renewed spirit. God's love flows through me, and I walk in His purpose.

Action Step:
Ask God to reveal one area of your heart that needs renewal. Write it down, pray over it, and invite the Holy Spirit to work in that area this week.

Prayer:
Father, thank You for renewing my heart. Replace anything in me that is not of You, and fill me with Your Spirit. Amen.

January 3rd, 2025: Forgetting What Lies Behind

Scripture:
"*Forgetting what lies behind and straining forward to what lies ahead, I press on toward the goal for the prize of the upward call of God in Christ Jesus.*" (Philippians 3:13-14, ESV)

Reflection:
The past can often feel like a prison. Mistakes, missed opportunities, or hurts can replay in your mind, holding you back from the future God has for you. Paul's words in Philippians remind us that we cannot move forward while clinging to what's behind.

Forgetting the past doesn't mean erasing it. It means surrendering it to God. Trust that He has redeemed your missteps and can use even your pain for His glory. The upward call of Christ is worth pursuing—He offers purpose, healing, and hope in every season.

Each day is a chance to press forward, step by step, into the life God has planned for you. Don't let yesterday's baggage weigh you down. Look ahead, run your race, and keep your eyes fixed on Jesus.

Affirmation:
I release the past and embrace the future God has for me. I press forward with faith and purpose.

Action Step:
Write down one regret, failure, or hurt you're holding onto. Pray over it, then tear up the paper as a symbolic act of releasing it to God.

Prayer:
Lord, thank You for releasing me from my past. Help me walk boldly into the future You have prepared for me. Amen.

January 4th, 2025: The God of New Things

Scripture:
"Forget the former things; do not dwell on the past. See, I am doing a new thing! Now it springs up; do you not perceive it?" (Isaiah 43:18-19, NIV)

Reflection:
God specializes in newness. He turns wilderness into pathways and deserts into rivers. Yet sometimes, we are so focused on past disappointments or old ways of thinking that we fail to see what God is doing right now.

The new thing God is doing may look different than what you expected. It might be a new opportunity, a restored relationship, or a deeper understanding of His Word. Trust that whatever He's doing is for your good and His glory.

Take a moment today to ask God to open your spiritual eyes. Don't get stuck in what was; step into what is—and what's to come.

Affirmation:
I am open to the new things God is doing in my life. I trust His plans and walk forward in faith.

Action Step:
Spend five minutes in silence today, asking God to reveal the "new thing" He is doing in your life. Journal what you sense or feel in prayer.

Prayer:
Lord, help me to see the new things You are doing. Open my heart to Your plans and give me courage to embrace them fully. Amen.

January 5th, 2025: Walking in Newness of Life

Scripture:
"We were buried therefore with Him by baptism into death, in order that, just as Christ was raised from the dead by the glory of the Father, we too might walk in newness of life." (Romans 6:4, ESV)

Reflection:
When you gave your life to Christ, everything changed. Your old self was buried, and you were raised into newness of life. This transformation isn't just symbolic; it's a living reality. You are no longer defined by sin, shame, or what the world says about you.

Walking in newness of life means living each day with a renewed perspective. Instead of striving in your own strength, you rely on the power of the resurrection. Instead of clinging to old habits or fears, you embrace the freedom and joy Christ offers.

But walking in this newness takes intentionality. It's a daily choice to align your thoughts, actions, and heart with God's truth. As you step forward today, remember—you're walking in victory because Jesus has already conquered death for you.

Affirmation:
I am alive in Christ. I walk in freedom, purpose, and the power of His resurrection.

Action Step:
Reflect on one area of your life where you're still living as if the "old you" is in control. Surrender it to God and ask Him to help you walk in His newness today.

Prayer:
Lord, thank You for raising me into new life. Help me to walk

in Your freedom and reflect Your love and power in all I do. Amen.

January 6th, 2025: Daily Renewal

Scripture:
"So we do not lose heart. Though our outer self is wasting away, our inner self is being renewed day by day." (2 Corinthians 4:16, ESV)

Reflection:
Life can feel draining—physically, emotionally, and spiritually. But God promises daily renewal. Even when your outer self feels weak, your inner self can be strengthened by His Spirit.

Renewal isn't something we achieve through effort; it's something we receive through surrender. Each day, God invites you to come to Him for restoration. When you spend time in His presence, He refreshes your soul, recharges your faith, and equips you for the day ahead.

No matter how tired, discouraged, or overwhelmed you feel, know this: God is renewing you right now. Lean into His strength and let Him carry you.

Affirmation:
My strength comes from the Lord. He renews me daily, and I am equipped to face today with confidence.

Action Step:
Take five minutes today to sit quietly in God's presence. As you breathe, thank Him for renewing your spirit and ask Him for the strength you need.

Prayer:
Father, thank You for renewing me day by day. Help me to rest in Your presence and draw strength from Your endless grace. Amen.

January 7th 2025: Strength for a New Journey

Scripture:
"Have I not commanded you? Be strong and courageous. Do not be frightened, and do not be dismayed, for the Lord your God is with you wherever you go." (Joshua 1:9, ESV)

Reflection:
Starting something new can be daunting. Whether it's stepping into a new season, a new opportunity, or simply a new day, uncertainty can lead to fear. But God commands us to be strong and courageous—not because we have all the answers, but because He goes with us.

Just as God assured Joshua before leading Israel into the Promised Land, He assures you today: "I am with you." His presence is your source of strength. He has already prepared the way before you, and He promises never to leave you.

Courage isn't the absence of fear; it's trusting God in the face of it. So, whatever lies ahead, remember—you're not walking this path alone.

Affirmation:
I am strong and courageous because God is with me. He equips me for every step of this journey.

Action Step:
Identify one area of your life where you need God's courage. Write a prayer asking Him for strength and take a small step of faith today.

Prayer:
Lord, thank You for being with me in every season. Help me to walk boldly into this new journey, trusting that You are by my side. Amen.

January 8th, 2025: Be Transformed

Scripture:
"Do not be conformed to this world, but be transformed by the renewal of your mind, that by testing you may discern what is the will of God, what is good and acceptable and perfect." (Romans 12:2, ESV)

Reflection:
The world constantly pushes us to conform—to follow its patterns, chase its values, and measure success by its standards. But as believers, we are called to a higher way. Transformation begins when we stop letting the world shape us and start letting God renew our minds.

Renewing your mind is not a one-time event; it's a daily process. As you spend time in God's Word and in His presence, He shifts your perspective, aligns your thoughts with His truth, and reveals His will for your life.

Today, take a moment to reflect on where your thoughts have been. Are they filled with fear or faith? Doubt or trust? Let God's truth shape your mindset and transform your heart.

Affirmation:
My mind is renewed by God's Word. I am being transformed daily to walk in His will and reflect His love.

Action Step:
Choose one worldly mindset you want to release (e.g., fear, comparison, or negativity). Write down a Scripture to replace it, and declare that truth over yourself throughout the day.

Prayer:
Father, transform me by renewing my mind. Help me to reject the world's patterns and embrace Your perfect will for my life. Amen.

January 9th, 2025: New Beginnings Through Grace

Scripture:
"For the grace of God has appeared, bringing salvation for all people, training us to renounce ungodliness and worldly passions, and to live self-controlled, upright, and godly lives in the present age." (Titus 2:11-12, ESV)

Reflection:
Grace is more than God's unmerited favor; it's His power working in you to live a life that honors Him. While the world's idea of a fresh start often relies on self-help or willpower, God offers something better: His grace.

His grace saves you, sustains you, and transforms you. It empowers you to leave behind ungodly habits and step into a life of purpose and holiness. This isn't about striving—it's about surrendering to His work in your life.

Let God's grace guide your new beginning. Whatever challenges you face, His grace is sufficient to help you overcome and thrive.

Affirmation:
I am saved, sustained, and strengthened by God's grace. I can face anything today because His grace is sufficient for me.

Action Step:
Identify one area where you feel weak or stuck. Ask God to help you rely on His grace, not your own strength, to make progress.

Prayer:
Lord, thank You for Your amazing grace. Help me to rely on You in every area of my life and live in a way that reflects Your love. Amen.

January 10th 2025: He Makes All Things New

Scripture:
"And He who was seated on the throne said, 'Behold, I am making all things new.' Also He said, 'Write this down, for these words are trustworthy and true.'" (Revelation 21:5, ESV)

Reflection:
God's promise to make all things new is not just for the distant future—it's a reality He's working out in your life today. Whether it's healing a broken heart, restoring a relationship, or giving fresh vision for the future, God's renewing power is always at work.

Newness doesn't always mean instant change. Sometimes, it's a gradual process as God refines, rebuilds, and restores. Trust His timing and His ability to bring beauty out of ashes.

Whatever feels broken or hopeless in your life, surrender it to God. He specializes in redemption and renewal, and He delights in making all things new.

Affirmation:
God is making all things new in my life. I trust His process and look forward to the beauty He is creating.

Action Step:
Take one area of your life that feels "old" or broken and pray specifically for God's renewal. Commit to trusting Him through the process, even if it takes time.

Prayer:
Lord, thank You for Your promise to make all things new. I trust You to restore and redeem every area of my life. Amen.

January 11th, 2025: Trusting God's Plan

Scripture:
"For I know the plans I have for you, declares the Lord, plans for welfare and not for evil, to give you a future and a hope." (Jeremiah 29:11, ESV)

Reflection:
It's easy to feel overwhelmed when life doesn't go as planned. But God's plans are not just good—they are perfect. Even when things seem chaotic or uncertain, you can trust that He is working all things together for your good.

God's plan includes a future filled with hope, but it also requires faith in the present. Trusting Him means letting go of the need to control every detail and believing that His wisdom far surpasses yours.

Today, surrender your plans to Him and ask for the faith to embrace His path, even when it's unexpected. His plans are always worth following.

Affirmation:
I trust in God's perfect plan for my life. He is leading me into a future filled with hope.

Action Step:
Write down one area where you're struggling to trust God's plan. Ask Him to give you peace and surrender it to His control.

Prayer:
Lord, thank You for having a perfect plan for my life. Help me to trust You completely and walk in the hope You have promised. Amen.

January 12th, 2025: Start Small, Stay Faithful

Scripture:
"*For whoever has despised the day of small things shall rejoice, and shall see the plumb line in the hand of Zerubbabel.*" (Zechariah 4:10, ESV)

Reflection:
Every great work of God starts with small beginnings. Whether it's rebuilding a temple, starting a ministry, or taking a step of faith in your personal life, God values your obedience in the small things.

The world often celebrates big results, but God celebrates faithfulness. When you remain faithful in the little assignments, He trusts you with greater things. The "small" steps you take today—praying, serving, forgiving—are laying a foundation for the future God has prepared for you.

Don't despise the process. Trust that every seed you plant in faith, no matter how small, will produce a harvest in God's perfect time.

Affirmation:
I will remain faithful in the small things, trusting that God is building something great in my life.

Action Step:
Identify one small, faithful action you can take today (e.g., reaching out to encourage someone, spending extra time in prayer, or serving where needed). Do it with joy and trust.

Prayer:
Lord, help me to see the value in small beginnings. Strengthen me to remain faithful in the little things, knowing You are working all things together for good. Amen.

January 13th, 2025: The Lord's Timing

Scripture:
"He has made everything beautiful in its time. Also, He has put eternity into man's heart, yet so that he cannot find out what God has done from the beginning to the end."
(Ecclesiastes 3:11, ESV)

Reflection:
Waiting on God's timing can be hard, but His timing is always perfect. He sees the bigger picture, while we often focus on immediate results. Trusting His timing means believing that He is preparing you for what's ahead—even if it feels like nothing is happening right now.

Sometimes, God's delays are opportunities for growth. He's shaping your character, strengthening your faith, and aligning circumstances for His glory. Don't rush the process; embrace the season you're in, knowing that He is making everything beautiful in its time.

Affirmation:
I trust God's perfect timing. He is making everything beautiful in my life according to His plan.

Action Step:
Take five minutes to reflect on an area where you've been impatient. Write a prayer asking God for peace as you wait on His timing.

Prayer:
Lord, thank You for Your perfect timing. Help me to trust Your process and remain patient as You work all things for my good. Amen.

January 14th, 2025: Renewing Your Mind

Scripture:
"*...to be renewed in the spirit of your minds, and to put on the new self, created after the likeness of God in true righteousness and holiness.*" (Ephesians 4:23-24, ESV)

Reflection:
Your thoughts shape your life. If your mind is filled with negativity, fear, or lies, those thoughts will influence your decisions and actions. But when you renew your mind with God's truth, you begin to see yourself and the world through His eyes.

Renewing your mind isn't a one-time event; it's a daily practice. It happens when you intentionally fill your heart and mind with God's Word and reject the lies of the enemy. Over time, you'll notice a shift—old patterns of thinking will fade, and new, God-honoring thoughts will take root.

Today, invite God to transform your thinking. Let His truth guide your day.

Affirmation:
My mind is renewed by God's Word. I think His thoughts, live in His truth, and walk in His righteousness.

Action Step:
Identify one recurring negative thought and replace it with a promise from Scripture. Speak that promise over yourself throughout the day.

Prayer:
Lord, renew my mind today. Help me to reject lies and embrace the truth of who I am in You. Amen.

January 15th 2025: A Firm Foundation

Scripture:
"He drew me up from the pit of destruction, out of the miry bog, and set my feet upon a rock, making my steps secure." (Psalm 40:2, ESV)

Reflection:
Life can feel shaky at times, but when God is your foundation, you can stand firm no matter what comes your way. He lifts you out of the mess, places your feet on solid ground, and gives you the strength to keep moving forward.

Building your life on Christ means trusting Him as your foundation, not just in theory, but in practice. When storms come, you don't have to fear. His promises are unshakable, His love is constant, and His presence is your safe place.

Today, lean into the security of God's foundation. He will not let you fall.

Affirmation:
My life is built on Christ, my solid rock. No storm can shake me because I stand on His promises.

Action Step:
Think of one "storm" or challenge you're facing. Meditate on God's promise to be your foundation, and declare His faithfulness over your situation.

Prayer:
Lord, thank You for being my firm foundation. Help me to trust You in every storm and build my life on Your unshakable promises. Amen.

January 16th, 2025: The Power of Today

Scripture:
"Therefore do not worry about tomorrow, for tomorrow will worry about itself. Each day has enough trouble of its own." (Matthew 6:34, NIV)

Reflection:
It's easy to get caught up in what's next—planning for tomorrow, worrying about next week, or stressing over the future. But Jesus reminds us to focus on today. Why? Because today is where your strength, grace, and opportunities are.

Worry about tomorrow robs you of the joy and purpose God has for you right now. Instead of trying to solve tomorrow's problems, ask God for the wisdom and strength to conquer today. When you trust Him with your future, you can fully embrace the present.

Affirmation:
I live in the grace of today. God gives me the strength I need for this moment, and I trust Him with my future.

Action Step:
Take a deep breath and list three things you're grateful for today. Commit to focusing on those blessings and letting go of tomorrow's worries.

Prayer:
Lord, help me to live in the moment and trust You with my future. Give me the grace to embrace today with faith and gratitude. Amen.

January 17th 2025: A Fresh Start Through Forgiveness

Scripture:
"If we confess our sins, He is faithful and just to forgive us our sins and to cleanse us from all unrighteousness." (1 John 1:9, ESV)

Reflection:
Have you ever spilled something on a white shirt—maybe coffee or ketchup—and thought, "There's no way this will ever come clean"? That's how sin can feel: like a permanent stain. But God promises something incredible—through confession and His forgiveness, He makes us clean again.

Forgiveness isn't just about removing guilt; it's about restoring relationship. When we bring our sins to God, He doesn't just wipe the slate clean—He gives us a fresh start.

Too often, we let shame hold us back from confessing to God, but His forgiveness is never withheld. He is faithful and just, ready to cleanse you fully, no matter the stain. Today is a new beginning—step into the freedom and joy of forgiveness.

Affirmation:
I am forgiven, restored, and made new in Christ. His mercy removes my guilt and gives me a fresh start.

Action Step:
Take 5 minutes to confess your sins to God. Be honest and specific. Then thank Him for His forgiveness and write down how it feels to know you've been made clean.

Prayer:
Father, thank You for forgiving me and cleansing me from all unrighteousness. Help me to walk in the freedom of Your grace and extend forgiveness to others. Amen.

January 18th, 2025: God's Word as a Lamp

Scripture:
"*Your word is a lamp to my feet and a light to my path.*"
(Psalm 119:105, ESV)

Reflection:
Have you ever walked through a dark room, trying to avoid stubbing your toe? That's what life can feel like without God's Word. It's easy to trip, get lost, or feel overwhelmed when you don't have the light of His guidance.

God's Word isn't just a set of instructions; it's a lamp for your journey. It illuminates the steps you need to take today and shines a light on the path ahead. Even when the way forward seems unclear, Scripture helps you walk with confidence, knowing God is leading you.

Today, treat God's Word as your guide. Instead of trying to figure out everything on your own, let His truth direct your thoughts, decisions, and actions.

Affirmation:
God's Word lights my path. I walk confidently in His truth and trust His guidance for my life.

Action Step:
Read one chapter of the Bible today, focusing on how it applies to your current season. Write down one verse that stands out and meditate on it throughout the day.

Prayer:
Lord, thank You for Your Word, which guides me in every step. Help me to walk in the light of Your truth today and trust You fully. Amen.

January 19th, 2025: Trust in the Lord

Scripture:
"*Trust in the Lord with all your heart, and do not lean on your own understanding. In all your ways acknowledge Him, and He will make straight your paths.*" (Proverbs 3:5-6, ESV)

Reflection:
Trusting God sounds simple—until life feels uncertain. It's tempting to rely on your own understanding, analyzing every detail and trying to control the outcome. But Scripture reminds us to lean on God instead of ourselves.

Trust means surrender. It's choosing to believe that God's wisdom, love, and timing are better than yours. When you acknowledge Him in every area of your life, He promises to direct your path—not just vaguely, but with clarity and purpose.

Let today be a day of trust. Whatever is weighing on your heart, release it to God. He is faithful to lead you.

Affirmation:
I trust God with all my heart. He is leading me, and His plans for me are good.

Action Step:
Write down one decision or challenge you're facing. Pray over it, asking God for wisdom, and commit to trusting Him with the outcome.

Prayer:
Lord, help me to trust You with my whole heart. I surrender my plans to You and believe that You are making my path straight. Amen.

January 20th, 2025: Born Again to a Living Hope

Scripture:
"Blessed be the God and Father of our Lord Jesus Christ! According to His great mercy, He has caused us to be born again to a living hope through the resurrection of Jesus Christ from the dead." (1 Peter 1:3, ESV)

Reflection:
Hope is a powerful thing. But the world's version of hope often feels fragile, based on wishful thinking or circumstances that can change in an instant. In Christ, however, we have a **living hope**—one that is alive, unshakable, and eternal.

This living hope is rooted in the resurrection of Jesus. Because He conquered death, we can live with confidence, knowing that no matter what happens in life, our ultimate victory is secure. Hope isn't just a feeling; it's a reality anchored in God's promises.

Today, let the truth of this living hope refresh your soul. Whatever you're facing, remember that Christ has already overcome, and He's working all things for your good.

Affirmation:
I have a living hope in Christ. His resurrection power sustains me, and His promises give me strength.

Action Step:
Think about an area in your life where you've lost hope. Spend time in prayer, asking God to fill you with His living hope and renew your trust in His promises.

Prayer:
Lord, thank You for giving me a living hope through Your resurrection. Help me to trust in Your promises and live with bold confidence in Your victory. Amen.

January 21st, 2025: God's Plans Are Good

Scripture:
"*The counsel of the Lord stands forever, the plans of His heart to all generations.*" (Psalm 33:11, ESV)

Reflection:
It's comforting to know that God's plans are not temporary or shaky—they are eternal, unchanging, and rooted in His heart for His people. No matter how unpredictable life feels, God's purposes remain firm.

Sometimes, His plans might not look like what we envisioned. Disappointments and detours can make us question His goodness. But the truth is, God's plans are always for our ultimate good, even when we don't understand them in the moment.

Trust that He is working behind the scenes, orchestrating something greater than you can imagine. His plans are not only good—they are perfect.

Affirmation:
God's plans for my life are good and eternal. I trust His purpose and follow His leading.

Action Step:
Reflect on a time when God's plans turned out better than what you had hoped. Write down that testimony as a reminder of His faithfulness.

Prayer:
Lord, thank You that Your plans for me are good and eternal. Help me to trust You in every season and rest in the assurance of Your purpose. Amen.

January 22nd, 2025: Seek First His Kingdom

Scripture:
"But seek first the kingdom of God and His righteousness, and all these things will be added to you." (Matthew 6:33, ESV)

Reflection:
Life is full of competing priorities—work, family, goals, and worries. It's easy to let these things consume your focus, but Jesus calls us to seek His kingdom first. This doesn't mean ignoring your responsibilities; it means making God your ultimate priority.

When you put God first, everything else falls into place. He knows your needs better than you do, and He's faithful to provide. Seeking His kingdom means aligning your heart with His, living according to His values, and trusting Him with the rest.

Today, pause and ask yourself: Am I putting God first? If not, it's never too late to realign.

Affirmation:
I seek first God's kingdom. He provides for my needs and leads me in His righteousness.

Action Step:
Take 10 minutes today to pray and ask God to help you prioritize Him in your thoughts, time, and actions.

Prayer:
Lord, I choose to seek Your kingdom first. Help me to trust You with my needs and live in a way that honors You. Amen.

January 23rd: Faith in the New Season

Scripture:
"Now faith is the assurance of things hoped for, the conviction of things not seen." (Hebrews 11:1, ESV)

Reflection:
Faith is trusting God even when you can't see the whole picture. It's stepping into a new season with confidence, knowing that He's already gone before you. While fear focuses on what's uncertain, faith focuses on God's promises.

New beginnings often come with challenges, but they're also opportunities to deepen your trust in God. Each step of faith you take today strengthens your relationship with Him and moves you closer to His plans for your life.

Remember, faith isn't about having all the answers—it's about trusting the One who does.

Affirmation:
I walk by faith, not by sight. I trust God's promises for my new season.

Action Step:
Identify one step of faith you can take today, no matter how small. Commit to taking that step, trusting God with the outcome.

Prayer:
Lord, increase my faith as I step into this new season. Help me to trust Your promises and walk boldly in Your purpose. Amen.

January 24th, 2025: A New Song

Scripture:
"*Oh sing to the Lord a new song; sing to the Lord, all the earth!*" (Psalm 96:1, ESV)

Reflection:
A new beginning deserves a new song. Just as God renews your heart and mind, He also invites you to worship Him in fresh and creative ways. Your "new song" doesn't have to be literal—it could be a new way of serving, a new prayer of gratitude, or a new testimony of His faithfulness.

When you focus on what God is doing now, your worship becomes alive and personal. Today, take time to reflect on His goodness and let it overflow in praise.

Affirmation:
I will sing a new song to the Lord. My life is a testimony of His faithfulness and love.

Action Step:
Write down three ways God has blessed you this week. Spend time thanking Him for each one, and let it inspire your worship.

Prayer:
Father, thank You for giving me a new song. Help me to worship You with a heart full of gratitude and joy. Amen.

January 25th: God's Grace Is Sufficient

Scripture:
"But He said to me, 'My grace is sufficient for you, for My power is made perfect in weakness.'" (2 Corinthians 12:9, ESV)

Reflection:
There will be days when you feel inadequate, weak, or overwhelmed. But God reminds us that His grace is enough. It's in our moments of weakness that His power shines the brightest.

God's grace isn't just about salvation—it's about daily sustenance. It's His strength meeting you in your need, His peace calming your fears, and His presence carrying you through challenges.

When you feel like you don't have enough, remember that His grace is always more than enough.

Affirmation:
God's grace is sufficient for me. His power is made perfect in my weakness.

Action Step:
Think of an area where you feel weak or overwhelmed. Ask God to show you how His grace is sustaining you in that area today.

Prayer:
Lord, thank You for Your all-sufficient grace. Help me to rely on Your strength and not my own. Amen.

January 26th, 2025: New Strength for the Weary

Scripture:
"But they who wait for the Lord shall renew their strength; they shall mount up with wings like eagles; they shall run and not be weary; they shall walk and not faint." (Isaiah 40:31, ESV)

Reflection:
We all face seasons of weariness. Life's demands can leave you feeling drained and overwhelmed. But God promises that when you wait on Him, He will renew your strength.

Waiting doesn't mean doing nothing—it means trusting God, resting in His presence, and leaning on His promises. It's in the waiting that He equips you to soar, to run your race with endurance, and to keep moving forward when you feel like giving up.

Today, let God renew your strength. He has everything you need to keep going.

Affirmation:
My strength is renewed as I wait on the Lord. I run with endurance and rise above every challenge.

Action Step:
Spend 10 minutes in quiet prayer, asking God to renew your strength and refresh your spirit for the day ahead.

Prayer:
Lord, thank You for renewing my strength when I feel weary. Help me to trust You in every season and rely on Your power. Amen.

January 27th, 2025: Peace in the New Year

Scripture:
"Peace I leave with you; My peace I give to you. Not as the world gives do I give to you. Let not your hearts be troubled, neither let them be afraid." (John 14:27, ESV)

Reflection:
The peace Jesus offers is unlike anything the world can provide. It's not based on circumstances or fleeting emotions —it's rooted in His presence and promises. This peace guards your heart, calms your fears, and carries you through uncertainty.

As you move forward in the new year, choose to embrace His peace. Don't let worry or fear take control. Instead, fix your eyes on Jesus, the Prince of Peace, and let His presence fill your heart and mind.

Affirmation:
I have the peace of Christ. My heart is untroubled, and my mind is at rest in Him.

Action Step:
Write down one thing that's been troubling you. Surrender it to God in prayer, and ask Him to fill you with His peace.

Prayer:
Jesus, thank You for the gift of Your peace. Help me to release my fears and rest in Your presence today. Amen.

January 28th, 2025: Restoring What's Broken

Scripture:
"I will restore to you the years that the swarming locust has eaten." (Joel 2:25, ESV)

Reflection:
God is in the business of restoration. Whether it's broken relationships, lost opportunities, or a weary heart, He has the power to redeem and restore what feels beyond repair.

His restoration doesn't just return things to the way they were—it makes them better. What the enemy meant for harm, God uses for good. Trust Him to work in the broken places of your life and to bring beauty out of ashes.

Affirmation:
God is restoring what's broken in my life. He brings beauty from ashes and hope from despair.

Action Step:
Reflect on an area of your life where you need restoration. Pray specifically for God's redeeming work in that area.

Prayer:
Lord, thank You for being a God of restoration. I trust You to bring healing and renewal to every broken place in my life. Amen.

January 29th, 2025: The Good Work in You

Scripture:
"And I am sure of this, that He who began a good work in you will bring it to completion at the day of Jesus Christ."
(Philippians 1:6, ESV)

Reflection:
God doesn't leave things unfinished. The good work He began in you—whether it's a calling, a transformation, or a season of growth—He promises to complete.

Even when progress feels slow or you struggle with doubt, know this: God is still working. He's molding you into the person He's called you to be, one step at a time. Trust His process and be patient with yourself.

Affirmation:
God is completing the good work He began in me. I trust His process and timing.

Action Step:
Write down one area where you see God working in your life. Thank Him for His faithfulness to complete it.

Prayer:
Father, thank You for the good work You are doing in me. Help me to trust Your process and walk in faith. Amen.

January 30th: God's Mercies Endure Forever

Scripture:
"Give thanks to the Lord, for He is good, for His steadfast love endures forever." (Psalm 136:1, ESV)

Reflection:
No matter how uncertain life feels, one truth remains: God's love and mercy endure forever. His faithfulness isn't temporary or conditional—it's eternal. From generation to generation, His steadfast love remains unchanged.

When you feel overwhelmed, pause and reflect on the ways God has shown His goodness in your life. Gratitude shifts your perspective, reminding you that even in difficult seasons, God's mercy is present and His love never fails.

Let today be filled with thanksgiving. Not because everything is perfect, but because His love is.

Affirmation:
God's steadfast love and mercy are with me always. I live with gratitude for His goodness in my life.

Action Step:
Write a list of five things you're thankful for today. Reflect on how each one is a reminder of God's enduring love.

Prayer:
Lord, thank You for Your mercy that never ends. Help me to live with a heart full of gratitude, trusting in Your steadfast love. Amen.

January 31st, 2025: The Lord Will Finish It

Scripture:
"*Looking to Jesus, the founder and perfecter of our faith, who for the joy that was set before Him endured the cross, despising the shame, and is seated at the right hand of the throne of God.*" (Hebrews 12:2, ESV)

Reflection:
As January comes to a close, remember this: the same God who began a good work in you will bring it to completion. Jesus is the author of your faith, but He's also the finisher. He doesn't leave things undone.

When you feel weary or unsure about the future, look to Jesus. His endurance on the cross was driven by joy—the joy of bringing you into His eternal family. That same joy is available to you today as you run the race set before you.

Fix your eyes on Him. Trust that He is writing a beautiful story in your life, and He will finish what He started.

Affirmation:
Jesus is the author and finisher of my faith. I trust Him to complete the good work He began in me.

Action Step:
Spend time reflecting on what God has done in your life this month. Write down one area where you see His faithfulness and one area where you're trusting Him to finish the work.

Prayer:
Jesus, thank You for being the author and finisher of my faith. Help me to run my race with endurance, trusting that You will complete the good work in me. Amen.

FEBRUARY: LOVE WITHOUT MEASURE

February is a month to reflect on the greatest love story of all —God's unfailing love for you. This love is unconditional, sacrificial, and boundless, demonstrated fully through Jesus Christ. As you grow in understanding His love, you'll be empowered to love others with the same grace and compassion. February's devotionals will explore God's love, the call to love others, and how forgiveness transforms relationships. Open your heart to experience and share the limitless love of God each day.

Day	Title	Scripture
Feb 1	God's Love Never Fails	1 Corinthians 13:8
Feb 2	Perfect Love Casts Out Fear	1 John 4:18
Feb 3	The Greatest Commandment	Matthew 22:37-39
Feb 4	God Demonstrates His Love	Romans 5:8
Feb 5	Love Is Patient, Love Is Kind	1 Corinthians 13:4-7

Feb 6	A Love That Forgives	Colossians 3:13
Feb 7	Nothing Can Separate Us	Romans 8:38-39
Feb 8	Love Your Enemies	Matthew 5:44
Feb 9	Love in Action	1 John 3:18
Feb 10	Rooted and Grounded in Love	Ephesians 3:17-19
Feb 11	The Father's Lavish Love	1 John 3:1
Feb 12	Loving with Humility	Philippians 2:3-4
Feb 13	A Covenant of Love	Deuteronomy 7:9
Feb 14	God's Love Letter	John 3:16
Feb 15	Love Covers a Multitude of Sins	1 Peter 4:8
Feb 16	Bearing Each Other's Burdens	Galatians 6:2
Feb 17	Speak the Truth in Love	Ephesians 4:15
Feb 18	Love and Obedience	John 14:15
Feb 19	A Friend Who Loves at All Times	Proverbs 17:17
Feb 20	A Love That Sacrifices	John 15:13
Feb 21	Love as Christ Loved	Ephesians 5:2
Feb 22	Loving the Least of These	Matthew 25:40

Feb 23	Love Is Not Self-Seeking	1 Corinthians 13:5
Feb 24	A Love That Builds Others Up	1 Thessalonians 5:11
Feb 25	Love That Never Quits	Galatians 6:9
Feb 26	Abide in My Love	John 15:9-10
Feb 27	A Love That Multiplies	1 Thessalonians 3:12
Feb 28	Love Beyond Measure	Ephesians 2:4-5

February 1st, 2025: God's Love Never Fails

Scripture:
"*Love never fails.*" (1 Corinthians 13:8, NIV)

Reflection:
Everything in life has an expiration date—trends fade, relationships can falter, and even the strongest human commitments can fall short. But God's love? It never fails. It's unshakable, unchanging, and eternal.

Think of a time when someone's love or loyalty didn't meet your expectations. It may have left you feeling disappointed, hurt, or even alone. God's love is the opposite—it's constant and completely dependable. His love isn't based on your performance or circumstances; it's rooted in who He is.

No matter what you're facing today, you can stand secure in this truth: God's love will never fail you.

Affirmation:
God's love for me never fails. I am secure, cherished, and held by His unchanging love.

Action Step:
Take a moment to reflect on areas where you've felt unloved or forgotten. Replace those feelings with this truth: God's love never fails. Write this Scripture somewhere visible to remind you throughout the day.

Prayer:
Lord, thank You for Your unfailing love. Help me to rest in the security of knowing that You are always faithful and that Your love never ends. Amen.

February 2nd, 2025: Perfect Love Casts Out Fear

Scripture:
"There is no fear in love, but perfect love casts out fear." (1 John 4:18, ESV)

Reflection:
Fear has a way of gripping us—fear of failure, rejection, the unknown. But God's perfect love drives out fear. His love reassures you that you are never alone, never forgotten, and always cared for.

When fear tries to take over, remember that it cannot coexist with the love of God. His love covers every insecurity and silences every "what if." You don't have to live in the shadow of fear when you're walking in the light of His love.

Today, lean into His perfect love. Let it fill the spaces where fear tries to creep in and remind you that you are safe in His arms.

Affirmation:
God's perfect love fills my heart and casts out all fear. I am bold, secure, and free in His love.

Action Step:
Identify one fear you've been holding onto. Write it down and surrender it to God in prayer. Speak this affirmation over yourself whenever that fear arises.

Prayer:
Father, thank You for Your perfect love that drives out fear. Help me to trust You more deeply and walk in boldness, knowing that I am secure in You. Amen.

February 3rd, 2025: The Greatest Commandment

Scripture:
"You shall love the Lord your God with all your heart and with all your soul and with all your mind. This is the great and first commandment. And a second is like it: You shall love your neighbor as yourself." (Matthew 22:37-39, ESV)

Reflection:
Jesus summed up all of God's commandments with one word: love. Loving God with everything you have and loving others as yourself isn't just a suggestion—it's the foundation of a life well-lived.

Loving God means putting Him first in your thoughts, decisions, and actions. Loving your neighbor means showing kindness, forgiveness, and patience, even when it's hard. This kind of love is active, not passive. It's something you do intentionally every day.

When you live out these two commandments, you reflect God's heart to the world around you. Today, ask yourself: How can I love God more deeply and love others more intentionally?

Affirmation:
I love the Lord my God with all my heart, soul, and mind. His love overflows in me to bless others.

Action Step:
Choose one way to show love to God today (e.g., extra prayer time, worship, or obedience in a specific area). Then find one way to love your neighbor, such as offering encouragement or lending a helping hand.

Prayer:
Lord, help me to love You with all my heart, soul, and mind. Teach me to love others as You have loved me. Amen.

February 4th 2025: God Demonstrates His Love

Scripture:
"But God demonstrates His own love for us in this: While we were still sinners, Christ died for us." (Romans 5:8, NIV)

Reflection:
God didn't wait for you to clean yourself up or earn His approval—He loved you at your lowest. He proved it by sending His Son to die for you. That's the ultimate demonstration of love: sacrificing everything for someone who doesn't deserve it.

When you question your worth or wonder if God truly loves you, look to the cross. It's the eternal reminder of His commitment to you. His love isn't just words—it's action.

Let that truth sink in today: You are fully loved, fully accepted, and fully valued by the Creator of the universe.

Affirmation:
God demonstrated His love for me through Jesus Christ. I am deeply loved and eternally valued.

Action Step:
Spend a few moments in gratitude, reflecting on what Jesus' sacrifice means for you. Write down one way you can demonstrate selfless love to someone else today.

Prayer:
Father, thank You for loving me even when I was unworthy. Help me to live in gratitude for Your sacrifice and reflect Your love to others. Amen.

February 5th, 2025: Love Is Patient, Love Is Kind

Scripture:
"*Love is patient and kind; love does not envy or boast; it is not arrogant.*" (1 Corinthians 13:4, ESV)

Reflection:
True love is more than a feeling—it's an action. Patience and kindness are two of love's defining characteristics, and they require intentional effort. Being patient means choosing to endure inconvenience without frustration. Being kind means looking for ways to bless others, even when it's not reciprocated.

Think about the people in your life who test your patience or challenge your kindness. Loving them isn't always easy, but it reflects God's love for us—a love that is patient with our flaws and kind in His mercy.

Today, ask God to help you love others the way He loves you.

Affirmation:
Love is patient and kind, and I choose to reflect God's love in all I do.

Action Step:
Identify one person in your life who needs extra patience or kindness. Commit to showing them God's love in a practical way today.

Prayer:
Lord, thank You for loving me with patience and kindness. Teach me to extend that same love to others, even when it's difficult. Amen.

February 6th, 2025: A Love That Forgives

Scripture:
"*...bearing with one another and, if one has a complaint against another, forgiving each other; as the Lord has forgiven you, so you also must forgive.*" (Colossians 3:13, ESV)

Reflection:
Forgiveness is one of the hardest expressions of love, especially when someone has hurt you deeply. Yet God calls us to forgive others as He has forgiven us—freely, fully, and without holding a grudge.

Think about what it cost Jesus to forgive you: His life. If He can forgive your sins, past and present, surely He can help you forgive others. Forgiveness doesn't mean condoning the wrong or ignoring the pain; it means releasing the bitterness that holds you captive.

When you forgive, you reflect the heart of God. And in that moment, you set yourself free.

Affirmation:
I forgive others as God has forgiven me. His love sets me free to live without bitterness.

Action Step:
Think of someone you need to forgive. Write their name in your journal and pray for them, asking God to help you release the hurt and extend forgiveness.

Prayer:
Father, thank You for forgiving me completely. Help me to forgive others with the same love and grace You've shown me. Amen.

February 7th, 2025: Nothing Can Separate Us

Scripture:
"*For I am sure that neither death nor life, nor angels nor rulers, nor things present nor things to come, nor powers, nor height nor depth, nor anything else in all creation, will be able to separate us from the love of God in Christ Jesus our Lord.*" (Romans 8:38-39, ESV)

Reflection:
Have you ever felt like God's love was out of reach? Maybe life's challenges have made you feel distant from Him, or your own mistakes have filled you with shame. But God's Word promises that nothing—not your circumstances, failures, or fears—can separate you from His love.

His love is unshakable. It's constant in your highs and unrelenting in your lows. No power, person, or situation can break the bond between you and your heavenly Father.

Rest in this truth today: You are always and forever loved.

Affirmation:
Nothing can separate me from God's love. I am secure in His everlasting arms.

Action Step:
Write down this verse and carry it with you today. Whenever you feel overwhelmed or unworthy, speak it aloud and remind yourself of God's unbreakable love.

Prayer:
Lord, thank You for Your love that never lets me go. Help me to trust in Your unchanging promises and rest in Your security. Amen.

February 8th, 2025: Love Your Enemies

Scripture:
"*But I say to you, Love your enemies and pray for those who persecute you.*" (Matthew 5:44, ESV)

Reflection:
Loving those who hurt you goes against every instinct. The natural response is to seek revenge or harbor resentment. But Jesus calls us to a radical kind of love—a love that extends even to our enemies.

Loving your enemies doesn't mean tolerating abuse or ignoring boundaries, but it does mean choosing to respond with grace instead of hatred. When you pray for those who wrong you, you invite God into the situation, and He begins to work not only in their hearts but in yours as well.

This kind of love reflects Jesus Himself, who prayed for the very people who nailed Him to the cross.

Affirmation:
I choose to love and pray for my enemies. God's love empowers me to respond with grace.

Action Step:
Think of someone who has wronged or hurt you. Pray for them by name today, asking God to bless them and work in their lives.

Prayer:
Father, help me to love my enemies as You love them. Give me the strength to pray for them and trust You to work in their lives and mine. Amen.

February 9th, 2025: Love in Action

Scripture:
"*Little children, let us not love in word or talk but in deed and in truth.*" (1 John 3:18, ESV)

Reflection:
Love isn't just something you say; it's something you do. Words are important, but actions speak louder. True love shows itself through kindness, sacrifice, and a willingness to meet the needs of others.

Think about the ways God shows His love for you—not just through promises, but through action. He provides for your needs, comforts you in trials, and sent His Son to die for you. Now, He calls you to reflect that same active love to the people around you.

Today, let your actions speak louder than your words. Be intentional about showing love in a tangible way.

Affirmation:
My love is shown through action. I reflect God's love by serving others with kindness and truth.

Action Step:
Look for one practical way to love someone today. It could be a kind word, an act of service, or simply listening to someone who needs to be heard.

Prayer:
Lord, thank You for demonstrating Your love through action. Help me to reflect Your love by serving others in tangible ways today. Amen.

February 10th 2025: Rooted and Grounded in Love

Scripture:
"*So that Christ may dwell in your hearts through faith—that you, being rooted and grounded in love, may have strength to comprehend... the love of Christ.*" (Ephesians 3:17-19, ESV)

Reflection:
Roots are what give a tree stability. Without them, the slightest wind could knock it over. In the same way, being rooted in God's love gives you the strength to stand firm in life's storms.

When you're deeply rooted in His love, you can face challenges with confidence, knowing that you're grounded in something unshakable. His love isn't just something you receive; it's the foundation that shapes your identity and empowers you to grow.

Today, remind yourself that God's love is your anchor. Let it ground you and give you the strength to flourish.

Affirmation:
I am rooted and grounded in God's love. His love is my strength and foundation.

Action Step:
Spend time meditating on the depth of God's love for you. Write down three ways His love has shaped your life and given you strength.

Prayer:
Father, thank You for grounding me in Your love. Help me to stand firm in that love and share it with the world around me. Amen.

February 11th, 2025: The Father's Lavish Love

Scripture:
"See what great love the Father has lavished on us, that we should be called children of God! And that is what we are!" (1 John 3:1, NIV)

Reflection:
God's love for you isn't stingy or hesitant—it's lavish. He calls you His child, not because of anything you've done, but because of His overwhelming grace. Being a child of God means you are deeply loved, fully accepted, and part of His eternal family.

Think about the word "lavished." It means poured out generously, without holding back. That's how God loves you —without limits. When you fully grasp His love, it transforms the way you see yourself and the world around you.

Let today be a reminder of your identity: You are His beloved child, cherished beyond measure.

Affirmation:
I am a child of God, loved lavishly by my heavenly Father. His love defines who I am.

Action Step:
Spend five minutes reflecting on what it means to be a child of God. Write down one way His love gives you confidence in your identity.

Prayer:
Father, thank You for loving me so lavishly and calling me Your child. Help me to live each day secure in Your love and to share it with others. Amen.

February 12th 2025: Loving with Humility

Scripture:
"Do nothing from selfish ambition or conceit, but in humility count others more significant than yourselves." (Philippians 2:3, ESV)

Reflection:
Humility is the foundation of true love. It means putting others before yourself, not because you're less valuable, but because you recognize their worth through God's eyes.

Jesus is the ultimate example of humble love. He left the glory of heaven to serve and sacrifice for humanity. Loving with humility doesn't come naturally—it requires intentionality and a heart surrendered to God.

Today, look for ways to prioritize someone else's needs over your own. In doing so, you reflect the heart of Christ.

Affirmation:
I love with humility, putting others first and reflecting the heart of Jesus in all I do.

Action Step:
Find one way to serve someone selflessly today, whether it's through encouragement, a kind gesture, or meeting a specific need.

Prayer:
Jesus, thank You for showing me what humble love looks like. Help me to put others before myself and reflect Your love through my actions. Amen.

February 13th, 2025: A Covenant of Love

Scripture:
"*Know therefore that the Lord your God is God, the faithful God who keeps covenant and steadfast love with those who love Him and keep His commandments, to a thousand generations.*" (Deuteronomy 7:9, ESV)

Reflection:
God's love is more than an emotion—it's a covenant. A covenant is an unbreakable promise, and God's steadfast love extends to all who love Him. His faithfulness isn't dependent on your performance; it's rooted in His nature.

When life feels uncertain, you can anchor yourself in this truth: God's covenant love never fails. He is faithful to every promise, and His love extends not only to you but to generations to come.

Today, rest in the assurance of His covenant. His love is unshakable and eternal.

Affirmation:
God's covenant love is faithful and steadfast. I am secure in His promises.

Action Step:
Take time to reflect on God's faithfulness in your life. Write down one way He has kept His promises to you, and thank Him for His unchanging love.

Prayer:
Lord, thank You for Your covenant of love that never fails. Help me to trust in Your faithfulness and walk in obedience to Your Word. Amen.

February 14th, 2025: God's Love Letter

Scripture:
"For God so loved the world, that He gave His only Son, that whoever believes in Him should not perish but have eternal life." (John 3:16, ESV)

Reflection:
John 3:16 is more than a verse—it's God's love letter to the world. In just a few words, it captures the depth of His love and the lengths He went to redeem you.

God's love isn't passive. It's active, sacrificial, and personal. He didn't just say He loves you—He proved it by giving His Son to die in your place. This act of love opened the door to eternal life, an invitation extended to anyone who believes.

Today, let this verse remind you of the immeasurable love God has for you. It's a love that changes everything.

Affirmation:
I am loved by God, who gave His Son for me. His love gives me life and purpose.

Action Step:
Share John 3:16 with someone today, whether in conversation, a text, or on social media. Let it be a reminder of God's love for them.

Prayer:
Father, thank You for loving me so much that You gave Your Son for me. Help me to share Your love with others today. Amen.

February 15th 2025: Love Covers a Multitude of Sins

Scripture:
"Above all, keep loving one another earnestly, since love covers a multitude of sins." (1 Peter 4:8, ESV)

Reflection:
Love doesn't deny or ignore sin, but it covers it with grace and forgiveness. When we love one another earnestly, we reflect God's own love—a love that forgives freely and chooses reconciliation over resentment.

Think about the people in your life who may have wronged you. Instead of letting bitterness take root, choose to cover those offenses with love. This doesn't mean excusing harmful behavior, but it does mean extending the same grace that God has shown you.

Earnest love has the power to heal wounds and restore relationships. Today, let love be your first response.

Affirmation:
I choose to love earnestly, covering offenses with grace and reflecting God's forgiveness.

Action Step:
Think of someone who has hurt you. Pray for them and ask God to help you respond with love and grace.

Prayer:
Lord, thank You for covering my sins with Your love. Help me to extend that same grace to others and to love earnestly in all situations. Amen.

February 16th, 2025: Bearing Each Other's Burdens

Scripture:
"*Bear one another's burdens, and so fulfill the law of Christ.*" (Galatians 6:2, ESV)

Reflection:
Love isn't just about words; it's about action. One of the most powerful ways to love others is by helping carry their burdens —whether emotional, physical, or spiritual.

When you come alongside someone in their struggles, you reflect the heart of Christ. He carried the ultimate burden—our sin—on the cross. In the same way, when we share in each other's trials, we become tangible reminders of God's love and faithfulness.

Today, look for someone who could use your support. A listening ear, a helping hand, or a prayer offered in faith can make a world of difference.

Affirmation:
I reflect Christ's love by bearing the burdens of others. His strength flows through me to bless those in need.

Action Step:
Identify one person in your life who is carrying a heavy burden. Reach out to them today and offer specific support, whether through prayer, encouragement, or practical help.

Prayer:
Lord, thank You for carrying my burdens. Help me to love others by sharing in their struggles and pointing them to You. Amen.

February 17th, 2025: Speak the Truth in Love

Scripture:
"Rather, speaking the truth in love, we are to grow up in every way into Him who is the head, into Christ." (Ephesians 4:15, ESV)

Reflection:
Truth without love can wound, and love without truth can mislead. But when truth is spoken in love, it becomes a tool for growth and transformation.

God calls us to be honest with one another, but that honesty should always be rooted in kindness and a desire to build up, not tear down. Loving someone enough to speak truth requires courage, but it also requires wisdom and grace.

Today, let your words reflect both truth and love, pointing others closer to Christ.

Affirmation:
I speak the truth in love, building others up and reflecting the heart of Christ.

Action Step:
Think of someone who needs encouragement or guidance. Pray for wisdom, then reach out to them with words of truth spoken in love.

Prayer:
Father, thank You for Your truth that sets us free. Help me to speak truth in love, bringing encouragement and growth to those around me. Amen.

February 18th, 2025: Love and Obedience

Scripture:
"*If you love Me, you will keep My commandments.*" (John 14:15, ESV)

Reflection:
Loving God isn't just about feelings or words; it's about action. When you obey His commandments, you show Him that His will matters more than your own.

Obedience isn't always easy. It requires trust and surrender, especially when His commands challenge your comfort zone. But every step of obedience deepens your relationship with Him and aligns your life with His perfect plan.

Today, let your love for God be reflected in your choices. When you walk in obedience, you walk in love.

Affirmation:
I show my love for God through obedience. His commands guide me and bring life to my soul.

Action Step:
Reflect on one area of your life where God is calling you to greater obedience. Take a step of faith today to align your actions with His will.

Prayer:
Lord, I love You, and I want my life to reflect that love. Help me to obey Your Word and trust in Your perfect plan. Amen.

February 19th 2025: A Friend Who Loves at All Times

Scripture:
"A friend loves at all times, and a brother is born for adversity." (Proverbs 17:17, ESV)

Reflection:
True friendship is a gift from God. A friend who loves at all times is someone who sticks with you through every season —celebrating your victories and standing by you in your struggles.

This kind of love reflects the heart of Jesus, the ultimate Friend who never leaves or forsakes us. As you think about your friendships, consider how you can embody this kind of steadfast love. Be the friend who shows up, who listens, and who loves unconditionally.

Today, thank God for the friends in your life and look for ways to be a reflection of His love to them.

Affirmation:
I am a friend who loves at all times. God's love flows through me to strengthen and bless others.

Action Step:
Reach out to a friend today—especially one who might be struggling. Offer words of encouragement or make time to listen to them.

Prayer:
Lord, thank You for the gift of friendship. Help me to be a faithful and loving friend, reflecting Your steadfast love. Amen.

February 20th, 2025: A Love That Sacrifices

Scripture:
"*Greater love has no one than this, that someone lay down his life for his friends.*" (John 15:13, ESV)

Reflection:
True love requires sacrifice. Jesus demonstrated this when He laid down His life for you—a selfless, ultimate act of love that secured your salvation.

While you may not be called to physically lay down your life, you are called to love sacrificially. This might mean giving your time, resources, or comfort to serve others. When you love with this kind of selflessness, you reflect the heart of Christ.

Today, ask God to help you love sacrificially, even when it's inconvenient.

Affirmation:
I love with the heart of Christ, willing to sacrifice for the good of others.

Action Step:
Identify one small sacrifice you can make today to show love to someone else. Whether it's your time, attention, or resources, let it be an offering of love.

Prayer:
Jesus, thank You for laying down Your life for me. Help me to love others with the same selfless heart, putting their needs above my own. Amen.

February 21st, 2025: Love as Christ Loved

Scripture:
"And walk in love, as Christ loved us and gave Himself up for us, a fragrant offering and sacrifice to God." (Ephesians 5:2, ESV)

Reflection:
Jesus didn't just talk about love—He lived it. His love was active, sacrificial, and unconditional. He calls you to walk in that same kind of love, letting it shape your words, actions, and attitude toward others.

Walking in love means imitating Christ. It's choosing grace over judgment, service over selfishness, and forgiveness over resentment. It's a daily decision to reflect His love in everything you do.

Today, let Christ's love inspire the way you walk through your day.

Affirmation:
I walk in love, following the example of Christ and reflecting His heart to the world.

Action Step:
Think of one way you can imitate Christ's love today—whether through kindness, forgiveness, or service—and commit to living it out.

Prayer:
Jesus, thank You for showing me how to love through Your life and sacrifice. Help me to walk in love today, reflecting Your heart in all I do. Amen.

February 22nd, 2025: Loving the Least of These

Scripture:
"Truly I tell you, whatever you did for one of the least of these brothers and sisters of mine, you did for Me." (Matthew 25:40, NIV)

Reflection:
Love is more than grand gestures—it's found in the small, everyday acts of kindness toward those who are often overlooked. When you serve the "least of these," whether it's through a listening ear, a warm meal, or a kind word, you're not just helping them; you're showing love to Jesus Himself.

Sometimes, the people who need love the most are the hardest to see. It could be the lonely coworker, the struggling neighbor, or the stranger in need. God invites you to open your heart and hands to reflect His love in these moments.

Today, ask Him to help you notice and care for the "least of these" in your life.

Affirmation:
I love others with the heart of Christ, serving the overlooked and reflecting His care.

Action Step:
Find one way to serve someone in need today. Whether it's a simple act of kindness or offering your time, let it be an expression of God's love.

Prayer:
Lord, help me to see the people You see—the lonely, the hurting, the overlooked. Give me the heart to love them as You do. Amen.

February 23rd, 2025: Love Is Not Self-Seeking

Scripture:
"*[Love] is not self-seeking, it is not easily angered, it keeps no record of wrongs.*" (1 Corinthians 13:5, NIV)

Reflection:
In a world that often says "put yourself first," God's definition of love flips the script. Real love is not self-seeking —it looks out for the needs of others and lets go of personal agendas.

Selfless love isn't always easy. It requires humility and a willingness to prioritize someone else's well-being. But this is the love Jesus demonstrated: a love that gave without expecting anything in return.

Today, practice putting someone else first. Let your love reflect the selfless heart of Christ.

Affirmation:
I love selflessly, putting others first and reflecting the humility of Christ.

Action Step:
Look for one opportunity today to put someone else's needs before your own. It could be as simple as letting someone go first or offering help without being asked.

Prayer:
Lord, thank You for loving me selflessly. Help me to reflect Your love by serving others with humility and grace. Amen.

February 24th, 2025: A Love That Builds Others Up

Scripture:
"Therefore encourage one another and build one another up, just as you are doing." (1 Thessalonians 5:11, ESV)

Reflection:
Love builds up—it doesn't tear down. Whether through words, actions, or attitudes, your love has the power to encourage others and help them grow closer to God.

Think about the people in your life. How often do you take the time to encourage them? A kind word, a thoughtful act, or a prayer can make a lasting impact. When you intentionally build others up, you reflect the heart of Jesus, who always lifted others with His words and actions.

Today, let your love leave a legacy of encouragement.

Affirmation:
My love encourages and builds others up. I am a reflection of Christ's kindness and care.

Action Step:
Reach out to at least one person today with words of encouragement. Send a message, make a call, or pray for them. Let them know how much they matter.

Prayer:
Lord, thank You for encouraging me daily through Your Word. Help me to build others up and reflect Your love through my actions. Amen.

February 25th, 2025: Love That Never Quits

Scripture:
"*And let us not grow weary of doing good, for in due season we will reap, if we do not give up.*" (Galatians 6:9, ESV)

Reflection:
Love that lasts requires perseverance. There will be times when loving others feels hard, inconvenient, or even unappreciated. But God calls us to keep going, trusting that every seed of love we plant will bear fruit in His time.

Jesus demonstrated a love that never quits. Even when faced with betrayal, rejection, and the cross, His love endured. When you're tempted to give up on loving someone, remember His example.

Today, commit to loving with persistence. The harvest is coming.

Affirmation:
I love with perseverance, trusting that God is working through every act of love.

Action Step:
Think of someone you've been tempted to give up on. Pray for renewed strength and commit to showing them love again today.

Prayer:
Jesus, thank You for loving me with a steadfast love that never quits. Help me to love others with the same perseverance, even when it's difficult. Amen.

February 26th, 2025: Abide in My Love

Scripture:
"*As the Father has loved Me, so have I loved you. Abide in My love.*" (John 15:9, ESV)

Reflection:
To abide means to remain, to dwell, to stay connected. Jesus invites you to abide in His love, not as a fleeting experience but as a daily way of life.

When you stay connected to His love, you're nourished, strengthened, and filled with peace. It's His love that empowers you to love others, even when your own strength runs out. Abiding isn't about striving; it's about resting in the truth of who He is and what He's done for you.

Let today be a day of abiding—staying rooted in His love and letting it flow through you.

Affirmation:
I abide in Christ's love. His love sustains and empowers me every day.

Action Step:
Set aside 10 minutes today to sit quietly in God's presence. Reflect on His love and ask Him to fill you with His peace.

Prayer:
Lord, help me to abide in Your love, staying connected to You in every moment. Thank You for the strength and joy that comes from dwelling in Your presence. Amen.

February 27th, 2025: A Love That Multiplies

Scripture:
"May the Lord make your love increase and overflow for each other and for everyone else." (1 Thessalonians 3:12, NIV)

Reflection:
God's love isn't meant to stay stagnant—it's designed to multiply and overflow. The more you experience His love, the more you can pour it out to others, creating a ripple effect that transforms lives.

When love overflows, it doesn't just bless the people close to you; it reaches strangers, communities, and even generations. This is the kind of love that changes the world, one heart at a time.

Today, ask God to fill you so completely with His love that it overflows to everyone you encounter.

Affirmation:
God's love overflows in me, blessing everyone I encounter.

Action Step:
Look for ways to extend your love beyond your immediate circle. Show kindness to someone new or go the extra mile to serve someone in need.

Prayer:
Lord, thank You for a love that overflows. Help me to share Your love freely and multiply it through my actions today. Amen.

February 28th 2025: Love Beyond Measure

Scripture:
"But because of His great love for us, God, who is rich in mercy, made us alive with Christ even when we were dead in transgressions—it is by grace you have been saved." (Ephesians 2:4-5, NIV)

Reflection:
God's love is truly beyond measure. It's not something you can earn or deserve—it's a gift of grace, poured out lavishly through Jesus Christ. His love reaches into the darkest places, transforms the most broken hearts, and offers new life.

When you fully grasp the depth of His love, it changes everything. It fills you with gratitude, strengthens your faith, and compels you to share it with others.

Let today be a celebration of God's immeasurable love.

Affirmation:
God's love for me is beyond measure. I live in His grace and share His love with the world.

Action Step:
Spend time thanking God for His great love. Share your testimony of His love with someone who needs encouragement.

Prayer:
Father, Your love is more than I can comprehend. Thank You for saving me and giving me new life. Help me to live in gratitude and reflect Your love to the world. Amen.

MARCH: FAITH THAT MOVES MOUNTAINS

Faith is the foundation of the Christian walk. It empowers us to trust God's promises, overcome obstacles, and take bold steps into the unknown. In this month, we'll explore what it means to live by faith, deepen our trust in God, and step confidently into His plans.

Day	Title	Scripture
Mar 1	Faith That Moves Mountains	Matthew 17:20
Mar 2	The Author and Perfecter of Faith	Hebrews 12:2
Mar 3	Faith Comes by Hearing	Romans 10:17
Mar 4	Walking by Faith, Not by Sight	2 Corinthians 5:7
Mar 5	Trusting God in the Unknown	Genesis 12:1-2
Mar 6	Faith Tested, Faith Strengthened	James 1:3
Mar 7	Faith Like a Child	Matthew 18:3
Mar 8	The Reward of Faith	Hebrews 11:6

Mar 9	Standing Firm in Faith	1 Corinthians 16:13
Mar 10	Faith in the Storm	Mark 4:39-40
Mar 11	God is Faithful	Lamentations 3:22-23
Mar 12	Overcoming Doubt	Mark 9:24
Mar 13	Faith to Step Out	Matthew 14:28-29
Mar 14	Faith Without Works is Dead	James 2:17
Mar 15	Faith for the Impossible	Luke 1:37
Mar 16	The Shield of Faith	Ephesians 6:16
Mar 17	Faith in God's Promises	2 Peter 1:4
Mar 18	Faith for Healing	Mark 5:34
Mar 19	Faith That Grows	2 Thessalonians 1:3
Mar 20	Bold Faith in Prayer	Mark 11:24
Mar 21	Faith That Sees the Unseen	Hebrews 11:1
Mar 22	Faithful Through the Fire	Daniel 3:17-18
Mar 23	Faith When You're Waiting	Psalm 27:14
Mar 24	The Joy of Faith	Philippians 1:25
Mar 25	Faith That Stays the Course	Galatians 6:9

Mar 26	A Legacy of Faith	2 Timothy 1:5
Mar 27	Faith That Pleases God	Hebrews 11:6
Mar 28	Faith That Overcomes	1 John 5:4
Mar 29	Faith Anchored in Christ	Colossians 2:6-7
Mar 30	Faith That Restores	Joel 2:25
Mar 31	The Victory of Faith	1 Corinthians 15:57

March 1st, 2025: Faith That Moves Mountains

Scripture:
"Truly I tell you, if you have faith as small as a mustard seed, you can say to this mountain, 'Move from here to there,' and it will move. Nothing will be impossible for you." (Matthew 17:20, NIV)

Reflection:
Have you ever faced a "mountain" in your life? Maybe it's a challenge that feels insurmountable, a prayer that seems unanswered, or a dream that feels out of reach. Jesus reminds us that even the smallest amount of faith has the power to move mountains.

Faith isn't about how big or perfect it is—it's about who your faith is in. The mustard seed is tiny, but it carries the potential for growth. Similarly, your faith, no matter how small, has the power to activate God's promises.

What mountain are you facing today? Speak to it in faith. Trust that God is working behind the scenes, even when you can't see it yet.

Affirmation:
With faith in God, I can overcome any mountain. His power is at work in my life.

Action Step:
Write down one "mountain" you're facing. Spend time in prayer, declaring God's promises over that situation and trusting Him to move.

Prayer:
Lord, thank You for the gift of faith. Help me to trust You with the mountains in my life and believe that nothing is impossible with You. Amen.

March 2nd, 2025: The Author and Perfecter of Faith

Scripture:
"*Fixing our eyes on Jesus, the author and perfecter of faith.*" (Hebrews 12:2, NASB)

Reflection:
Faith begins and grows with Jesus. He is the author who writes faith into your story, and He's also the perfecter who strengthens it through every season.

When life gets overwhelming, it's easy to fix your eyes on your problems instead of your Savior. But faith flourishes when you look to Jesus—when you remember who He is, what He's done, and the victory He's already secured for you.

Let today be a day of refocusing. Shift your gaze from the chaos of life to the One who holds it all together. He is faithful to perfect the faith He's placed in you.

Affirmation:
Jesus is the author and perfecter of my faith. I keep my eyes fixed on Him.

Action Step:
Spend five minutes meditating on who Jesus is. Write down one way He has strengthened your faith in the past, and thank Him for being faithful.

Prayer:
Jesus, thank You for being the author and perfecter of my faith. Help me to keep my eyes on You and trust You in every season. Amen.

March 3rd, 2025: Faith Comes by Hearing

Scripture:
"*So faith comes from hearing, and hearing through the word of Christ.*" (Romans 10:17, ESV)

Reflection:
Faith isn't something you manufacture—it's something that grows as you hear God's Word. When you fill your heart and mind with Scripture, you're reminded of God's character, promises, and power.

Think about a time when hearing the Word of God strengthened your faith. It could have been a sermon, a verse that spoke to you during devotion, or even a friend's encouragement. God's Word is alive, and it's always working to build your trust in Him.

Today, take time to intentionally hear God's Word. Let it water the seeds of faith in your heart and watch them grow.

Affirmation:
My faith grows as I hear God's Word. His promises strengthen and sustain me.

Action Step:
Listen to a Scripture-based podcast, sermon, or audio Bible today. Write down one promise that resonates with you and meditate on it throughout the day.

Prayer:
Lord, thank You for speaking through Your Word. Let it strengthen my faith and draw me closer to You today. Amen.

March 4th, 2025: Walking by Faith, Not by Sight

Scripture:
"*For we walk by faith, not by sight.*" (2 Corinthians 5:7, ESV)

Reflection:
Faith often calls us to step into the unknown. It's easy to trust God when you can see the path ahead, but true faith requires trusting Him even when the way is unclear.

Walking by faith means relying on God's promises, not your perceptions. It's trusting that His plans are good, even when circumstances seem uncertain. Like Peter stepping out of the boat onto the water, faith invites you to fix your eyes on Jesus and trust that He will carry you.

Today, take one step forward in faith, even if you can't see the full picture. God's hand is steady, and He won't let you fall.

Affirmation:
I walk by faith, trusting in God's promises even when I cannot see the way.

Action Step:
Think of one area in your life where you're struggling to trust God. Surrender it to Him in prayer, and commit to taking one small step of faith today.

Prayer:
Lord, help me to walk by faith and not by sight. Give me the courage to trust You fully, even when the path is unclear. Amen.

March 5th, 2025: Trusting God in the Unknown

Scripture:
"Now the Lord said to Abram, 'Go from your country and your kindred and your father's house to the land that I will show you.'" (Genesis 12:1, ESV)

Reflection:
Imagine leaving everything familiar to follow God into the unknown. That's exactly what Abraham did. He didn't know where he was going, but he trusted the One who was leading him.

Trusting God in the unknown requires surrender. It means letting go of control and believing that God's plans are better than your own. You may not see the full picture, but you can trust the One who holds it.

Today, take comfort in knowing that God sees the end from the beginning. He is faithful to guide you every step of the way.

Affirmation:
I trust God in the unknown, knowing His plans for me are good and His guidance is perfect.

Action Step:
Write down one area where you feel uncertain. Spend time in prayer, asking God to guide you and give you peace as you follow Him.

Prayer:
Lord, thank You for leading me, even when I can't see the full picture. Help me to trust You in the unknown and walk in faith every step of the way. Amen.

March 6th, 2025: Faith Tested, Faith Strengthened

Scripture:
"*For you know that the testing of your faith produces steadfastness.*" (James 1:3, ESV)

Reflection:
Faith doesn't grow in comfort—it grows in the fire. When your faith is tested, it's an opportunity for God to strengthen and refine it.

Think of testing as a workout for your spirit. Just as muscles grow stronger through resistance, your faith becomes more resilient through challenges. Trials aren't meant to break you; they're meant to build you up, preparing you for greater things.

Whatever you're facing today, remember that God is using it to produce steadfastness in you. Trust that He is working for your good, even in the hardest moments.

Affirmation:
My faith is strengthened through trials. God is working in me to produce steadfastness.

Action Step:
Identify one challenge you're facing. Instead of focusing on the difficulty, ask God to show you how He's using it to strengthen your faith.

Prayer:
Lord, thank You for using every trial to strengthen my faith. Help me to trust You in the process and remain steadfast in Your promises. Amen.

March 7th, 2025: Faith Like a Child

Scripture:
"Truly I tell you, unless you change and become like little children, you will never enter the kingdom of heaven."
(Matthew 18:3, NIV)

Reflection:
Children have a remarkable ability to trust. They believe without overanalyzing, and they approach life with wonder and dependence. That's the kind of faith Jesus calls us to have —a faith that trusts God fully and rests in His care.

Faith like a child isn't naive; it's confident in the goodness of the Father. It's a faith that says, "I don't need to understand everything—I just need to trust that my Father does."

Today, let go of striving and overthinking. Approach God with the simplicity and trust of a child, knowing that He delights in taking care of you.

Affirmation:
I have childlike faith, trusting in my heavenly Father's goodness and care.

Action Step:
Spend time in prayer today, telling God your needs with the honesty and simplicity of a child. Trust that He hears and delights in answering you.

Prayer:
Father, thank You for being so good and faithful. Help me to approach You with the trust and simplicity of a child, resting in Your care. Amen.

March 8th, 2025: The Reward of Faith

Scripture:
"*And without faith it is impossible to please God, because anyone who comes to Him must believe that He exists and that He rewards those who earnestly seek Him.*" (Hebrews 11:6, NIV)

Reflection:
God delights in faith. When you believe in Him and seek Him earnestly, He rewards you—not just with material blessings, but with His presence, peace, and purpose.

Faith is the foundation of your relationship with God. It's what draws you closer to Him and allows you to experience the fullness of His love and power. The reward of faith is not just what God gives you—it's who He is to you.

Today, seek God with all your heart. Trust that He is a rewarder of those who come to Him in faith.

Affirmation:
I seek God with faith, knowing that He rewards those who trust and believe in Him.

Action Step:
Spend time seeking God today. Read a passage of Scripture, journal your thoughts, and ask Him to reveal Himself to you in a fresh way.

Prayer:
Lord, thank You for rewarding those who seek You in faith. Help me to draw closer to You and trust You with my whole heart. Amen.

March 9th, 2025: Standing Firm in Faith

Scripture:
"*Be on your guard; stand firm in the faith; be courageous; be strong*." (1 Corinthians 16:13, NIV)

Reflection:
Faith doesn't waver in the face of adversity—it stands firm. But standing firm requires intentionality. It means staying grounded in God's Word, surrounding yourself with encouragement, and holding onto His promises even when circumstances are hard.

There will be days when your faith is tested, but God gives you the strength to stand. Courage isn't the absence of fear; it's choosing to trust God in spite of it.

Today, plant your feet firmly in faith. Let God's promises be the anchor that keeps you steady.

Affirmation:
I stand firm in my faith, trusting God's promises and walking with courage.

Action Step:
Write down a Scripture that strengthens your faith. Keep it with you and declare it when challenges arise.

Prayer:
Lord, thank You for giving me the strength to stand firm in faith. Help me to be courageous and unwavering, trusting in Your promises. Amen.

March 10th, 2025: Faith in the Storm

Scripture:
"And He awoke and rebuked the wind and said to the sea, 'Peace! Be still!' And the wind ceased, and there was a great calm. He said to them, 'Why are you so afraid? Have you still no faith?'" (Mark 4:39-40, ESV)

Reflection:
Storms in life can feel overwhelming, leaving you anxious and afraid. But Jesus reminds us that no storm is greater than His power. When the disciples panicked in the storm, Jesus spoke peace over the chaos. He can do the same for you.

Faith in the storm doesn't deny the reality of the waves; it rests in the reality of who Jesus is. He is your protector, provider, and peace. The winds may rage, but His presence is your anchor.

Today, trust Jesus to calm the storms in your life. He has the authority to bring peace.

Affirmation:
I have faith in Jesus, who calms the storms of my life and fills me with His peace.

Action Step:
Identify a "storm" in your life. Spend time in prayer, asking Jesus to speak peace over that situation and trusting Him to carry you through.

Prayer:
Jesus, thank You for being my peace in the storm. Help me to trust Your power and rest in Your presence. Amen.

March 11th, 2025: God is Faithful

Scripture:
"*The steadfast love of the Lord never ceases; His mercies never come to an end; they are new every morning; great is Your faithfulness.*" (Lamentations 3:22-23, ESV)

Reflection:
Faith isn't just about your ability to trust—it's about God's ability to be faithful. His love is steadfast, His mercy is endless, and His promises never fail.

When you reflect on His faithfulness in the past, it strengthens your faith for the future. He has carried you before, and He will carry you again. His faithfulness is your firm foundation, no matter what life brings.

Let today be a reminder of God's unchanging faithfulness. He is with you and for you.

Affirmation:
God is faithful to His promises. His love and mercy sustain me every day.

Action Step:
Write down one way God has been faithful to you recently. Keep it as a reminder of His goodness and let it strengthen your faith.

Prayer:
Lord, thank You for Your faithfulness that never fails. Help me to trust You more deeply and rest in Your steadfast love. Amen.

March 12th, 2025: Overcoming Doubt

Scripture:
"Immediately the boy's father exclaimed, 'I do believe; help me overcome my unbelief!'" (Mark 9:24, NIV)

Reflection:
Faith doesn't mean you never experience doubt—it means bringing your doubts to God and asking Him to strengthen your belief. The father in this verse desperately wanted healing for his son, but he struggled with unbelief. Instead of hiding it, he brought it to Jesus, and Jesus responded with compassion and power.

God isn't intimidated by your doubts. He invites you to bring them to Him, trusting that He can turn your uncertainty into unshakable faith.

Today, let your doubts be a bridge to deeper faith as you seek God's help.

Affirmation:
I bring my doubts to God, trusting Him to strengthen my faith and guide me in truth.

Action Step:
Write down one doubt or fear you've been wrestling with. Pray over it, asking God to help you trust Him more deeply.

Prayer:
Lord, I believe—help my unbelief. Thank You for meeting me in my doubts and growing my faith in You. Amen.

March 13th, 2025: Faith to Step Out

Scripture:
"And Peter answered Him, 'Lord, if it is You, command me to come to You on the water.' He said, 'Come.' So Peter got out of the boat and walked on the water." (Matthew 14:28-29, ESV)

Reflection:
Faith often requires stepping out of your comfort zone. Peter experienced the miraculous because he was willing to step out of the boat at Jesus' command.

Stepping out in faith doesn't mean you won't feel fear—it means trusting Jesus enough to move forward despite it. The same Jesus who called Peter is calling you today. He's inviting you to trust Him with your fears and step into the unknown.

What "boat" is God calling you to step out of today?

Affirmation:
I have the faith to step out of my comfort zone, trusting Jesus to guide and sustain me.

Action Step:
Think of one area where you feel God is calling you to step out in faith. Take one small action today to move forward, trusting Him with the outcome.

Prayer:
Jesus, give me the faith to step out of my comfort zone and follow where You lead. Thank You for holding me up every step of the way. Amen.

March 14th, 2025: Faith Without Works is Dead

Scripture:
"So also faith by itself, if it does not have works, is dead."
(James 2:17, ESV)

Reflection:
Faith isn't just what you believe—it's how you live. True faith shows itself through action, whether it's serving others, stepping out in obedience, or trusting God with your decisions.

Think of faith as a seed. If you plant it but never water or nurture it, it won't grow. In the same way, your faith grows and bears fruit when it's accompanied by action.

Today, let your faith move you to action. Show your trust in God through the way you live and love.

Affirmation:
My faith is alive and active, bearing fruit through my words and actions.

Action Step:
Choose one way to act on your faith today—whether it's serving someone, taking a step of obedience, or sharing your testimony.

Prayer:
Lord, help me to live out my faith through action. Let my life be a reflection of Your love and grace. Amen.

March 15th, 2025: Faith for the Impossible

Scripture:
"*For nothing will be impossible with God.*" (Luke 1:37, ESV)

Reflection:
God specializes in the impossible. Whether it's opening doors, bringing healing, or answering prayers in miraculous ways, His power knows no limits.

When you face something that feels impossible, remember this: It's not about what you can do—it's about what God can do through you. Faith invites you to believe in His power, even when the odds seem insurmountable.

Today, ask God for the faith to believe Him for the impossible. Trust that His plans are good, and His power is limitless.

Affirmation:
I believe in God's power to do the impossible. Nothing is too hard for Him.

Action Step:
Write down one "impossible" situation in your life. Pray over it, declaring God's power and promises over that situation.

Prayer:
Lord, thank You for being the God of the impossible. Help me to trust in Your power and believe in Your plans, even when the way seems uncertain. Amen.

March 16th, 2025: The Shield of Faith

Scripture:
"In all circumstances take up the shield of faith, with which you can extinguish all the flaming darts of the evil one." (Ephesians 6:16, ESV)

Reflection:
Faith isn't just something you have—it's something you use. Paul describes faith as a shield, a defense against the attacks of the enemy. Doubt, fear, and lies are the flaming darts the enemy throws, but faith extinguishes them.

When you hold up your shield of faith, you remind yourself of God's promises and His power. You choose to trust in His truth instead of the enemy's lies. No matter how fierce the battle, your faith is your protection.

Today, stand firm behind your shield of faith, knowing that God is fighting for you.

Affirmation:
My faith is my shield. It extinguishes every attack of the enemy and keeps me standing strong in Christ.

Action Step:
Write down one lie or fear the enemy has been attacking you with. Counter it with a Scripture that reflects God's truth, and speak it out loud in faith.

Prayer:
Lord, thank You for giving me the shield of faith. Help me to stand firm, trusting in Your promises and rejecting the lies of the enemy. Amen.

March 17th, 2025: Faith in God's Promises

Scripture:
"He has granted to us His precious and very great promises, so that through them you may become partakers of the divine nature." (2 Peter 1:4, ESV)

Reflection:
God's promises are a foundation for your faith. They're not just words—they're guarantees backed by His unchanging character. When you trust in His promises, you're not hoping for the best—you're standing on a certainty.

But faith in God's promises requires patience. Sometimes, the fulfillment doesn't come immediately. Yet every delay has a purpose, and every promise will come to pass in His perfect timing.

Today, anchor your faith in the promises of God. They are precious, powerful, and unbreakable.

Affirmation:
I trust in God's promises. They are unchanging and will be fulfilled in His perfect timing.

Action Step:
Pick one promise from Scripture that speaks to your current season. Meditate on it, and thank God for the assurance that He will fulfill it.

Prayer:
Father, thank You for Your precious promises. Help me to trust in them fully, even when I can't see the outcome yet. Amen.

March 18th, 2025: Faith for Healing

Scripture:
"And He said to her, 'Daughter, your faith has made you well; go in peace, and be healed of your disease.'" (Mark 5:34, ESV)

Reflection:
The woman with the issue of blood had faith that Jesus could heal her. She didn't wait for Him to notice her—she reached out in faith and touched the hem of His garment. Jesus honored her faith, and she was healed.

Faith for healing doesn't mean ignoring the pain or denying the struggle—it means trusting that God is greater. Whether you're praying for physical, emotional, or spiritual healing, know that God sees you, loves you, and responds to your faith.

Today, reach out to Him, believing that His power and love are more than enough to bring healing.

Affirmation:
I have faith in God's healing power. He sees me, loves me, and restores me.

Action Step:
If you or someone you know needs healing, spend time in prayer today, asking God for His touch and trusting Him with the outcome.

Prayer:
Lord, thank You for being my Healer. I bring my needs to You in faith, trusting in Your power to restore and make whole. Amen.

<u>March 19th, 2025: Faith That Grows</u>

Scripture:
"*We ought always to give thanks to God for you, brothers, as is right, because your faith is growing abundantly.*" (2 Thessalonians 1:3, ESV)

Reflection:
Faith isn't static—it's meant to grow. Just as a seed grows into a tree through care and nurturing, your faith grows through time in God's Word, prayer, and trusting Him in every season.

Growth often happens in the challenges. When you step out in faith or trust God in a trial, you're stretching your spiritual muscles. The more you rely on Him, the stronger your faith becomes.

Today, thank God for how far He's brought you and ask Him to help your faith grow even more.

Affirmation:
My faith is growing abundantly as I trust God in every season.

Action Step:
Reflect on one way your faith has grown recently. Write it down and thank God for His work in your life.

Prayer:
Lord, thank You for growing my faith. Help me to trust You more deeply and rely on Your strength in every situation. Amen.

March 20th, 2025: Bold Faith in Prayer

Scripture:
"Therefore I tell you, whatever you ask in prayer, believe that you have received it, and it will be yours." (Mark 11:24, ESV)

Reflection:
Prayer isn't just a ritual—it's a bold act of faith. When you pray, you're not just speaking into the air; you're communicating with the Creator of the universe, who invites you to bring your needs to Him.

Bold faith in prayer means trusting that God hears you and answers according to His will. It's not about manipulating outcomes—it's about aligning your heart with His and believing that He is able to do immeasurably more than you ask or imagine.

Today, approach God with boldness, knowing that He loves to hear from you.

Affirmation:
I pray with bold faith, trusting that God hears me and answers according to His perfect will.

Action Step:
Bring one specific request to God today. Pray boldly, believing in His power to answer, and trust His perfect timing.

Prayer:
Father, thank You for inviting me to come to You in prayer. Help me to pray with boldness and trust in Your power and wisdom. Amen.

March 21st, 2025: Faith That Sees the Unseen

Scripture:
"Now faith is the assurance of things hoped for, the conviction of things not seen." (Hebrews 11:1, ESV)

Reflection:
Faith gives you eyes to see what the natural eye cannot. It's the assurance that God's promises are true, even when you can't see the evidence yet.

Think of faith as the bridge between hope and reality. It's what keeps you steady while you wait for God to move. Even when circumstances seem unchanged, faith reminds you that God is at work behind the scenes.

Today, let your faith rise above what you can see. Trust in the unseen work of God.

Affirmation:
My faith gives me the confidence to trust in God's unseen plans and promises.

Action Step:
Write down one promise of God that you're waiting to see fulfilled. Speak it out loud, declaring your trust in His unseen work.

Prayer:
Lord, thank You for giving me faith to trust in what I cannot see. Help me to hold onto Your promises and rest in Your perfect timing. Amen.

March 22nd, 2025: Faithful Through the Fire

Scripture:
"If this be so, our God whom we serve is able to deliver us from the burning fiery furnace, and He will deliver us out of your hand, O king. But if not, be it known to you, O king, that we will not serve your gods." (Daniel 3:17-18, ESV)

Reflection:
Faith isn't just believing for deliverance—it's trusting God even when the outcome isn't what you hoped. Shadrach, Meshach, and Abednego had faith that God could save them, but they also trusted Him even if He didn't.

This is the kind of faith that honors God: steadfast, unwavering, and rooted in His sovereignty. When you face your own "fiery furnaces," remember that He is with you in the fire, and His purposes will prevail.

Faith through the fire doesn't always change your circumstances, but it always changes you.

Affirmation:
My faith is steadfast, trusting God to deliver me or sustain me, no matter the outcome.

Action Step:
Identify a challenging situation in your life. Declare your trust in God's faithfulness, regardless of the outcome, and ask Him to strengthen your faith.

Prayer:
Lord, thank You for being with me in every trial. Help me to trust Your plan, even when it's hard to see the outcome. Amen.

March 23rd, 2025: Faith When You're Waiting

Scripture:
"*Wait for the Lord; be strong, and let your heart take courage; wait for the Lord!*" (Psalm 27:14, ESV)

Reflection:
Waiting is one of the hardest parts of faith. It requires patience, trust, and the belief that God's timing is perfect, even when it feels delayed.

In the waiting, God is not inactive. He is working behind the scenes, preparing you and aligning circumstances for His glory. Waiting isn't wasted time—it's growth time.

If you're in a season of waiting, take heart. Be strong and courageous, knowing that God's promises are worth the wait.

Affirmation:
I trust God in the waiting. His timing is perfect, and His plans are for my good.

Action Step:
Write a prayer of surrender, giving your waiting season to God and trusting Him to work in His perfect timing.

Prayer:
Father, thank You for being with me in the waiting. Strengthen my heart and help me to trust in Your timing and purpose. Amen.

March 24th, 2025: The Joy of Faith

Scripture:
"*Knowing this, that I shall abide and continue with you all for your furtherance and joy of faith.*" (Philippians 1:25, KJV)

Reflection:
Faith is not just a struggle; it's a source of joy. When you trust in God, you experience the peace and happiness that comes from knowing He's in control. Faith brings joy because it connects you to the One who holds your future.

Even in trials, you can have joy because your faith reminds you of God's goodness, promises, and eternal love. Joy isn't the absence of hardship—it's the presence of God in the midst of it.

Today, let your faith be a source of joy, lifting your spirit and strengthening your heart.

Affirmation:
My faith fills me with joy, knowing that God is good and His promises are true.

Action Step:
Write down three things you're grateful for that demonstrate God's faithfulness in your life. Let gratitude fill your heart with joy.

Prayer:
Lord, thank You for the joy that comes from trusting You. Help me to find happiness in Your presence, even in difficult moments. Amen.

March 25th, 2025: Faith That Stays the Course

Scripture:
"*And let us not grow weary of doing good, for in due season we will reap, if we do not give up*." (Galatians 6:9, ESV)

Reflection:
Faith is about persistence. When the road gets long and results seem far off, it's tempting to give up. But God calls you to stay the course, trusting that His timing and harvest are worth the wait.

Every act of faith, no matter how small, is a seed sown in His kingdom. Don't let weariness steal your harvest. Trust that God is working, even when you don't see the results yet.

Today, renew your commitment to stay the course in faith. The reward is coming.

Affirmation:
I will not grow weary in doing good. My faith keeps me strong, and my harvest is on the way.

Action Step:
Identify one area where you've been tempted to give up. Commit it to God in prayer and take one small action to keep moving forward in faith.

Prayer:
Lord, thank You for strengthening me when I feel weary. Help me to stay the course and trust that You will bring the harvest in due time. Amen.

March 26th, 2025: A Legacy of Faith

Scripture:
"I am reminded of your sincere faith, a faith that dwelt first in your grandmother Lois and your mother Eunice and now, I am sure, dwells in you as well." (2 Timothy 1:5, ESV)

Reflection:
Faith isn't just for you—it's a legacy you pass on to others. Timothy's faith was influenced by his grandmother and mother, who modeled trust in God. Your faith has the power to impact the next generation, shaping their understanding of God's love and faithfulness.

Think about the people in your life who are watching your faith. Whether it's your children, friends, or community, your trust in God can inspire them to trust Him too.

Today, ask God to help you leave a legacy of faith that lasts for generations.

Affirmation:
My faith leaves a lasting impact, pointing others to God's love and faithfulness.

Action Step:
Take a moment to pray for someone who looks up to you. Ask God to use your faith to inspire and encourage them.

Prayer:
Lord, thank You for the faith You've placed in me. Help me to live in a way that leaves a legacy of trust and love for You. Amen.

March 27th, 2025: Faith That Overcomes

Scripture:
"*For everyone born of God overcomes the world. This is the victory that has overcome the world—our faith.*" (1 John 5:4, NIV)

Reflection:
Faith is your victory. Through Christ, you have the power to overcome every challenge, fear, and temptation the world throws your way.

Your faith isn't rooted in your own strength—it's rooted in God's power and promises. When you stand firm in Him, nothing can defeat you. Victory doesn't mean life will be easy; it means you will endure and triumph because God is with you.

Today, walk in the confidence that your faith makes you an overcomer.

Affirmation:
My faith gives me victory over the world. Through Christ, I am an overcomer.

Action Step:
Think of a challenge you're currently facing. Declare your victory in Christ over that situation, and thank Him for His strength.

Prayer:
Lord, thank You for the victory that comes through faith in You. Help me to overcome every challenge and stand strong in Your promises. Amen.

March 28th, 2025: Faith Anchored in Christ

Scripture:
"*Therefore, as you received Christ Jesus the Lord, so walk in Him, rooted and built up in Him and established in the faith.*" (Colossians 2:6-7, ESV)

Reflection:
Faith needs an anchor, and that anchor is Jesus Christ. When your faith is rooted in Him, it's steady, unshakable, and secure, no matter what storms come your way.

Walking in faith means living daily in the truth of who Jesus is and what He's done for you. It's about letting His love, grace, and power shape every step you take.

Today, make Christ your foundation and let your faith grow deeper in Him.

Affirmation:
My faith is rooted in Christ. He is my anchor, my foundation, and my strength.

Action Step:
Spend time reflecting on what it means to walk in Christ daily. Write down one area where you want your faith to grow deeper in Him.

Prayer:
Jesus, thank You for being my anchor and foundation. Help me to walk in You every day, growing deeper in faith and trust. Amen.

APRIL: RESURRECTION POWER

April centers on the resurrection of Jesus and the transformative power it brings to our lives. Each day focuses on new life, hope, and victory—living in the reality of Christ's triumph over sin and death.

Day	Title	Scripture
Apr 1	The Power of the Resurrection	Philippians 3:10
Apr 2	Made Alive in Christ	Ephesians 2:4-5
Apr 3	Victory Over Death	1 Corinthians 15:55-57
Apr 4	A New Creation	2 Corinthians 5:17
Apr 5	The Empty Tomb	Luke 24:5-6
Apr 6	Abundant Life in Christ	John 10:10
Apr 7	The Stone Was Rolled Away	Mark 16:4
Apr 8	Christ's Love Compels Us	2 Corinthians 5:14-15
Apr 9	Alive in the Spirit	Romans 8:11
Apr 10	The Hope of Glory	Colossians 1:27
Apr 11	Raised with Christ	Colossians 3:1-2

Apr 12	Living in Freedom	Galatians 5:1
Apr 13	The Same Power Lives in You	Ephesians 1:19-20
Apr 14	Living Stones	1 Peter 2:5
Apr 15	Strength in Weakness	2 Corinthians 12:9-10
Apr 16	Clothed with Power	Luke 24:49
Apr 17	Overcoming Through Christ	Romans 8:37
Apr 18	Dead to Sin, Alive to God	Romans 6:11
Apr 19	A Living Hope	1 Peter 1:3
Apr 20	Restored and Redeemed	Joel 2:25-26
Apr 21	The Risen Christ	Matthew 28:6
Apr 22	No Condemnation in Christ	Romans 8:1
Apr 23	Resurrected Dreams	Ezekiel 37:5
Apr 24	The Light of the World	Matthew 5:14-16
Apr 25	The Joy of Salvation	Psalm 51:12
Apr 26	Living in the Power of Grace	Titus 2:11-12
Apr 27	The Kingdom is Advancing	Matthew 11:12

Apr 28	From Glory to Glory	2 Corinthians 3:18
Apr 29	The Name Above Every Name	Philippians 2:9-10
Apr 30	The Victory is Won	Revelation 1:18

April 1st, 2025: The Power of the Resurrection

Scripture:
"*I want to know Christ—yes, to know the power of His resurrection and participation in His sufferings.*" (Philippians 3:10, NIV)

Reflection:
The resurrection of Jesus isn't just a historical event—it's the very power that transforms your life. This power defeated death, conquered sin, and brought hope to the hopeless. And it's the same power that's at work in you today.

To know Christ and the power of His resurrection means embracing both victory and surrender. It's letting go of old ways and stepping into new life. This resurrection power gives you strength for today, hope for tomorrow, and victory over every obstacle.

What area of your life needs resurrection power today? Surrender it to Jesus and watch Him bring new life.

Affirmation:
The power of Christ's resurrection is alive in me. I walk in victory, hope, and new life.

Action Step:
Reflect on one area where you feel defeated or stuck. Pray, inviting the resurrection power of Christ to bring transformation and renewal.

Prayer:
Lord, thank You for the power of Your resurrection. Help me to live in that power daily, walking in the victory You have secured for me. Amen.

April 2nd, 2025: Made Alive in Christ

Scripture:
"*But because of His great love for us, God, who is rich in mercy, made us alive with Christ even when we were dead in transgressions—it is by grace you have been saved.*" (Ephesians 2:4-5, NIV)

Reflection:
Before Christ, we were spiritually dead—lost in sin and without hope. But because of His great love, God made us alive in Christ. This isn't just about future eternity; it's about a transformed life here and now.

Being alive in Christ means living with purpose, walking in freedom, and experiencing the fullness of His grace. It's leaving behind the old ways of death and stepping boldly into the new life He offers.

Today, thank God for His mercy and let His grace shape how you live.

Affirmation:
I am alive in Christ. His mercy and grace have transformed my life.

Action Step:
Spend time reflecting on what it means to be "alive in Christ." Write down one way you can walk in the new life He's given you today.

Prayer:
Father, thank You for making me alive in Christ. Help me to live each day in the freedom and grace You've given me. Amen.

April 3rd, 2025: Victory Over Death

Scripture:
"Where, O death, is your victory? Where, O death, is your sting?" (1 Corinthians 15:55, NIV)

Reflection:
Through the resurrection, Jesus conquered death once and for all. For believers, death is not the end—it's the doorway to eternal life with Christ. This victory takes away the sting of fear and replaces it with hope.

You can live each day with confidence, knowing that even life's hardest challenges can't separate you from His love. Victory isn't just about eternity; it's about living in the freedom and boldness of Christ's triumph today.

Let the truth of His victory give you courage to face whatever comes.

Affirmation:
Through Christ, I have victory over death. I live in boldness, freedom, and hope.

Action Step:
Write down a fear or challenge you're facing. Declare the victory of Christ over it and pray for His peace to fill your heart.

Prayer:
Jesus, thank You for conquering death and giving me eternal life. Help me to live boldly in the freedom of Your victory. Amen.

April 4th, 2025: A New Creation

Scripture:
"Therefore, if anyone is in Christ, he is a new creation. The old has passed away; behold, the new has come." (2 Corinthians 5:17, ESV)

Reflection:
In Christ, you are not defined by your past. The resurrection power of Jesus makes you a new creation, completely transformed by His grace. The "old you"—the sin, the shame, the mistakes—is gone. God is doing a new thing in your life.

Sometimes, it's easy to feel stuck in old patterns or defined by past failures. But Jesus invites you to see yourself through His eyes: redeemed, renewed, and restored. Embrace the new life He has given you, and live in the freedom of His grace.

Affirmation:
I am a new creation in Christ. My past is redeemed, and my future is filled with hope.

Action Step:
Write down one "old" mindset, habit, or fear that you want to leave behind. Surrender it to God and step into the new identity He's given you.

Prayer:
Father, thank You for making me a new creation in Christ. Help me to walk in the freedom of my new life and leave the past behind. Amen.

April 5th, 2025: The Empty Tomb

Scripture:
"Why do you look for the living among the dead? He is not here; He has risen!" (Luke 24:5-6, NIV)

Reflection:
The empty tomb is the ultimate symbol of hope. It reminds us that Jesus defeated death, and because of Him, we can walk in victory. The resurrection is proof that nothing—not sin, not death, not despair—is beyond God's power to overcome.

Yet how often do we look for life in dead places? Whether it's old habits, toxic relationships, or worldly distractions, these "dead things" can't bring the life we're seeking. The empty tomb invites us to turn our focus to the living Savior and find our hope in Him.

Affirmation:
Jesus is alive, and His resurrection gives me hope and victory.

Action Step:
Reflect on an area in your life where you've been seeking fulfillment in "dead places." Ask God to help you turn your focus to Him and experience His life-giving power.

Prayer:
Lord, thank You for the hope of the empty tomb. Help me to leave behind what's dead and find life and purpose in You. Amen.

April 6th, 2025: Abundant Life in Christ

Scripture:
"*I have come that they may have life, and have it to the full.*" (John 10:10, NIV)

Reflection:
Jesus didn't just come to give you eternal life—He came to give you abundant life here and now. This doesn't mean life will be without challenges, but it does mean you can live with purpose, joy, and peace, no matter what comes your way.

Abundant life is about living in the fullness of God's love, grace, and power. It's about trusting Him to meet your needs, fill your heart, and guide your steps.

Today, ask yourself: Am I living the abundant life Jesus promised? If not, what's holding you back?

Affirmation:
I live the abundant life Jesus promised, filled with His love, peace, and purpose.

Action Step:
Write down one way you can embrace the abundant life Jesus offers today. It could be choosing joy, stepping out in faith, or resting in His peace.

Prayer:
Jesus, thank You for offering me life to the full. Help me to live in the abundance of Your love and grace today. Amen.

April 7th, 2025: The Stone Was Rolled Away

Scripture:
"But when they looked up, they saw that the stone, which was very large, had been rolled away." (Mark 16:4, NIV)

Reflection:
The stone was a physical barrier, sealing the tomb and symbolizing the finality of death. But when the women arrived, they found it rolled away, revealing the empty tomb and the victory of Jesus.

Sometimes, we face "stones" in our own lives—obstacles that feel immovable. But just as God rolled away the stone from Jesus' tomb, He can remove the barriers in your life. No obstacle is too large for His power.

Whatever "stone" you're facing today, trust that God is able to roll it away and bring victory into your situation.

Affirmation:
God is removing the barriers in my life. Nothing is too hard for Him.

Action Step:
Identify one "stone" in your life that feels like an obstacle. Pray, asking God to move it, and trust Him to work in His perfect timing.

Prayer:
Father, thank You for rolling away the stones in my life. Help me to trust in Your power to overcome every obstacle. Amen.

April 8th, 2025: Christ's Love Compels Us

Scripture:
"*For Christ's love compels us, because we are convinced that one died for all, and therefore all died.*" (2 Corinthians 5:14, NIV)

Reflection:
The love of Christ isn't passive—it's active, compelling us to live differently. His sacrificial love inspires us to love others selflessly, serve boldly, and live with purpose.

When you reflect on the depth of Jesus' love for you, how can you not share it with others? His love transforms not only your heart but also how you see the world around you. It calls you to action—to love, forgive, and serve as He did.

Today, let Christ's love be the driving force behind everything you do.

Affirmation:
Christ's love compels me to live with purpose, love others selflessly, and reflect His heart.

Action Step:
Think of one person you can show Christ's love to today. It could be through a kind word, an act of service, or forgiveness.

Prayer:
Jesus, thank You for Your love that transforms my heart and compels me to live for You. Help me to reflect Your love to the world around me. Amen.

April 9th, 2025: Alive in the Spirit

Scripture:
"If the Spirit of Him who raised Jesus from the dead dwells in you, He who raised Christ Jesus from the dead will also give life to your mortal bodies through His Spirit who dwells in you." (Romans 8:11, ESV)

Reflection:
The same Spirit that raised Jesus from the dead lives in you. Think about that for a moment—the power that overcame death and the grave is at work in your life.

Being alive in the Spirit means living with the confidence and power of God within you. It's not about striving in your own strength but allowing the Holy Spirit to guide, empower, and transform you daily.

Today, ask the Spirit to renew your strength and fill you with His life-giving power.

Affirmation:
The Spirit of God lives in me, giving me life, strength, and power.

Action Step:
Spend a few moments in quiet prayer, inviting the Holy Spirit to work in your heart and guide you today.

Prayer:
Holy Spirit, thank You for living in me and giving me life. Fill me with Your power and help me to walk in step with You. Amen.

April 10th, 2025: The Hope of Glory

Scripture:
"To them God has chosen to make known among the Gentiles the glorious riches of this mystery, which is Christ in you, the hope of glory." (Colossians 1:27, NIV)

Reflection:
Christ in you is the hope of glory. This profound truth means that Jesus lives within you, bringing hope, purpose, and the promise of eternal glory.

Hope isn't wishful thinking—it's a confident expectation rooted in who Jesus is. When life feels uncertain, this hope anchors your soul and reminds you that God's glory is your future.

Let the hope of Christ in you give you strength and courage today, no matter what you face.

Affirmation:
Christ in me is the hope of glory. I live with confidence and expectation of His promises.

Action Step:
Take a moment to reflect on how the hope of Christ has sustained you in challenging times. Thank Him for being your constant source of strength.

Prayer:
Jesus, thank You for being the hope of glory within me. Help me to live with confidence in Your promises and share that hope with others. Amen.

April 11th, 2025: Raised with Christ

Scripture:
"If then you have been raised with Christ, seek the things that are above, where Christ is, seated at the right hand of God." (Colossians 3:1, ESV)

Reflection:
When you are raised with Christ, your focus shifts from earthly things to heavenly ones. This doesn't mean ignoring the world around you, but it does mean living with eternity in mind.

Being raised with Christ invites you to live differently—seeking His will, loving others, and reflecting His character. Your identity is no longer rooted in this world but in the resurrection power of Jesus.

Today, let your actions reflect the reality of being raised with Christ.

Affirmation:
I have been raised with Christ. My heart and mind are set on things above.

Action Step:
Spend time today reflecting on what it means to live with eternity in mind. Write down one way you can seek "things above" in your daily life.

Prayer:
Lord, thank You for raising me with Christ. Help me to set my heart and mind on things above and live in the power of His resurrection. Amen.

April 12th, 2025: Living in Freedom

Scripture:
"For freedom Christ has set us free; stand firm therefore, and do not submit again to a yoke of slavery." (Galatians 5:1, ESV)

Reflection:
The resurrection of Jesus brings freedom—freedom from sin, shame, and the chains that once held you captive. In Christ, you are no longer a slave to your past or to fear.

But freedom requires stewardship. Paul reminds us to stand firm and resist falling back into old patterns. Living in freedom means daily choosing Christ over the things that once enslaved you.

Today, walk boldly in the freedom Christ has given you.

Affirmation:
I am free in Christ. I stand firm in His grace and live in the freedom He has given me.

Action Step:
Identify one area in your life where you feel stuck or bound. Pray for God's help to walk in freedom and take one practical step toward breaking free.

Prayer:
Jesus, thank You for setting me free. Help me to live boldly in that freedom and resist anything that would pull me back into bondage. Amen.

April 13th, 2025: The Same Power Lives in You

Scripture:
"*...and His incomparably great power for us who believe. That power is the same as the mighty strength He exerted when He raised Christ from the dead.*" (Ephesians 1:19-20, NIV)

Reflection:
The same power that raised Jesus from the dead lives in you. This truth isn't just comforting—it's empowering. It means that no challenge, no temptation, no obstacle is too great for the power of God within you.

God's resurrection power equips you to live boldly, love deeply, and walk victoriously. It reminds you that you are never alone—His Spirit is your strength every step of the way.

Today, ask God to help you live in the reality of His power.

Affirmation:
The same power that raised Jesus from the dead lives in me. I am victorious through Christ.

Action Step:
Think of one area in your life where you need God's power. Pray specifically for strength and guidance in that area, trusting His Spirit to work through you.

Prayer:
Lord, thank You for the resurrection power that lives in me. Help me to walk in victory and rely on Your strength each day. Amen.

April 14th, 2025: Living Stones

Scripture:
"*You also, like living stones, are being built into a spiritual house to be a holy priesthood.*" (1 Peter 2:5, NIV)

Reflection:
Did you know that you're part of something much bigger than yourself? God calls you a "living stone," uniquely designed to be part of the spiritual house He's building. Every prayer you pray, every act of love, and every step of faith becomes part of this masterpiece.

Sometimes, it's easy to feel small or insignificant, but God sees you as essential to His kingdom. He's shaping you, refining you, and fitting you into His grand design.

Today, rest in the knowledge that your life matters deeply to God. You're a vital piece of His work.

Affirmation:
I am a living stone, shaped by God and part of His eternal masterpiece.

Action Step:
Take a moment to thank God for the unique role He's given you in His kingdom. Ask Him to show you how you can build up others as part of His spiritual house.

Prayer:
Lord, thank You for making me a living stone in Your house. Help me to trust Your plan and embrace the unique role You've given me. Amen.

April 15th, 2025: Strength in Weakness

Scripture:
"But He said to me, 'My grace is sufficient for you, for My power is made perfect in weakness.'" (2 Corinthians 12:9, ESV)

Reflection:
We've all been there—feeling like we don't have enough strength to face what's ahead. But God meets us in those moments. His grace doesn't just cover your weakness; it transforms it.

When you feel inadequate, God's power shows up. He doesn't expect you to have it all together—He asks you to lean on Him. Your weakness becomes the stage for His strength.

What part of your life feels heavy right now? Invite God into that space and let His grace sustain you.

Affirmation:
God's grace is enough for me. His strength carries me when I feel weak.

Action Step:
Think of an area where you're feeling stretched or overwhelmed. Pause and pray, asking God to show His strength through your weakness.

Prayer:
Lord, thank You for Your grace that's enough for every moment. I surrender my weakness to You and trust in Your strength today. Amen.

April 16th, 2025: Clothed with Power

Scripture:
"I am going to send you what My Father has promised; but stay in the city until you have been clothed with power from on high." (Luke 24:49, NIV)

Reflection:
Have you ever felt unequipped for what lies ahead? Jesus promised His disciples they wouldn't have to walk in their own strength. The Holy Spirit would come, clothing them with power to live boldly for Him.

That same Spirit is available to you today. He empowers you to love, serve, and face every challenge with courage. You're not on your own—God's Spirit is your strength, your guide, and your helper.

Take a moment to invite Him to clothe you with His power today.

Affirmation:
I am clothed with power from on high. God's Spirit equips me for everything I face.

Action Step:
Before you begin your day, spend a few moments inviting the Holy Spirit to fill and empower you. Ask Him to guide your steps and strengthen your heart.

Prayer:
Holy Spirit, thank You for clothing me with power. Fill me today and help me walk boldly in Your strength. Amen.

April 17th, 2025: Overcoming Through Christ

Scripture:
"*In all these things we are more than conquerors through Him who loved us.*" (Romans 8:37, NIV)

Reflection:
Do you ever feel like life is a constant uphill climb? You're not alone. But here's the truth: In Christ, you're not just surviving—you're overcoming.

Because of His love, you're more than a conqueror. That doesn't mean life will be easy, but it does mean you have the strength to rise above every challenge. Jesus has already won the ultimate victory, and His Spirit lives in you.

Whatever you're facing today, remember this: You're not fighting alone, and the victory is already yours.

Affirmation:
I am more than a conqueror through Christ who loves me. His victory is my victory.

Action Step:
Identify one challenge in your life where you need God's help to overcome. Pray and declare His victory over that situation.

Prayer:
Jesus, thank You for making me more than a conqueror. Help me to trust in Your strength and walk boldly in the victory You've already won. Amen.

April 18th, 2025: Dead to Sin, Alive to God

Scripture:
"*So you also must consider yourselves dead to sin and alive to God in Christ Jesus.*" (Romans 6:11, ESV)

Reflection:
Sometimes, it's easy to feel stuck in old habits or weighed down by guilt. But here's the good news: In Christ, you're no longer a slave to sin. His resurrection means you've been set free to live a new life, alive to God's purpose and grace.

Living alive to God doesn't mean you'll never stumble, but it does mean that sin no longer defines you. Each day is a fresh start to walk in His freedom and power.

What does it mean for you to be alive to God today?

Affirmation:
I am dead to sin and alive to God. His grace empowers me to live in freedom.

Action Step:
Reflect on one area where you've felt stuck. Surrender it to God in prayer, asking Him to help you live in His freedom and grace.

Prayer:
Lord, thank You for making me alive to Your purpose and grace. Help me to leave sin behind and walk in the freedom of new life. Amen.

April 19th, 2025: A Living Hope

Scripture:
"In His great mercy, He has given us new birth into a living hope through the resurrection of Jesus Christ from the dead." (1 Peter 1:3, NIV)

Reflection:
Hope isn't just a feeling—it's alive because Jesus is alive. His resurrection gives you a hope that doesn't fade or falter, no matter what you're facing.

This living hope anchors you through life's storms, reminding you that God's promises are unshakable. It's the assurance that your future is secure, and His plans for you are good.

Today, let this hope fill your heart and give you peace.

Affirmation:
Jesus is my living hope. His resurrection fills me with confidence and peace.

Action Step:
Write down one area of your life where you need hope. Pray, asking God to fill that space with His living hope.

Prayer:
Father, thank You for the living hope I have through Jesus. Help me to trust in Your promises and find peace in Your presence. Amen.

April 20th, 2025: Restored and Redeemed

Scripture:
"*I will restore to you the years that the swarming locust has eaten.*" (Joel 2:25, ESV)

Reflection:
Have you ever felt like you've lost time or opportunities? Maybe you look back on a season of life and wonder if it was wasted. But God is a restorer. He takes what seems broken or lost and turns it into something beautiful.

His promise to restore isn't just about returning what was taken—it's about redeeming it, making it better than before. Whether it's relationships, dreams, or time, God can renew and redeem in ways you never imagined.

Today, trust Him to restore the areas of your life that feel empty or broken.

Affirmation:
God is restoring what's been lost in my life. His redemption brings beauty and hope.

Action Step:
Identify one area of your life where you need restoration. Pray, asking God to redeem that situation and trusting in His timing.

Prayer:
Father, thank You for being a God of restoration. I surrender my losses to You, trusting You to redeem and restore them for Your glory. Amen.

<u>**April 21st, 2025: The Risen Christ**</u>

Scripture:
"*He is not here; He has risen, just as He said.*" (Matthew 28:6, NIV)

Reflection:
The resurrection of Jesus changed everything. It proved His power over sin and death and opened the door for you to live in victory. When the women found the empty tomb, they were reminded of Jesus' promise: "just as He said."

Jesus always keeps His word. If He promised resurrection and delivered, you can trust every other promise He's made. Whatever you're walking through today, let the risen Christ remind you that He's faithful, powerful, and with you always.

Affirmation:
Jesus is alive, and His promises never fail. I live in the power of His resurrection.

Action Step:
Spend time today thanking Jesus for His resurrection and reflecting on what it means for your life.

Prayer:
Jesus, thank You for rising from the grave and giving me eternal life. Help me to trust in Your promises and live in the power of Your resurrection. Amen.

April 22nd, 2025: No Condemnation in Christ

Scripture:
"*There is therefore now no condemnation for those who are in Christ Jesus.*" (Romans 8:1, ESV)

Reflection:
Guilt and shame can weigh you down, making you feel like you're not enough. But the resurrection of Jesus declares this truth: you are no longer condemned. In Christ, you are forgiven, loved, and set free.

Living in this freedom means letting go of the past and walking boldly in God's grace. When guilt tries to creep in, remind yourself that Jesus has already paid the price for your sins.

You are fully accepted by God—no condemnation, no shame.

Affirmation:
There is no condemnation for me in Christ. I am forgiven, loved, and free.

Action Step:
Take a moment to release any lingering guilt or shame to God in prayer. Walk forward today in the freedom of His grace.

Prayer:
Lord, thank You for freeing me from condemnation through Christ. Help me to live in the freedom of Your grace and leave the past behind. Amen.

April 23rd, 2025: Resurrected Dreams

Scripture:
"This is what the Sovereign Lord says to these bones: 'I will make breath enter you, and you will come to life.'" (Ezekiel 37:5, NIV)

Reflection:
Have you ever felt like a dream God placed in your heart has died? Maybe time, disappointment, or fear caused you to let it go. But just as God brought life to dry bones, He can resurrect the dreams He's given you.

God's timing is perfect, and His power is limitless. When He breathes new life into your dreams, it's always for His glory and your good.

If there's a dream you've let go of, bring it back to Him in prayer. Trust that He can bring it back to life in His way and time.

Affirmation:
God is breathing new life into my dreams. His plans for me are good and full of purpose.

Action Step:
Think of a dream or calling you've set aside. Pray, asking God to renew your vision and give you wisdom for the next step.

Prayer:
Lord, thank You for being the God of resurrection. Breathe new life into my dreams and help me trust in Your perfect timing. Amen.

April 24th, 2025: The Light of the World

Scripture:
"*You are the light of the world. A town built on a hill cannot be hidden.*" (Matthew 5:14, NIV)

Reflection:
Jesus calls you the light of the world. Just as He brought light into the darkness through His resurrection, you're called to shine His love and truth in a world that desperately needs it.

Being a light doesn't mean you have to be perfect. It means letting God's love shine through your imperfections, pointing others to Him.

Today, think about how you can reflect His light. Even a small act of kindness can make a big impact.

Affirmation:
I am the light of the world, shining God's love and truth wherever I go.

Action Step:
Look for one simple way to reflect God's light today—whether through encouragement, generosity, or kindness.

Prayer:
Jesus, thank You for calling me to be the light of the world. Help me to reflect Your love and truth in everything I do. Amen.

April 25th, 2025: The Joy of Salvation

Scripture:
"*Restore to me the joy of Your salvation and grant me a willing spirit, to sustain me.*" (Psalm 51:12, NIV)

Reflection:
Salvation is the greatest gift you'll ever receive. It's the foundation of your hope, joy, and purpose. But sometimes, life's challenges can overshadow the joy of what Jesus has done for you.

Take a moment today to reflect on the incredible gift of salvation. Let it renew your heart with gratitude and joy. The same God who saved you is walking with you, sustaining you every step of the way.

Affirmation:
The joy of my salvation fills my heart with gratitude and hope.

Action Step:
Spend time thanking God for the gift of salvation. Write down three ways it has transformed your life.

Prayer:
Father, thank You for the joy of salvation. Help me to live with a heart full of gratitude and a spirit that reflects Your love. Amen.

April 26th, 2025: Living in the Power of Grace

Scripture:
"For the grace of God has appeared that offers salvation to all people. It teaches us to say 'No' to ungodliness and worldly passions, and to live self-controlled, upright, and godly lives in this present age." (Titus 2:11-12, NIV)

Reflection:
God's grace is more than forgiveness—it's power. It's the power to live differently, to say no to the things that once held you captive, and to walk in freedom. His grace doesn't just cover your past; it transforms your present and future.

Living in the power of grace means embracing the strength God gives you to live a life that honors Him. It's not about striving—it's about surrendering to His Spirit and letting His grace work in you.

Today, lean into His grace. Let it empower you to live fully for Him.

Affirmation:
God's grace empowers me to live a life that honors Him. I walk in His strength and freedom.

Action Step:
Identify one area where you need God's grace to strengthen you. Ask Him for help and take one step forward in His power today.

Prayer:
Lord, thank You for the power of Your grace. Help me to live in it daily, relying on Your strength to walk in freedom and purpose. Amen.

April 27th, 2025: The Kingdom is Advancing

Scripture:
"*From the days of John the Baptist until now, the kingdom of heaven has been forcefully advancing, and forceful people lay hold of it.*" (Matthew 11:12, NIV)

Reflection:
The resurrection of Jesus marked the unstoppable advance of God's kingdom. It's not a distant hope—it's a present reality, breaking into the world through lives transformed by Christ.

You're invited to be part of this movement. Every prayer you pray, every act of love you show, and every step of faith you take is part of advancing His kingdom. Even in moments that feel small, God is working through you to bring His light and love to the world.

Today, step boldly into your role in His advancing kingdom.

Affirmation:
I am part of God's advancing kingdom. Through Christ, I bring His love and light into the world.

Action Step:
Ask God to show you one way you can advance His kingdom today—whether through prayer, serving someone in need, or sharing your faith.

Prayer:
Father, thank You for inviting me to be part of Your kingdom. Help me to live boldly for You, bringing Your love and truth to the world. Amen.

April 28th, 2025: From Glory to Glory

Scripture:
"*And we all, who with unveiled faces contemplate the Lord's glory, are being transformed into His image with ever-increasing glory, which comes from the Lord, who is the Spirit.*" (2 Corinthians 3:18, NIV)

Reflection:
Your journey with God is a process. He's transforming you, shaping you, and taking you from glory to glory. It's not about perfection; it's about progress—becoming more like Jesus each day.

This transformation happens as you spend time with Him, reflect on His Word, and let His Spirit work in you. Even when it feels slow or messy, trust that He's doing a beautiful work in your life.

Today, celebrate the progress you've made and the God who's bringing you into ever-increasing glory.

Affirmation:
I am being transformed into the image of Christ. God is taking me from glory to glory.

Action Step:
Spend a few moments reflecting on how God has transformed you over the past year. Thank Him for His work in your life and ask Him to continue shaping you.

Prayer:
Lord, thank You for transforming me daily into the image of Christ. Help me to trust Your process and celebrate the progress You're making in my life. Amen.

April 29th, 2025: The Name Above Every Name

Scripture:
"Therefore God exalted Him to the highest place and gave Him the name that is above every name, that at the name of Jesus every knee should bow, in heaven and on earth and under the earth." (Philippians 2:9-10, NIV)

Reflection:
The name of Jesus carries unmatched power. It's the name that silences storms, breaks chains, heals hearts, and defeats darkness. His resurrection exalted Him to the highest place, giving Him authority over all things.

When you pray in His name, you're not just speaking words —you're invoking the power of the risen Savior. Whatever you're facing today, speak the name of Jesus over it. There's no situation too great or too small for Him to handle.

Affirmation:
The name of Jesus is my strength and victory. I trust in His unmatched power and authority.

Action Step:
Take a moment to pray over a specific situation in your life, speaking the name of Jesus with faith and confidence.

Prayer:
Jesus, Your name is above every name. Thank You for the power and authority You bring into my life. Help me to trust in You fully and declare Your victory over every situation. Amen.

<u>**April 30th, 2025: The Victory is Won**</u>

Scripture:
"I am the Living One; I was dead, and now look, I am alive forever and ever! And I hold the keys of death and Hades." (Revelation 1:18, NIV)

Reflection:
Jesus' resurrection isn't just a story—it's the ultimate declaration of victory. He defeated sin, conquered death, and opened the way for eternal life. When He rose from the grave, He secured the victory not just for Himself but for you.

Because He lives, you can face tomorrow. Because He holds the keys of death, you can live without fear. Whatever battles you're facing today, remember: The ultimate victory is already won.

Affirmation:
The victory is mine in Christ. Jesus is alive, and I live in the power of His resurrection.

Action Step:
Reflect on what Christ's victory means for your daily life. Write down one area where you need to live more fully in that victory and commit it to prayer.

Prayer:
Jesus, thank You for Your victory over sin and death. Help me to live boldly in the power of Your resurrection, trusting You in all things. Amen.

MAY: WALKING IN THE SPIRIT

May focuses on living a Spirit-filled life, walking in step with the Holy Spirit, and experiencing His power, guidance, and fruit in daily life. It's about cultivating intimacy with God, growing in character, and stepping into Spirit-empowered living.

Day	Title	Scripture
May 1	Life in the Spirit	Romans 8:2
May 2	The Fruit of the Spirit	Galatians 5:22-23
May 3	Keeping in Step with the Spirit	Galatians 5:25
May 4	Hearing God's Voice	John 10:27
May 5	Spirit of Power, Love, and Self-Control	2 Timothy 1:7
May 6	The Spirit Guides Us	John 16:13
May 7	The Comforter	John 14:16-17
May 8	Filled with the Spirit	Ephesians 5:18

May 9	Quench Not the Spirit	1 Thessalonians 5:19
May 10	Boldness Through the Spirit	Acts 4:31
May 11	Gifts of the Spirit	1 Corinthians 12:4-7
May 12	The Spirit as Our Helper	Romans 8:26
May 13	Walking by Faith and Not by Sight	2 Corinthians 5:7
May 14	The Spirit of Truth	John 14:26
May 15	Freedom in the Spirit	2 Corinthians 3:17
May 16	Strengthened in the Inner Man	Ephesians 3:16
May 17	The Spirit Brings Life	Ezekiel 37:14
May 18	The Spirit and Prayer	Jude 1:20
May 19	Empowered for Witness	Acts 1:8
May 20	Sealed with the Spirit	Ephesians 1:13-14
May 21	Rest in the Spirit	Isaiah 63:14
May 22	The Spirit of Unity	Ephesians 4:3
May 23	The Spirit Produces Righteousness	Romans 14:17
May 24	Led by the Spirit	Romans 8:14

May 25	Overcoming by the Spirit	Zechariah 4:6
May 26	The Spirit of Sonship	Romans 8:15
May 27	Abiding in the Spirit	1 John 2:27
May 28	The Spirit is our Helper	Romans 8:27
May 29	Spirit-Led Transformation	2 Corinthians 3:18
May 30	Thirsting for the Spirit	John 7:37-39
May 31	Living in Spirit-Filled Joy	Romans 15:13

May 1st, 2025: Life in the Spirit

Scripture:
"For the law of the Spirit of life has set you free in Christ Jesus from the law of sin and death." (Romans 8:2, ESV)

Reflection:
Life in the Spirit is a life of freedom. Through Jesus, the Holy Spirit sets you free from the power of sin and death, offering you a life filled with hope, joy, and purpose.

Sometimes, though, it's easy to fall back into old patterns or feel weighed down by guilt. But the Spirit reminds you that you're no longer a slave—you're free. You don't have to live under the weight of what once held you captive.

Today, take a deep breath and remind yourself: You're free in Christ. Walk in that freedom, knowing the Spirit is your constant companion.

Affirmation:
The Spirit of life has set me free. I walk in the freedom and joy of Christ.

Action Step:
Think about one area in your life where you're not living in freedom. Spend time in prayer, asking the Holy Spirit to guide you into the truth of His freedom.

Prayer:
Holy Spirit, thank You for setting me free through Christ. Help me to live in that freedom every day and trust You to guide my steps. Amen.

May 2nd, 2025: The Fruit of the Spirit

Scripture:
"But the fruit of the Spirit is love, joy, peace, forbearance, kindness, goodness, faithfulness, gentleness, and self-control." (Galatians 5:22-23, NIV)

Reflection:
The Holy Spirit produces fruit in your life—not through striving, but through abiding. As you spend time with God and allow the Spirit to work in you, these qualities naturally grow and overflow into your relationships and actions.

It's not about trying harder to be kind or patient—it's about letting the Spirit do the work in you. The fruit is evidence of His presence, shaping you to reflect the character of Christ.

Which fruit of the Spirit do you feel God is growing in you today?

Affirmation:
The Holy Spirit is producing fruit in my life. I am becoming more like Christ every day.

Action Step:
Pick one fruit of the Spirit you'd like to grow in. Pray, asking the Holy Spirit to nurture that fruit in your heart, and look for an opportunity to practice it today.

Prayer:
Holy Spirit, thank You for working in me to produce fruit that reflects Your love and character. Help me to grow in the areas You are nurturing today. Amen.

May 3rd, 2025: Keeping in Step with the Spirit

Scripture:
"*Since we live by the Spirit, let us keep in step with the Spirit.*" (Galatians 5:25, NIV)

Reflection:
Walking with the Spirit is like walking with a close friend. It requires attentiveness, trust, and a willingness to match your steps to His. Sometimes, life's pace can pull you ahead, or distractions might cause you to fall behind. But the Spirit gently calls you back, inviting you to walk in sync with Him.

Keeping in step with the Spirit isn't about perfection—it's about connection. It's about tuning your heart to His voice and letting Him guide you one step at a time.

Today, take a moment to pause and ask: Am I walking in step with the Spirit, or am I rushing ahead or falling behind?

Affirmation:
I walk in step with the Spirit, trusting Him to guide me each day.

Action Step:
Find a quiet moment today to pray, "Holy Spirit, help me align my steps with Yours." Listen for His gentle direction, and let Him lead you.

Prayer:
Holy Spirit, thank You for walking with me. Help me to stay close to You and follow Your leading in every step I take today. Amen.

May 4th, 2025: Hearing God's Voice

Scripture:
"My sheep listen to My voice; I know them, and they follow Me." (John 10:27, NIV)

Reflection:
Hearing God's voice is one of the greatest joys of walking with Him. As His sheep, you're designed to recognize His voice amid the noise of the world.

God speaks through His Word, His Spirit, and sometimes through others or circumstances. The more time you spend with Him, the more you'll recognize the unique way He communicates with you.

Have you been longing to hear from God? Take time to quiet your heart today and listen. He's always speaking, and He delights in guiding you.

Affirmation:
I am God's child, and I hear His voice. He leads me in love and truth.

Action Step:
Spend five minutes in silence today, asking God to speak to your heart. Write down anything that comes to mind, whether a Scripture, thought, or sense of His presence.

Prayer:
Lord, thank You for speaking to me. Help me to quiet my heart, recognize Your voice, and follow where You lead. Amen.

May 5th, 2025: Spirit of Power, Love, and Self-Control

Scripture:
"For God gave us a spirit not of fear but of power and love and self-control." (2 Timothy 1:7, ESV)

Reflection:
Fear can feel paralyzing, but the Spirit of God brings power, love, and self-control to help you move forward with courage. His power strengthens you, His love grounds you, and His self-control steadies you.

When fear whispers lies, the Spirit reminds you of truth: You are empowered by God, loved deeply, and equipped to handle whatever comes your way.

What would your day look like if you walked in this Spirit instead of fear?

Affirmation:
God's Spirit fills me with power, love, and self-control. I walk in courage and peace.

Action Step:
Identify one area where fear has been holding you back. Pray for the Spirit's power to move forward with love and confidence today.

Prayer:
Holy Spirit, thank You for filling me with courage, love, and wisdom. Help me to walk boldly in Your strength and leave fear behind. Amen.

May 6th, 2025: The Spirit Guides Us

Scripture:
"But when He, the Spirit of truth, comes, He will guide you into all the truth." (John 16:13, NIV)

Reflection:
Life can feel uncertain at times, but the Holy Spirit is your guide. He knows the way forward, even when you can't see it. His guidance may not always come as a loud declaration—it might be a gentle nudge, a quiet assurance, or a verse that speaks to your heart.

Trusting the Spirit's guidance requires surrender. It's about letting go of your need to control and allowing Him to lead. When you do, you'll find His way is always better than your own.

Today, invite the Spirit to guide you in your decisions, big or small.

Affirmation:
The Holy Spirit is my guide. I trust Him to lead me into truth and show me the way forward.

Action Step:
Pray over one decision you're facing today, asking the Spirit for wisdom and clarity. Trust His guidance, even if it feels small or subtle.

Prayer:
Holy Spirit, thank You for guiding me into truth. Help me to trust Your leading and follow Your wisdom in every area of my life. Amen.

May 7th, 2025: The Comforter

Scripture:
"And I will ask the Father, and He will give you another Helper, to be with you forever—even the Spirit of truth." (John 14:16-17, ESV)

Reflection:
The Holy Spirit is your Helper, your Comforter, and your constant companion. When life feels overwhelming, He's there to bring peace. When you're unsure what to do, He's there to offer guidance. When you're hurting, He's there to comfort you.

You don't have to carry your burdens alone. The Spirit is with you forever, ready to strengthen and sustain you. Today, let Him be your source of comfort and rest.

Affirmation:
The Holy Spirit is my Helper and Comforter. I find peace and strength in His presence.

Action Step:
Spend time reflecting on one area where you need the Spirit's comfort. Pray and invite Him to fill that space with His peace and reassurance.

Prayer:
Holy Spirit, thank You for being my Comforter and Helper. Fill me with Your peace and remind me that I'm never alone. Amen.

<u>May 8th, 2025: Filled with the Spirit</u>

Scripture:
"*Do not get drunk on wine, which leads to debauchery. Instead, be filled with the Spirit.*" (Ephesians 5:18, NIV)

Reflection:
What does it mean to be filled with the Spirit? It's not a one-time experience—it's a daily surrender to His presence and power. Just as a vessel needs to be refilled with water, your heart needs to be continually filled with the Spirit.

When you're filled with the Spirit, His peace calms you, His wisdom guides you, and His power strengthens you for whatever comes your way. It's an invitation to live fully connected to God.

Today, pause and ask: Am I running on empty, or am I letting the Spirit fill and refresh me?

Affirmation:
I am filled with the Spirit, empowered to live with purpose, peace, and joy.

Action Step:
Set aside a few minutes today to ask the Holy Spirit to fill you afresh. Reflect on areas where you need His presence, and invite Him to work in your heart.

Prayer:
Holy Spirit, I open my heart to You. Fill me afresh with Your presence and empower me to live fully for You today. Amen.

May 9th, 2025: Quench Not the Spirit

Scripture:
"*Do not quench the Spirit.*" (1 Thessalonians 5:19, ESV)

Reflection:
The Holy Spirit speaks and works in your life, but His voice is often gentle. When you ignore His promptings or choose your own way over His, it's like pouring water on a flame.

Quenching the Spirit isn't about big acts of disobedience—it's the small moments where you hesitate to follow His leading. But the good news is that He's always ready to rekindle the fire in your heart.

Today, pay attention to the Spirit's voice. Is there something He's prompting you to do? Don't wait—step out in faith.

Affirmation:
I honor the Holy Spirit in my life. I listen to His voice and follow His leading.

Action Step:
Think back to a recent moment when you felt the Spirit prompting you. Reflect on how you can respond now and commit to taking action today.

Prayer:
Holy Spirit, forgive me for the times I've ignored Your voice. Help me to stay sensitive to Your leading and walk in step with You. Amen.

May 10th, 2025: Boldness Through the Spirit

Scripture:
"*And when they had prayed, the place in which they were gathered together was shaken, and they were all filled with the Holy Spirit and continued to speak the word of God with boldness.*" (Acts 4:31, ESV)

Reflection:
Boldness isn't about personality—it's about the Spirit's power. When the early church faced persecution, they didn't shrink back. Instead, they prayed for boldness, and the Spirit gave them the courage to proclaim the gospel fearlessly.

You might not face the same challenges they did, but the Spirit gives you boldness to live out your faith, share God's love, and stand firm in truth.

Is there an area in your life where you need boldness? Ask the Spirit to strengthen you today.

Affirmation:
The Spirit gives me boldness to live and speak for Christ with courage and love.

Action Step:
Identify one situation where you've felt hesitant to live out your faith. Pray for boldness and take a small step forward in courage today.

Prayer:
Holy Spirit, thank You for giving me boldness. Strengthen me to live and speak with courage and love, trusting in Your power. Amen.

May 11th, 2025: Gifts of the Spirit

Scripture:
"There are different kinds of gifts, but the same Spirit distributes them." (1 Corinthians 12:4, NIV)

Reflection:
The Holy Spirit has uniquely gifted you to serve others and glorify God. Whether it's teaching, encouragement, hospitality, or another gift, your role in the body of Christ is vital.

Sometimes it's easy to compare your gifts to others, but the Spirit has given you exactly what you need to fulfill your calling. Your gifts are a reflection of His creativity and love.

Today, ask God to help you use your gifts for His kingdom.

Affirmation:
The Holy Spirit has gifted me uniquely to serve others and glorify God.

Action Step:
Take a moment to reflect on your gifts. How are you currently using them? Ask God to show you one new way to use your gifts this week.

Prayer:
Holy Spirit, thank You for the gifts You've placed in my life. Help me to use them faithfully to serve others and bring glory to You. Amen.

May 12th, 2025: The Spirit as Our Helper

Scripture:
"*The Spirit helps us in our weakness. We do not know what we ought to pray for, but the Spirit Himself intercedes for us through wordless groans.*" (Romans 8:26, NIV)

Reflection:
Have you ever felt so overwhelmed that you didn't even know how to pray? In those moments, the Spirit is there to help. He takes your unspoken thoughts and deepest struggles and brings them before the Father.

You don't have to have the perfect words. The Spirit knows your heart, and He intercedes on your behalf with compassion and power.

Whatever you're facing today, rest in the knowledge that the Spirit is your Helper. You're not alone.

Affirmation:
The Holy Spirit helps me in my weakness. He intercedes for me with love and power.

Action Step:
If you're feeling unsure how to pray, simply sit in God's presence. Let the Spirit lead your heart and trust Him to carry your needs to the Father.

Prayer:
Holy Spirit, thank You for being my Helper. When I don't know how to pray, I trust You to intercede for me and guide my heart. Amen.

May 13th, 2025: Walking by Faith and Not by Sight

Scripture:
"*For we walk by faith, not by sight.*" (2 Corinthians 5:7, ESV)

Reflection:
Walking by faith means trusting God even when you can't see the whole picture. The Spirit helps you take steps of faith, reminding you that God's promises are sure, even when your circumstances feel uncertain.

Faith isn't about having all the answers—it's about trusting the One who does. The Spirit gives you the courage to move forward, one step at a time, even when the path feels unclear.

Today, let the Spirit guide you as you take steps of faith, trusting that God is with you.

Affirmation:
I walk by faith and not by sight. The Spirit leads me with confidence and peace.

Action Step:
Reflect on one area where you've been hesitant to step out in faith. Ask the Spirit to give you courage, and take a small step forward today.

Prayer:
Holy Spirit, thank You for leading me in faith. Help me to trust You even when I can't see the whole picture. Guide my steps and strengthen my heart. Amen.

May 14th, 2025: The Spirit of Truth

Scripture:
"*But the Advocate, the Holy Spirit, whom the Father will send in My name, will teach you all things and will remind you of everything I have said to you.*" (John 14:26, NIV)

Reflection:
The Holy Spirit is your personal teacher, guiding you into truth. He not only reveals the truth of God's Word but also helps you apply it to your daily life. When doubts arise or the world's voices grow loud, the Spirit reminds you of what Jesus has said.

He's not just a guide—He's an Advocate, standing with you and for you. You don't have to navigate life's questions alone; the Spirit is always ready to lead you into clarity and peace.

Today, ask the Spirit to teach you something new and remind you of the truths you need to hold onto.

Affirmation:
The Holy Spirit teaches me and reminds me of God's truth. I am never without His guidance.

Action Step:
Spend time reading a passage of Scripture, and ask the Spirit to help you understand it in a fresh way. Listen for how it applies to your life today.

Prayer:
Holy Spirit, thank You for being my Advocate and teacher. Guide me into truth and remind me of what Jesus has spoken. Amen.

May 15th, 2025: Freedom in the Spirit

Scripture:
"Now the Lord is the Spirit, and where the Spirit of the Lord is, there is freedom." (2 Corinthians 3:17, NIV)

Reflection:
True freedom comes from living in the Spirit. It's not about doing whatever you want—it's about being free from the chains of sin, fear, and condemnation. The Spirit gives you the ability to live in joy, peace, and purpose.

Where the Spirit is, freedom flourishes. You no longer have to carry the weight of trying to earn God's love or prove your worth. You're already fully accepted and deeply loved.

Let the Spirit's freedom fill your heart today, releasing you from anything that feels heavy or binding.

Affirmation:
Where the Spirit is, there is freedom. I live in the joy and peace of His presence.

Action Step:
Think of one area where you feel weighed down or bound. Surrender it to God, and ask the Spirit to help you walk in freedom.

Prayer:
Holy Spirit, thank You for bringing freedom into my life. Help me to trust in Your love and live fully in the peace You provide. Amen.

May 16th, 2025: Strengthened in the Inner Man

Scripture:
"*I pray that out of His glorious riches He may strengthen you with power through His Spirit in your inner being.*" (Ephesians 3:16, NIV)

Reflection:
Life can sometimes leave you feeling drained, but the Holy Spirit renews and strengthens you from the inside out. His power isn't just for outward achievements—it's for the core of who you are, giving you endurance, peace, and resilience.

When you feel weary, remember this: The Spirit's power is greater than anything you face. He fills you with the strength to persevere and the confidence to stand firm.

Today, invite the Spirit to refresh and strengthen your inner being.

Affirmation:
I am strengthened by the Spirit in my inner being. His power sustains me every day.

Action Step:
Set aside five minutes to sit quietly and ask the Spirit to fill you with renewed strength. Reflect on His ability to carry you through every challenge.

Prayer:
Holy Spirit, thank You for strengthening me from the inside out. Fill me with Your power and peace today. Amen.

May 17th, 2025: The Spirit Brings Life

Scripture:
"*I will put My Spirit in you and you will live, and I will settle you in your own land. Then you will know that I the Lord have spoken, and I have done it, declares the Lord.*" (Ezekiel 37:14, NIV)

Reflection:
The Spirit doesn't just sustain life—He brings it. When you feel dry, weary, or stuck, the Spirit breathes new life into you, just as He did with the dry bones in Ezekiel's vision.

No situation is too far gone for God. His Spirit can restore what feels lost, renew your heart, and fill you with hope. If there's an area in your life that feels lifeless, invite the Spirit to breathe His life into it today.

Affirmation:
The Spirit brings life and hope into every area of my life. Nothing is too far gone for Him.

Action Step:
Think about an area of your life where you need renewal. Pray and ask the Spirit to bring fresh life and hope into that situation.

Prayer:
Lord, thank You for being the giver of life. Breathe Your Spirit into the areas where I need renewal and fill me with hope. Amen.

May 18th, 2025: Empowered for Witness

Scripture:
"But you will receive power when the Holy Spirit comes on you; and you will be My witnesses in Jerusalem, and in all Judea and Samaria, and to the ends of the earth." (Acts 1:8, NIV)

Reflection:
The Holy Spirit empowers you not just for your own journey but to share the love and truth of Jesus with others. Witnessing isn't about having all the answers—it's about being a vessel for God's love and light.

When the Spirit fills you, He gives you the boldness to share your faith and the wisdom to speak truth with love. You don't have to do it in your own strength—the Spirit equips you for every opportunity.

Today, ask the Spirit to open doors for you to share His love.

Affirmation:
The Spirit empowers me to share God's love and truth with boldness and wisdom.

Action Step:
Pray for one specific opportunity to be a witness today, whether through your words, actions, or encouragement to someone in need.

Prayer:
Holy Spirit, thank You for empowering me to share Your love. Open doors for me to be a witness today and give me the courage to step through them. Amen.

May 19th, 2025: Sealed with the Spirit

Scripture:
"*When you believed, you were marked in Him with a seal, the promised Holy Spirit, who is a deposit guaranteeing our inheritance.*" (Ephesians 1:13-14, NIV)

Reflection:
The Holy Spirit is God's seal on your life—a mark of ownership and a promise of what's to come. You belong to Him, and nothing can change that.

This seal is a daily reminder that you're secure in God's love and His plans for your future. The Spirit is your guarantee of eternal life and a constant companion in your walk with Christ.

When doubts creep in, remember that you're sealed by the Spirit, fully known and fully loved.

Affirmation:
I am sealed with the Spirit, secure in God's love and His promises for my life.

Action Step:
Reflect on what it means to be sealed by the Spirit. Write down one promise of God that gives you confidence in His faithfulness.

Prayer:
Holy Spirit, thank You for sealing me in Christ. Help me to rest in Your promises and walk confidently in Your love. Amen.

May 20th, 2025: Rest in the Spirit

Scripture:
"*Like cattle that go down to the plain, they were given rest by the Spirit of the Lord.*" (Isaiah 63:14, NIV)

Reflection:
Life can feel like a constant race, but the Spirit invites you into rest. His rest isn't just physical—it's a deep, soul-level peace that comes from knowing you're fully loved and cared for.

Resting in the Spirit means letting go of the need to strive and trusting God to carry you. It's an act of surrender, a reminder that He is your shepherd and provider.

Today, let the Spirit lead you beside still waters and renew your soul.

Affirmation:
I find rest in the Spirit. His peace renews my soul and restores my strength.

Action Step:
Take 10 minutes today to pause and rest in God's presence. Let the Spirit refresh your heart and quiet your mind.

Prayer:
Holy Spirit, thank You for offering me true rest. Help me to surrender my burdens to You and find peace in Your presence. Amen.

<u>May 21st, 2025: The Spirit of Unity</u>

Scripture:
"*Make every effort to keep the unity of the Spirit through the bond of peace.*" (Ephesians 4:3, NIV)

Reflection:
The Holy Spirit creates unity among believers, knitting us together as one body in Christ. This unity isn't about agreeing on everything—it's about valuing love, peace, and the shared purpose of glorifying God.

In a divided world, the Spirit empowers you to be a peacemaker. By walking in humility, forgiveness, and grace, you reflect God's heart and strengthen the bond of unity with others.

Today, ask the Spirit to guide you in building bridges of love and peace.

Affirmation:
The Spirit of God unites us. I am a peacemaker, reflecting His love and grace.

Action Step:
Think of one relationship where unity could grow. Pray for wisdom and take a step toward peace, whether through a kind word, reconciliation, or encouragement.

Prayer:
Holy Spirit, thank You for bringing unity through Your love. Help me to live as a peacemaker, strengthening the bond of peace with others. Amen.

May 22nd, 2025: The Spirit Produces Righteousness

Scripture:
"*For the kingdom of God is not a matter of eating and drinking, but of righteousness, peace, and joy in the Holy Spirit.*" (Romans 14:17, NIV)

Reflection:
The Spirit shapes your heart to reflect God's righteousness, not through striving but through surrender. He empowers you to make choices that align with His will, filling your life with peace and joy.

Righteousness isn't about perfection—it's about allowing the Spirit to lead you daily. As you lean on Him, your actions and attitudes begin to mirror Christ more and more.

Today, ask the Spirit to guide your heart toward righteousness, bringing peace and joy in every step.

Affirmation:
The Spirit produces righteousness in my life, bringing peace and joy in every season.

Action Step:
Reflect on one decision you're facing. Ask the Spirit to guide you toward righteousness and trust His leading.

Prayer:
Holy Spirit, thank You for shaping my heart to reflect God's righteousness. Lead me today, and fill me with Your peace and joy. Amen.

May 23rd, 2025: Led by the Spirit

Scripture:
"*For those who are led by the Spirit of God are the children of God.*" (Romans 8:14, NIV)

Reflection:
Being led by the Spirit is a daily invitation to trust God's direction. Like a loving parent, He guides you with wisdom, patience, and care. When you listen for His voice, He leads you along the best paths for your life.

Sometimes His leading feels clear, and other times it requires stepping out in faith. Either way, you can trust that He's with you, working all things for your good.

Today, surrender your plans and let the Spirit lead you step by step.

Affirmation:
I am a child of God, led by His Spirit into wisdom and purpose.

Action Step:
Pray for guidance in a specific area of your life. Pause and listen for the Spirit's leading, trusting Him to show you the way forward.

Prayer:
Holy Spirit, thank You for leading me as Your child. Help me to trust Your guidance and follow wherever You lead. Amen.

May 24th, 2025: Overcoming by the Spirit

Scripture:
"*'Not by might nor by power, but by My Spirit,' says the Lord Almighty.*" (Zechariah 4:6, NIV)

Reflection:
When life feels overwhelming, the Spirit reminds you that victory doesn't come from your strength but from His. He gives you the courage, wisdom, and power to overcome challenges that seem impossible.

By relying on the Spirit, you can face anything with confidence. He's your source of strength, working in ways you might not see but can always trust.

Whatever you're facing today, remember: It's not by might, not by power, but by His Spirit.

Affirmation:
I overcome by the power of the Holy Spirit. His strength carries me through every challenge.

Action Step:
Think about a challenge you're currently facing. Pray, asking the Spirit for strength, and take one practical step forward in faith today.

Prayer:
Holy Spirit, thank You for being my strength in every situation. Help me to rely on You and trust in Your power to overcome. Amen.

May 25th, 2025: The Spirit of Sonship

Scripture:
"The Spirit you received brought about your adoption to sonship. And by Him we cry, 'Abba, Father.'" (Romans 8:15, NIV)

Reflection:
The Spirit confirms your identity as God's beloved child. Through Him, you have direct access to the Father, able to approach Him with confidence, love, and trust.

Calling God "Abba" isn't just a formal acknowledgment—it's an intimate cry of relationship. The Spirit reminds you that you're not a servant or a stranger but a cherished member of God's family.

Let this truth sink into your heart today: You are deeply loved and fully accepted by your heavenly Father.

Affirmation:
I am a child of God, deeply loved and fully accepted by my Father.

Action Step:
Spend a few moments in prayer, calling God "Abba, Father." Thank Him for His love and ask the Spirit to deepen your understanding of your identity in Him.

Prayer:
Holy Spirit, thank You for reminding me of my identity as God's child. Help me to rest in His love and trust Him as my Father. Amen.

May 26th, 2025: Abiding in the Spirit

Scripture:
"As for you, the anointing you received from Him remains in you, and you do not need anyone to teach you. But as His anointing teaches you about all things and as that anointing is real, not counterfeit—just as it has taught you, remain in Him." (1 John 2:27, NIV)

Reflection:
Abiding in the Spirit means staying connected to God's presence, allowing Him to guide and sustain you throughout the day. It's not about doing more—it's about being with Him.

The Spirit's anointing is a constant reminder that you're never alone. He teaches, comforts, and strengthens you as you remain in Him.

Today, focus on abiding in the Spirit. Let Him fill every moment with His peace and power.

Affirmation:
I abide in the Spirit, resting in His presence and walking in His peace.

Action Step:
Pause during your day to reconnect with the Spirit. Take a deep breath, whisper a prayer, and let His presence refresh you.

Prayer:
Holy Spirit, thank You for being with me always. Help me to remain in You and draw strength from Your presence today. Amen.

May 27th, 2025: Spirit-Led Transformation

Scripture:
"*And we all, who with unveiled faces contemplate the Lord's glory, are being transformed into His image with ever-increasing glory, which comes from the Lord, who is the Spirit.*" (2 Corinthians 3:18, NIV)

Reflection:
The Spirit doesn't just help you; He transforms you. Day by day, He's shaping you into the image of Christ, making you more loving, patient, and full of grace.

This transformation isn't instant—it's a journey. Some days you'll see growth, and other days you may feel stuck. But the Spirit is faithful, and He never stops working in you.

Trust His process and celebrate the small steps of transformation in your life.

Affirmation:
The Spirit is transforming me into the image of Christ. I am a work in progress, loved and guided by God.

Action Step:
Reflect on one area of your life where you've seen growth recently. Thank the Spirit for His transforming work and ask Him to continue shaping you.

Prayer:
Holy Spirit, thank You for transforming me into the image of Christ. Help me to trust Your work and celebrate the progress You're making in my life. Amen.

May 28th, 2025: The Spirit as Our Helper

Scripture:
"But the Helper, the Holy Spirit, whom the Father will send in My name, He will teach you all things, and bring to your remembrance all that I said to you." (John 14:26, NASB)

Reflection:
The Holy Spirit is your constant Helper, sent by the Father to guide, teach, and remind you of the truth. He illuminates Scripture, provides wisdom, and equips you to live a life that honors God. No matter what challenges you face, the Spirit is present to empower and comfort you.

As your Helper, the Spirit doesn't simply solve problems—He shapes you into the image of Christ, teaching you to rely on God and trust His timing. In moments of confusion or need, His guidance is always available.

Today, lean on the Spirit as your Helper, trusting Him to teach you, remind you of God's promises, and guide your steps.

Affirmation:
The Holy Spirit is my Helper, teaching me truth and guiding me in every area of my life.

Action Step:
Think of a situation where you need guidance or clarity. Ask the Holy Spirit to help you discern God's will and to remind you of His Word.

Prayer:
Holy Spirit, thank You for being my Helper. Teach me Your truth, guide my steps, and help me to live in a way that honors Christ. Amen.

May 29th, 2025: Spirit-Led Transformation

Scripture:
"*And we all, who with unveiled faces contemplate the Lord's glory, are being transformed into His image with ever-increasing glory, which comes from the Lord, who is the Spirit.*" (2 Corinthians 3:18, NIV)

Reflection:
The Holy Spirit works in you to bring transformation, changing you into the likeness of Christ. This isn't a one-time event but an ongoing process of growth and renewal. As you spend time in God's presence, contemplating His glory, the Spirit removes barriers and reshapes your character to reflect Jesus.

Transformation by the Spirit requires surrender. It's about allowing Him to lead, trusting Him to refine you, and embracing His work in every area of your life. The more you yield to Him, the more His glory shines through you.

Today, invite the Holy Spirit to continue His transformative work in your life, making you more like Christ.

Affirmation:
I am being transformed by the Spirit into the image of Christ, reflecting His glory in my life.

Action Step:
Take time to reflect on an area where you've seen the Spirit's transformation in your life. Thank Him and ask for His continued work.

Prayer:
Holy Spirit, thank You for transforming me into the image of Christ. Help me to surrender fully to Your work and to reflect Your glory in all I do. Amen.

May 30th, 2025: Thirsting for the Spirit

Scripture:
"*On the last and greatest day of the festival, Jesus stood and said in a loud voice, 'Let anyone who is thirsty come to Me and drink. Whoever believes in Me, as Scripture has said, rivers of living water will flow from within them.' By this He meant the Spirit.*" (John 7:37-39, NIV)

Reflection:
Jesus invites all who thirst to come to Him and be filled with the Spirit, the source of living water. This thirst represents a deep longing for God's presence, power, and guidance. When you come to Him in faith, He satisfies your soul and overflows His Spirit into every part of your life.

The living water of the Spirit is not just for you—it flows through you to bless others. As you thirst for more of Him, He fills you to the point of overflow, empowering you to bring His love, joy, and truth to the world.

Today, bring your thirst to Jesus, asking Him to fill you with the living water of the Spirit.

Affirmation:
I thirst for the Spirit, and Jesus fills me with rivers of living water that overflow into every area of my life.

Action Step:
Spend time in prayer, asking Jesus to quench your spiritual thirst. Reflect on ways His Spirit can overflow into the lives of those around you.

Prayer:
Jesus, thank You for the living water of the Spirit. I bring my thirst to You, trusting You to fill me and use me to bless others. Amen.

May 31st, 2025: Living in Spirit-Filled Joy

Scripture:
"*May the God of hope fill you with all joy and peace as you trust in Him, so that you may overflow with hope by the power of the Holy Spirit.*" (Romans 15:13, NIV)

Reflection:
Joy is a hallmark of the Spirit's presence in your life. It's not dependent on circumstances but flows from trusting in God and being filled with His hope. The Holy Spirit empowers you to live in this joy, bringing peace and strength to face every situation.

When you live in Spirit-filled joy, it overflows to those around you, offering encouragement and hope. This joy is a testimony of God's goodness and a reminder that He is always at work, bringing His purposes to pass.

Today, let the Holy Spirit fill you with His joy and peace, trusting in the God of hope.

Affirmation:
I live in Spirit-filled joy, overflowing with hope and peace by the power of the Holy Spirit.

Action Step:
Identify one way you can share the Spirit's joy with someone today—through encouragement, a kind act, or a prayer.

Prayer:
Holy Spirit, thank You for filling me with joy and hope. Help me to live in Your peace and to overflow with encouragement to those around me. Amen.

JUNE: GROWING IN GOD'S WISDOM

June's theme is centered on growing in God's wisdom—understanding His Word, walking in discernment, and making decisions that align with His will. Wisdom isn't just knowledge; it's applying God's truth to daily life. This month invites readers to embrace a lifestyle of seeking God's guidance and growing in their understanding of His ways.

Day	Title	Scripture
June 1	The Beginning of Wisdom	Proverbs 9:10
June 2	Ask for Wisdom	James 1:5
June 3	Wisdom from Above	James 3:17
June 4	Walking in Understanding	Proverbs 4:7
June 5	The Treasure of Wisdom	Colossians 2:3
June 6	The Fear of the Lord	Proverbs 1:7
June 7	Discernment in Every Decision	Philippians 1:9-10
June 8	God's Word Lights the Way	Psalm 119:105

June 9	Wise Counsel	Proverbs 15:22
June 10	A Heart of Wisdom	Psalm 90:12
June 11	Wisdom Through the Spirit	1 Corinthians 2:13
June 12	Wisdom in Trials	Job 28:28
June 13	Wisdom Builds the House	Proverbs 24:3
June 14	The Wise and Foolish Builders	Matthew 7:24-25
June 15	Trusting God's Plan	Proverbs 3:5-6
June 16	Humility Leads to Wisdom	Proverbs 11:2
June 17	Wisdom that Brings Peace	Proverbs 3:17
June 18	Avoiding the Way of Folly	Proverbs 14:12
June 19	The Wisdom of Waiting	Psalm 37:7
June 20	Wisdom and Generosity	Proverbs 11:25
June 21	Guarding Your Heart	Proverbs 4:23
June 22	Wisdom in Words	Proverbs 15:1
June 23	Wisdom for the Next Generation	Deuteronomy 6:6-7
June 24	Living by God's Truth	John 17:17
June 25	The Power of a Listening Ear	Proverbs 19:20

June 26	Wisdom for Daily Living	Psalm 37:30
June 27	Growing in Godly Knowledge	Proverbs 18:15
June 28	Wisdom is a Gift	Ecclesiastes 2:26
June 29	The Source of Wisdom	1 Corinthians 1:30
June 30	Living Out God's Wisdom	Colossians 4:5

June 1st, 2025: The Beginning of Wisdom

Scripture:
"The fear of the Lord is the beginning of wisdom, and knowledge of the Holy One is understanding." (Proverbs 9:10, NIV)

Reflection:
Wisdom begins with a reverent awe of God—recognizing His greatness, His holiness, and His love. When you honor God as the foundation of your life, every other piece begins to fall into place.

This fear isn't about being afraid of God; it's about standing in awe of Him. It's an attitude that says, "God, You are greater than I can imagine, and I trust Your ways above my own."

Today, take a moment to reflect on God's greatness. Let a deep respect for who He is shape the decisions you make.

Affirmation:
Wisdom begins with honoring God. I trust His ways and seek to walk in His truth.

Action Step:
Spend five minutes in worship today, focusing on God's greatness. Thank Him for His wisdom and ask Him to guide your decisions.

Prayer:
Lord, You are the source of all wisdom. Help me to live in awe of who You are and to seek Your guidance in everything I do. Amen.

June 2nd. 2025 : Ask for Wisdom

Scripture:
"If any of you lacks wisdom, you should ask God, who gives generously to all without finding fault, and it will be given to you." (James 1:5, NIV)

Reflection:
When life feels uncertain, God invites you to ask Him for wisdom. He doesn't withhold His guidance or make you feel unworthy for asking. Instead, He gives generously and graciously, equipping you to face any situation.

Asking for wisdom isn't a sign of weakness—it's a declaration of trust. It says, "God, I need You, and I believe Your wisdom is greater than mine."

What decision or situation do you need wisdom for today? Bring it to God, trusting Him to provide clarity and direction.

Affirmation:
God gives me wisdom generously. I trust Him to guide me in every situation.

Action Step:
Write down one area where you need wisdom. Spend time in prayer, specifically asking God for His guidance and listening for His response.

Prayer:
Father, thank You for Your promise to give wisdom generously. I bring my needs to You today, trusting You to lead me with clarity and grace. Amen.

June 3: Wisdom from Above

Scripture:
"But the wisdom that comes from heaven is first of all pure; then peace-loving, considerate, submissive, full of mercy and good fruit, impartial and sincere." (James 3:17, NIV)

Reflection:
Worldly wisdom often prioritizes self-interest, but God's wisdom is pure and selfless. It leads to peace, compassion, and actions that bear good fruit. This heavenly wisdom transforms how you think, speak, and act.

When you seek God's wisdom, it shapes your character to reflect Christ. It helps you navigate difficult conversations with grace, make decisions that promote peace, and show kindness in every interaction.

Today, ask God to fill you with His wisdom, so your life can bear the fruit of His love.

Affirmation:
God's wisdom is pure and peace-loving. I reflect His heart in my words and actions.

Action Step:
Think of a recent situation where you struggled to act wisely. Ask God to help you approach similar moments with His heavenly wisdom.

Prayer:
Lord, thank You for Your wisdom that brings peace and bears good fruit. Help me to live in a way that reflects Your love and grace. Amen.

June 4: Walking in Understanding

Scripture:
"The beginning of wisdom is this: Get wisdom. Though it cost all you have, get understanding." (Proverbs 4:7, NIV)

Reflection:
Wisdom and understanding go hand in hand. Wisdom helps you see what's right, and understanding helps you know why it's right. Together, they guide you in making decisions that honor God and bless others.

True understanding often requires humility and a willingness to learn. It's about seeking God's perspective and being open to His correction. The more you pursue understanding, the more equipped you are to walk in wisdom.

Today, ask God to deepen your understanding of His truth and how it applies to your life.

Affirmation:
I seek wisdom and understanding, trusting God to guide my steps and grow my faith.

Action Step:
Take time to reflect on a current challenge. Ask God for not only the right decision but also the deeper understanding of His purpose in it.

Prayer:
Lord, thank You for offering me wisdom and understanding. Help me to seek Your truth above all else and apply it faithfully in my life. Amen.

June 5: The Treasure of Wisdom

Scripture:
"*In Christ are hidden all the treasures of wisdom and knowledge.*" (Colossians 2:3, NIV)

Reflection:
Christ is the ultimate source of wisdom. Every treasure of knowledge and understanding is found in Him. When you seek wisdom, you're really seeking Him—and in knowing Him, you find everything you need.

Worldly wisdom may offer quick fixes, but true wisdom is eternal and rooted in Christ. He reveals His treasures to those who seek Him wholeheartedly, guiding you to live in alignment with His will.

Today, pursue Christ as the treasure of wisdom. Let Him lead your heart and renew your mind.

Affirmation:
Christ is my source of wisdom. In Him, I find all the treasures of knowledge and truth.

Action Step:
Spend time reading a passage about Jesus today (like John 1:1-18). Reflect on how He embodies wisdom and what that means for your life.

Prayer:
Jesus, You are the treasure of wisdom and knowledge. Help me to seek You above all else and trust in Your perfect understanding. Amen.

June 6: The Fear of the Lord

Scripture:
"The fear of the Lord is the beginning of knowledge, but fools despise wisdom and instruction." (Proverbs 1:7, NIV)

Reflection:
The "fear of the Lord" isn't about being afraid—it's about reverence, awe, and deep respect for who God is. It's the foundation of wisdom because it puts Him in His rightful place as the center of your life.

When you live with the fear of the Lord, you're guided by a desire to honor Him in all you do. It shapes your choices, your words, and your priorities.

Today, let the fear of the Lord draw you closer to His heart and deepen your trust in His ways.

Affirmation:
I honor and revere the Lord. He is the foundation of my life and the source of all wisdom.

Action Step:
Take a moment to reflect on God's greatness. Write down three attributes of God that inspire awe in your heart, and thank Him for who He is.

Prayer:
Lord, You are holy and worthy of all my reverence. Teach me to walk in the fear of You, letting it guide every part of my life. Amen.

June 7th, 2025: Discernment in Every Decision

Scripture:
"And this is my prayer: that your love may abound more and more in knowledge and depth of insight, so that you may be able to discern what is best." (Philippians 1:9-10, NIV)

Reflection:
Life is full of decisions, big and small. Discernment is the ability to see what's truly best—not just what's good or acceptable, but what aligns with God's will.

Discernment grows as your love for God deepens. The more you know Him and trust His Word, the more clearly you'll recognize His leading in your life.

Today, invite the Holy Spirit to sharpen your discernment, helping you make decisions that reflect God's heart.

Affirmation:
God gives me discernment to choose what is best and to walk in His will.

Action Step:
Think about a decision you're currently facing. Spend time in prayer, asking the Holy Spirit for clarity and wisdom to discern what is best.

Prayer:
Holy Spirit, thank You for guiding me with love and wisdom. Help me to discern what is best in every decision I make today. Amen.

June 8th, 2025: God's Word Lights the Way

Scripture:
"*Your word is a lamp to my feet and a light to my path.*" (Psalm 119:105, NIV)

Reflection:
God's Word is your guide, shining light on the path ahead. When life feels uncertain or confusing, Scripture offers clarity, direction, and hope. It illuminates your steps, showing you how to walk in truth and avoid stumbling blocks.

Spending time in God's Word isn't just a good habit—it's a lifeline. It equips you to navigate challenges, make wise decisions, and grow in faith.

Today, let Scripture light your path. Trust its wisdom to lead you in the right direction.

Affirmation:
God's Word is my guide, lighting my path and leading me in truth.

Action Step:
Read Psalm 119:105-112. Reflect on how God's Word has guided you in the past and how it can guide you today.

Prayer:
Lord, thank You for the gift of Your Word. Help me to rely on it as my light and to follow where it leads. Amen.

June 9th, 2025: Wise Counsel

Scripture:
"Plans fail for lack of counsel, but with many advisers, they succeed." (Proverbs 15:22, NIV)

Reflection:
God often uses wise counsel to guide you. Trusted friends, mentors, or spiritual leaders can offer perspective and insight that aligns with His Word. Seeking advice doesn't show weakness—it shows wisdom.

But not all advice is equal. True wisdom comes from those who love God and seek His truth. Surround yourself with people who will point you to Him and encourage you to walk in His ways.

Today, seek out wise counsel for an area where you need guidance.

Affirmation:
I value wise counsel and seek advice from those who love and follow God.

Action Step:
Identify someone you trust who can offer godly wisdom. Reach out to them today to discuss an area where you need guidance.

Prayer:
Lord, thank You for placing wise people in my life. Help me to seek counsel that honors You and guides me in Your truth. Amen.

June 10th, 2025: A Heart of Wisdom

Scripture:
"Teach us to number our days, that we may gain a heart of wisdom." (Psalm 90:12, NIV)

Reflection:
Life is a gift, and every day is an opportunity to grow in wisdom. When you live with an awareness of life's brevity, you focus on what truly matters—loving God, serving others, and pursuing eternal priorities.

A heart of wisdom values each moment, seeking God's purpose in both the ordinary and the extraordinary. It doesn't waste time on distractions but invests in what lasts forever.

Today, ask God to help you live intentionally, treasuring the time He's given you.

Affirmation:
I value the time God has given me. I seek His wisdom to live with purpose and intention.

Action Step:
Take a moment to reflect on your priorities. Write down one way you can better align your time with God's purpose for your life.

Prayer:
Lord, teach me to number my days and to live with a heart of wisdom. Help me to focus on what matters most and to walk in Your purpose. Amen.

June 11th, 2025: Wisdom Through the Spirit

Scripture:
"This is what we speak, not in words taught us by human wisdom but in words taught by the Spirit, explaining spiritual realities with Spirit-taught words." (1 Corinthians 2:13, NIV)

Reflection:
The Holy Spirit is your ultimate teacher. While human wisdom can offer insight, true spiritual understanding comes only through Him. He reveals the mysteries of God's Word and helps you apply His truth to your life.

When you feel uncertain about a decision or confused about Scripture, remember this: The Spirit is always ready to teach you. He speaks through God's Word, whispers to your heart in prayer, and uses everyday experiences to deepen your understanding.

Today, invite the Holy Spirit to teach you something new. Ask Him to open your eyes to spiritual truths you might have missed.

Affirmation:
The Holy Spirit is my teacher, guiding me into wisdom and revealing God's truth to my heart.

Action Step:
Spend a few minutes reflecting on a recent challenge or question. Ask the Holy Spirit to teach you how to see it through God's eyes, and write down what comes to mind.

Prayer:
Holy Spirit, thank You for being my teacher. Open my eyes to spiritual truths and help me to grow in understanding, wisdom, and faith. Amen.

June 12th, 2025: Wisdom in Trials

Scripture:
"And He said to the human race, 'The fear of the Lord—that is wisdom, and to shun evil is understanding.'" (Job 28:28, NIV)

Reflection:
Trials can feel overwhelming, but they also create opportunities to grow in wisdom. Job's journey reminds us that even in suffering, God is present, shaping us and teaching us to trust Him more deeply.

Wisdom in trials comes from fearing the Lord—not in a way that leads to dread, but in reverence and trust in His sovereignty. When you choose to lean on Him, He guides you through the storm and reveals purpose even in pain.

If you're facing a challenge today, remember that God's wisdom is available to you in the midst of it.

Affirmation:
In every trial, God's wisdom guides me. I trust Him to lead me through challenges with purpose and grace.

Action Step:
Think about a current or past trial. Reflect on what God may be teaching you through it. Write down one lesson or truth you've gained from that experience.

Prayer:
Lord, help me to see trials through Your eyes. Give me the wisdom to trust You, even when the way is unclear, and teach me to lean on Your strength. Amen.

June 13th, 2025: Wisdom Builds the House

Scripture:
"*By wisdom a house is built, and through understanding it is established.*" (Proverbs 24:3, NIV)

Reflection:
Wisdom isn't just for decisions—it's the foundation of a life, a family, and a legacy that honors God. Building your "house" with wisdom means establishing your life on His truth, making choices rooted in His guidance, and prioritizing His values.

When you rely on God's wisdom, you create stability and strength that can withstand life's storms. This wisdom influences not only your personal life but also your relationships, your family, and your impact on others.

Today, reflect on what kind of "house" you're building. Let God's wisdom shape its foundation.

Affirmation:
I build my life on God's wisdom, creating a foundation of strength, peace, and purpose.

Action Step:
Think about one area of your life—your family, career, or relationships. Ask God for wisdom to strengthen its foundation and take one intentional step toward that today.

Prayer:
Lord, thank You for being the foundation of my life. Help me to build my life, my relationships, and my legacy with Your wisdom and guidance. Amen.

June 14th, 2025: The Wise and Foolish Builders

Scripture:
"Therefore everyone who hears these words of Mine and puts them into practice is like a wise man who built his house on the rock." (Matthew 7:24, NIV)

Reflection:
It's not enough to hear God's Word—you need to act on it. Jesus' parable of the wise and foolish builders reminds us that wisdom is putting His teachings into practice.

The "rock" isn't just knowing Scripture; it's living by it. When storms come, the foundation you've built through obedience to God will keep you steady. The foolish builder may have known the right thing but chose not to follow through—and his house fell.

Today, ask yourself: Am I building on the rock or the sand? Let obedience to God's Word strengthen your foundation.

Affirmation:
I am a wise builder, living out God's Word and building my life on the solid foundation of His truth.

Action Step:
Reflect on a recent area where you heard God's Word but struggled to act on it. Pray for strength to apply His teachings and take one step of obedience today.

Prayer:
Lord, thank You for being my solid foundation. Help me not just to hear Your Word but to live by it, building my life on Your truth. Amen.

June 15th, 2025: Trusting God's Plan

Scripture:
"Trust in the Lord with all your heart and lean not on your own understanding; in all your ways submit to Him, and He will make your paths straight." (Proverbs 3:5-6, NIV)

Reflection:
Trusting God's plan often requires letting go of your own. It means surrendering control and choosing to believe that His ways are higher, even when they don't make sense.

When you submit your plans to Him, you invite His wisdom to guide you. He doesn't promise an easy path, but He does promise to make it straight—leading you to the purpose He's prepared for you.

Today, surrender your plans to God. Trust Him to guide your steps, knowing that His plans are always for your good.

Affirmation:
I trust in God's plan for my life. His wisdom guides my steps and leads me into His purpose.

Action Step:
Identify one area where you've been relying on your own understanding. Pray and release it to God, asking for His wisdom and direction.

Prayer:
Lord, I surrender my plans to You. Help me to trust Your wisdom and follow the path You've prepared for me. Amen.

June 16th, 2025: Humility Leads to Wisdom

Scripture:
"*When pride comes, then comes disgrace, but with humility comes wisdom.*" (Proverbs 11:2, NIV)

Reflection:
Pride tells you that you can handle everything on your own, but humility acknowledges your need for God. True wisdom begins when you humble yourself, admitting that His ways are higher than yours.

Humility isn't about thinking less of yourself; it's about thinking of yourself less. It creates space for God's wisdom to take root in your heart and guide your steps. When you let go of pride, you open the door to His leading.

Today, choose humility and invite God to fill you with His wisdom.

Affirmation:
I choose humility, trusting God's wisdom to guide me above my own understanding.

Action Step:
Reflect on an area where pride may be holding you back. Surrender it to God in prayer, asking Him to help you walk in humility.

Prayer:
Father, thank You for teaching me the value of humility. Help me to trust Your wisdom and walk in Your ways, putting pride aside. Amen.

June 17th, 2025: Wisdom that Brings Peace

Scripture:
"*Her ways are pleasant ways, and all her paths are peace.*" (Proverbs 3:17, NIV)

Reflection:
God's wisdom leads to peace, even in the middle of life's chaos. When you follow His guidance, you experience a calm assurance that you're walking the right path. His wisdom guards your heart, gives clarity to your decisions, and brings harmony to your relationships.

This peace doesn't mean the absence of challenges, but it does mean the presence of His Spirit. As you seek God's wisdom, let His peace guide your heart and mind today.

Affirmation:
God's wisdom fills my life with peace. I walk in His ways, trusting His guidance in every step.

Action Step:
Take a moment to identify any unrest in your heart. Ask God for His wisdom and peace to settle that area of your life.

Prayer:
Lord, thank You for the peace that comes from Your wisdom. Help me to trust in Your guidance and rest in Your presence today. Amen.

June 18th, 2025: Avoiding the Way of Folly

Scripture:
"There is a way that appears to be right, but in the end it leads to death." (Proverbs 14:12, NIV)

Reflection:
Not every path that looks good is from God. Folly often disguises itself as wisdom, promising quick fixes or easy rewards. But true wisdom seeks God's will and waits for His timing, even when it's hard.

Choosing the way of wisdom means saying no to what seems right in your own eyes and trusting God to lead you on the better path. His ways may take longer or look different, but they always lead to life and peace.

Today, pause and reflect on your choices. Are they aligned with God's wisdom?

Affirmation:
I trust in God's wisdom to guide my steps, avoiding the way of folly and walking in truth.

Action Step:
Think of a decision you're facing. Pray and ask God to show you if it aligns with His wisdom or if it's a path of folly.

Prayer:
Lord, help me to avoid the way of folly and to trust in Your wisdom, even when it's difficult. Guide my steps and keep me on the path that leads to life. Amen.

June 19th, 2025: The Wisdom of Waiting

Scripture:
"*Be still before the Lord and wait patiently for Him; do not fret when people succeed in their ways.*" (Psalm 37:7, NIV)

Reflection:
Waiting can feel like wasted time, but in God's hands, it's often the most productive season of your life. Wisdom teaches you to trust God's timing, knowing that He's working behind the scenes for your good.

When you rush ahead, you risk missing His best. But when you wait patiently, you experience His perfect plan unfolding. The wisdom of waiting is about trusting that God's delays are not denials—they're part of His loving purpose for you.

Today, embrace the stillness and trust that He is at work.

Affirmation:
I trust God's timing. His wisdom leads me to wait patiently and confidently in His promises.

Action Step:
Think about an area of your life where you're waiting on God. Surrender it to Him in prayer, asking for patience and trust.

Prayer:
Father, thank You for teaching me the wisdom of waiting. Help me to trust Your timing and to rest in the knowledge that You are working all things for my good. Amen.

June 20th, 2025: Wisdom and Generosity

Scripture:
"A generous person will prosper; whoever refreshes others will be refreshed." (Proverbs 11:25, NIV)

Reflection:
Wisdom understands the power of generosity. When you give to others—whether it's your time, resources, or encouragement—you're reflecting God's heart and inviting His blessings into your life.

Generosity isn't about how much you have; it's about trusting that God will provide as you pour into others. Wisdom teaches you that giving is never a loss—it's an investment in God's kingdom and in the lives of those around you.

Today, look for a way to refresh someone else, trusting that God will refresh you in return.

Affirmation:
I live generously, trusting God to provide for my needs and bless others through me.

Action Step:
Find one way to be generous today—whether through giving, serving, or encouraging someone. Let God's wisdom guide your generosity.

Prayer:
Lord, thank You for teaching me the value of generosity. Help me to reflect Your heart by giving freely and trusting You to meet every need. Amen.

June 21st, 2025: Guarding Your Heart

Scripture:
"*Above all else, guard your heart, for everything you do flows from it.*" (Proverbs 4:23, NIV)

Reflection:
Your heart is the wellspring of your life—it influences your thoughts, words, and actions. Wisdom teaches you to guard it carefully, protecting it from negativity, distractions, or anything that pulls you away from God.

Guarding your heart doesn't mean closing yourself off; it means filling your heart with God's truth and allowing His Spirit to direct your life. What you let in shapes who you become.

Today, ask God to help you guard your heart and fill it with His wisdom and love.

Affirmation:
I guard my heart with wisdom, allowing God's truth to shape my thoughts and actions.

Action Step:
Reflect on what you've been allowing into your heart lately. Pray for wisdom to remove anything unhelpful and to focus on what aligns with God's truth.

Prayer:
Lord, help me to guard my heart and fill it with Your wisdom and love. Let everything I do flow from a heart centered on You. Amen.

June 22nd, 2025: Wisdom in Words

Scripture:
"A gentle answer turns away wrath, but a harsh word stirs up anger." (Proverbs 15:1, NIV)

Reflection:
Words hold incredible power. They can heal or hurt, encourage or discourage, build up or tear down. Wisdom teaches you to choose your words carefully, letting them reflect God's love and truth.

A gentle answer doesn't mean avoiding hard conversations—it means speaking with grace and kindness, even when emotions run high. The Holy Spirit gives you the self-control to pause, pray, and respond wisely in every situation.

Today, ask God to guide your words so they bring peace and encouragement.

Affirmation:
My words reflect God's wisdom and love. I speak with grace, kindness, and truth.

Action Step:
Before responding to a challenging situation, pause and pray for wisdom. Ask God to help you speak words that bring healing and reflect His heart.

Prayer:
Lord, thank You for the power of words. Help me to use mine wisely, speaking with kindness and grace in every conversation. Amen.

June 23rd, 2025: Wisdom for the Next Generation

Scripture:
"These commandments that I give you today are to be on your hearts. Impress them on your children." (Deuteronomy 6:6-7, NIV)

Reflection:
Passing on wisdom to the next generation is one of the greatest callings you can fulfill. Whether you're raising children, mentoring someone, or leading by example, your life speaks louder than your words.

Wisdom is caught as much as it's taught. When others see you living with integrity, faith, and love, they're inspired to do the same. God invites you to invest in the next generation, pointing them to Him and equipping them for their journey.

Today, think about how you can leave a legacy of wisdom for those who come after you.

Affirmation:
I invest in the next generation, sharing God's wisdom through my words and example.

Action Step:
Identify one way to share wisdom with someone younger—whether through encouragement, teaching, or simply spending time together.

Prayer:
Lord, thank You for the privilege of investing in others. Help me to live in a way that reflects Your wisdom and inspires the next generation to follow You. Amen.

June 24th, 2025: Living by God's Truth

Scripture:
"*Sanctify them by the truth; Your word is truth.*" (John 17:17, NIV)

Reflection:
God's truth sets you apart, shaping your character and guiding your steps. In a world filled with conflicting messages, living by His truth requires courage and intentionality.

The more you immerse yourself in Scripture, the more your mind is renewed and your heart is aligned with His will. His truth is a foundation you can stand on, no matter what challenges you face.

Today, let God's truth be your anchor. Choose to live in a way that honors Him and reflects His Word.

Affirmation:
I am set apart by God's truth. His Word is my guide, shaping my life and renewing my mind.

Action Step:
Spend 10 minutes meditating on a passage of Scripture that speaks to your current situation. Write down how you can live out its truth today.

Prayer:
Father, thank You for the gift of Your truth. Help me to live by Your Word, standing firm in faith and reflecting Your love to the world. Amen.

June 25th, 2025: The Power of a Listening Ear

Scripture:
"*Listen to advice and accept discipline, and at the end you will be counted among the wise.*" (Proverbs 19:20, NIV)

Reflection:
Wisdom begins with listening—not just hearing, but truly paying attention with an open heart. Whether it's God's voice, wise counsel, or the needs of others, a listening ear invites growth and understanding.

It's easy to rush into decisions or respond without fully listening, but wisdom requires patience and humility. By taking time to listen, you not only gain insight but also show love and respect to those around you.

Today, ask God to help you listen well—to Him and to others.

Affirmation:
I listen with humility and patience, inviting God's wisdom into my life and relationships.

Action Step:
Make a conscious effort to listen deeply in one conversation today. Reflect on what you learn and how it influences your response.

Prayer:
Holy Spirit, help me to listen with an open heart and a patient spirit. Teach me to hear Your voice and honor others by truly listening. Amen.

June 26th, 2025: Wisdom for Daily Living

Scripture:
"*The mouths of the righteous utter wisdom, and their tongues speak what is just.*" (Psalm 37:30, NIV)

Reflection:
God's wisdom isn't just for big decisions—it's for every moment of your daily life. From how you speak to how you act, wisdom guides your thoughts and shapes your character.

When you commit each day to God, you invite His wisdom into everything you do. He helps you navigate challenges, respond with grace, and honor Him in both the small and significant.

Today, ask God to help you live wisely in every moment, reflecting His goodness in all you do.

Affirmation:
I live each day with God's wisdom, letting His truth guide my thoughts, words, and actions.

Action Step:
Before starting your day, pray for wisdom in specific tasks or interactions. Trust God to guide you moment by moment.

Prayer:
Lord, thank You for offering wisdom for every part of my life. Help me to live wisely today, honoring You in every word and action. Amen.

June 27th 2025: Growing in Godly Knowledge

Scripture:
"The heart of the discerning acquires knowledge, for the ears of the wise seek it out." (Proverbs 18:15, NIV)

Reflection:
Wisdom grows as you seek knowledge—not just information, but understanding rooted in God's truth. A discerning heart is eager to learn, constantly drawing closer to God and His Word.

Godly knowledge equips you to make better decisions, build stronger relationships, and live a life that honors Him. The more you seek Him, the more you'll find clarity and direction in every area of your life.

Today, commit to growing in knowledge that strengthens your faith and deepens your walk with God.

Affirmation:
I seek godly knowledge with a discerning heart, growing in wisdom and faith each day.

Action Step:
Choose a topic or Scripture to study this week that will deepen your understanding of God's Word. Start by setting aside time to explore it today.

Prayer:
Lord, thank You for the gift of knowledge that leads to wisdom. Help me to seek understanding that strengthens my faith and glorifies You. Amen.

June 28th, 2025: Wisdom is a Gift

Scripture:
"To the person who pleases Him, God gives wisdom, knowledge, and happiness." (Ecclesiastes 2:26, NIV)

Reflection:
Wisdom isn't something you earn—it's a gift from God. As you walk in obedience and delight in Him, He freely pours out wisdom to guide and bless you.

This gift isn't just for your benefit; it equips you to bless others and glorify God in every aspect of your life. When you seek His wisdom, you're opening yourself to receive His best for you.

Today, thank God for the gift of wisdom and ask Him to help you steward it well.

Affirmation:
God's wisdom is a gift in my life, equipping me to honor Him and bless others.

Action Step:
Reflect on an area where you've seen God's wisdom at work. Thank Him for this gift and pray for continued guidance.

Prayer:
Lord, thank You for the gift of wisdom. Help me to use it well, honoring You in all I do and pointing others to Your love. Amen.

June 29th, 2025: The Source of Wisdom

Scripture:
"It is because of Him that you are in Christ Jesus, who has become for us wisdom from God—that is, our righteousness, holiness, and redemption." (1 Corinthians 1:30, NIV)

Reflection:
Jesus is the ultimate source of wisdom. In Him, you find not only the answers to life's questions but also the fullness of righteousness, holiness, and redemption.

When you center your life on Christ, His wisdom shapes every decision, relationship, and purpose. You're no longer striving in your own strength—you're walking in the power of His truth.

Today, draw near to Jesus, the source of all wisdom, and let Him guide your steps.

Affirmation:
Christ is my source of wisdom. In Him, I find strength, purpose, and direction.

Action Step:
Spend time in prayer, asking Jesus to reveal His wisdom for a specific area of your life. Trust Him to lead you in His truth.

Prayer:
Jesus, thank You for being my wisdom and my strength. Help me to trust in Your guidance and to walk in Your truth every day. Amen.

June 30th, 2025: Living Out God's Wisdom

Scripture:
"*Be wise in the way you act toward outsiders; make the most of every opportunity.*" (Colossians 4:5, NIV)

Reflection:
God's wisdom isn't meant to stay hidden—it's meant to be lived out in the way you interact with others. Every conversation, decision, and action is an opportunity to reflect His love and grace.

When you live out God's wisdom, you become a light to those around you. Your life points others to His truth and opens doors for His kingdom to advance.

Today, ask God to help you live wisely, making the most of every opportunity He places before you.

Affirmation:
I live out God's wisdom, reflecting His love and truth in every opportunity.

Action Step:
Think about one interaction or opportunity you have today. Ask God for wisdom to handle it in a way that reflects His grace and purpose.

Prayer:
Lord, thank You for the wisdom You've given me. Help me to live it out boldly, reflecting Your love and truth in every moment. Amen.

JULY: WALKING IN GOD'S LOVE

July's theme centers on living in God's love and letting it flow through us to others. This month explores the depth of God's love for us, how it transforms our hearts, and how we can share that love with a world in need. It's a journey of growing in intimacy with God and becoming His vessels of grace and compassion.

Day	Title	Scripture
July 1	Loved with an Everlasting Love	Jeremiah 31:3
July 2	The Greatest Commandment	Matthew 22:37-39
July 3	God's Love Never Fails	1 Corinthians 13:8
July 4	Perfect Love Drives Out Fear	1 John 4:18
July 5	God So Loved the World	John 3:16
July 6	Nothing Can Separate Us	Romans 8:38-39
July 7	Love Covers a Multitude of Sins	1 Peter 4:8
July 8	Walking in Love	Ephesians 5:2

July 9	Love is Patient and Kind	1 Corinthians 13:4
July 10	The Greatest of These is Love	1 Corinthians 13:13
July 11	Abiding in Love	John 15:9-10
July 12	Love Your Enemies	Matthew 5:44
July 13	Love in Action	1 John 3:18
July 14	Loving the Unlovable	Luke 6:32-33
July 15	The Power of Forgiveness	Colossians 3:13
July 16	Love and Humility	Philippians 2:3-4
July 17	Love Builds Up	1 Corinthians 8:1
July 18	Love is the Fulfillment of the Law	Romans 13:10
July 19	God Delights in You	Zephaniah 3:17
July 20	Love is Sacrificial	John 15:13
July 21	God is Love	1 John 4:16
July 22	Love is the Mark of a Disciple	John 13:35
July 23	Compassion Like Christ	Matthew 9:36
July 24	A Love That Never Quits	Lamentations 3:22-23
July 25	Loving Through Service	Galatians 5:13

July 26	Love for the Lost	Luke 19:10
July 27	Sharing God's Love Boldly	2 Timothy 1:7
July 28	The Love of Christ Compels Us	2 Corinthians 5:14
July 29	Love Brings Unity	Colossians 3:14
July 30	Love Never Gives Up	1 Corinthians 13:7
July 31	Be Rooted in Love	Ephesians 3:17-18

July 1st, 2025: Loved with an Everlasting Love

Scripture:
"*I have loved you with an everlasting love; I have drawn you with unfailing kindness.*" (Jeremiah 31:3, NIV)

Reflection:
God's love for you is eternal and unchanging. It doesn't depend on your performance, your past, or your circumstances. His love is a constant, unwavering presence in your life.

When you feel unworthy or unloved, remember this truth: God chose to love you with an everlasting love. He draws you close with His kindness, offering grace and compassion that never run out.

Today, let His love fill your heart. Rest in the knowledge that you are deeply cherished by the Creator of the universe.

Affirmation:
I am loved with an everlasting love. God's kindness draws me closer to His heart.

Action Step:
Spend a few moments reflecting on how God has shown His love to you recently. Write down one way you can respond to His love by sharing it with someone else today.

Prayer:
Lord, thank You for loving me with a love that never ends. Help me to rest in Your kindness and share Your love with others. Amen.

July 2nd 2025: The Greatest Commandment

Scripture:
"Love the Lord your God with all your heart and with all your soul and with all your mind. This is the first and greatest commandment. And the second is like it: Love your neighbor as yourself." (Matthew 22:37-39, NIV)

Reflection:
Jesus simplified all of God's commandments into two: love God and love others. When your life is centered on these two things, everything else falls into place.

Loving God means giving Him your whole heart, prioritizing Him above all else. Loving others means extending grace, kindness, and compassion, even when it's hard. These aren't just commands—they're invitations to experience the fullness of life that comes from living in love.

Today, ask God to help you love Him and others more deeply.

Affirmation:
I love God with all my heart, soul, and mind. His love flows through me to others.

Action Step:
Think of one way you can show love to God today (e.g., through worship, prayer, or obedience) and one way to love someone else (e.g., an act of kindness or encouragement).

Prayer:
Lord, teach me to love You fully and to love others as You have loved me. Help me to live out the greatest commandment every day. Amen.

July 3rd, 2025: God's Love Never Fails

Scripture:
"*Love never fails.*" (1 Corinthians 13:8, NIV)

Reflection:
Human love can falter, but God's love never fails. It is steadfast, enduring, and perfect. Even when you feel distant from Him or unsure of your worth, His love remains constant.

This unfailing love isn't just a comfort—it's a call to reflect His love in your relationships. When you love with God's strength, you can overcome hurt, extend forgiveness, and build connections that reflect His heart.

Today, let God's unfailing love renew your spirit and inspire your actions.

Affirmation:
God's love for me never fails. His steadfast love empowers me to love others.

Action Step:
Reflect on a relationship where love feels strained. Pray for God's unfailing love to guide your heart and actions in that situation.

Prayer:
Father, thank You for Your love that never fails. Help me to trust in Your love and reflect it in my relationships. Amen.

July 4th, 2025: Perfect Love Drives Out Fear

Scripture:
"There is no fear in love. But perfect love drives out fear, because fear has to do with punishment. The one who fears is not made perfect in love." (1 John 4:18, NIV)

Reflection:
Fear can paralyze, but God's perfect love sets you free. His love reminds you that you are fully accepted, forgiven, and cherished. When you embrace this truth, fear loses its grip on your heart.

Perfect love doesn't mean life will be without challenges, but it does mean you can face those challenges with confidence, knowing God is with you. His love is greater than your fears, and His presence is your peace.

Today, let God's love drive out any fear in your heart, replacing it with faith and trust.

Affirmation:
God's perfect love fills my heart, casting out all fear and bringing peace.

Action Step:
Identify one fear you're holding onto. Bring it to God in prayer, and ask Him to replace it with the assurance of His love.

Prayer:
Father, thank You for Your perfect love that drives out fear. Help me to trust in Your love and walk boldly in faith. Amen.

July 5th, 2025: God So Loved the World

Scripture:
"For God so loved the world that He gave His one and only Son, that whoever believes in Him shall not perish but have eternal life." (John 3:16, NIV)

Reflection:
God's love isn't just for a select few—it's for the whole world. He loved you so much that He gave His most precious gift, His Son, to bring you into eternal life with Him.

This love isn't based on what you've done or how "good" you are. It's a gift freely given, an open invitation to everyone who believes. If you've experienced this love, you're also called to share it with others so they, too, can know the hope and joy of eternal life.

Today, reflect on the depth of God's love and how you can share it with someone else.

Affirmation:
I am deeply loved by God, and His love compels me to share His hope with the world.

Action Step:
Think of one person who might need to hear about God's love. Pray for them and look for an opportunity to share the hope of the gospel.

Prayer:
Lord, thank You for loving me so much that You gave Your Son for my salvation. Help me to share Your love with others and point them to You. Amen.

July 6th, 2025: Nothing Can Separate Us

Scripture:
"For I am convinced that neither death nor life, neither angels nor demons, neither the present nor the future, nor any powers, neither height nor depth, nor anything else in all creation, will be able to separate us from the love of God that is in Christ Jesus our Lord." (Romans 8:38-39, NIV)

Reflection:
God's love is unshakable and unbreakable. No force in heaven or on earth can separate you from His love. Even in your darkest moments, His love remains constant, holding you close.

This promise brings comfort and strength. When you face uncertainty, pain, or doubt, you can rest in the assurance that God's love is always with you.

Today, let the truth of God's unchanging love fill your heart with peace and courage.

Affirmation:
Nothing can separate me from God's love. His love sustains me through every season of life.

Action Step:
Write down one challenge or fear you're currently facing. As you pray, declare that God's love is greater than anything on that list.

Prayer:
Father, thank You for Your love that nothing can separate me from. Help me to rest in Your unchanging love and find peace in Your presence. Amen.

July 7th, 2025: Love Covers a Multitude of Sins

Scripture:
"*Above all, love each other deeply, because love covers over a multitude of sins.*" (1 Peter 4:8, NIV)

Reflection:
God's love has covered your sins through the sacrifice of Jesus, and now He calls you to extend that love to others. Love doesn't ignore sin, but it offers forgiveness, grace, and the chance for restoration.

Loving deeply means choosing patience over anger, understanding over judgment, and forgiveness over bitterness. It's not always easy, but the Spirit equips you to love as God has loved you.

Today, let God's love flow through you to cover and heal the hurts around you.

Affirmation:
God's love covers my sins and empowers me to love others with grace and compassion.

Action Step:
Think of a relationship where forgiveness is needed. Pray for God's love to fill your heart and give you the grace to extend forgiveness.

Prayer:
Lord, thank You for covering my sins with Your love. Help me to love others deeply, offering forgiveness and grace as You have done for me. Amen.

July 8th, 2025: Walking in Love

Scripture:
"And walk in the way of love, just as Christ loved us and gave Himself up for us as a fragrant offering and sacrifice to God." (Ephesians 5:2, NIV)

Reflection:
Walking in love means making love the defining characteristic of your life. It's not just something you feel—it's something you do. Jesus modeled this through His sacrificial love, and He calls you to follow in His footsteps.

When you walk in love, you reflect God's heart to the world. It might look like a kind word, an act of service, or forgiving someone who hurt you. Every step you take in love is an offering that brings glory to God.

Today, commit to walking in love, letting it guide your thoughts, words, and actions.

Affirmation:
I walk in the way of love, reflecting Christ's sacrificial love to those around me.

Action Step:
Choose one specific way to show love to someone today, whether through encouragement, kindness, or an act of service.

Prayer:
Jesus, thank You for showing me what it means to walk in love. Help me to reflect Your love in every step I take today. Amen.

July 9th, 2025: Love is Patient and Kind

Scripture:
"*Love is patient, love is kind. It does not envy, it does not boast, it is not proud.*" (1 Corinthians 13:4, NIV)

Reflection:
True love is patient—it doesn't rush or demand its own way. True love is kind—it looks for ways to bless, encourage, and uplift. These qualities reflect the character of God's love for you.

Patience and kindness can be challenging, especially in difficult situations. But as you rely on the Holy Spirit, He empowers you to love in ways that go beyond your own strength.

Today, ask God to help you practice patience and kindness, even when it's hard.

Affirmation:
I choose patience and kindness, letting God's love flow through me to others.

Action Step:
Reflect on a recent situation where you felt impatient or unkind. Pray for God's help to respond differently in the future, showing His love in action.

Prayer:
Lord, thank You for loving me with patience and kindness. Teach me to love others in the same way, even when it's not easy. Amen.

July 10th, 2025: The Greatest of These is Love

Scripture:
"*And now these three remain: faith, hope, and love. But the greatest of these is love.*" (1 Corinthians 13:13, NIV)

Reflection:
Faith gives you strength, hope keeps you moving forward, but love is the greatest because it's eternal. Love is the essence of who God is, and it's the foundation of His relationship with you.

When you prioritize love, you reflect God's heart. Everything you do—whether small or significant—takes on eternal value when it's done in love.

Today, let love be your motivation, shaping how you interact with God and with others.

Affirmation:
Love is the foundation of my life. I reflect God's love in everything I do.

Action Step:
Think of one way you can prioritize love in your daily interactions. Write it down and commit to practicing it throughout the day.

Prayer:
Father, thank You for making love the foundation of my life. Help me to prioritize love in all I do, reflecting Your heart to the world. Amen.

July 11th, 2025: Abiding in Love

Scripture:
"As the Father has loved Me, so have I loved you. Now remain in My love." (John 15:9, NIV)

Reflection:
Jesus invites you to remain in His love—not to visit occasionally, but to make it your home. Abiding in His love means staying connected to Him through prayer, His Word, and daily surrender.

When you abide in Jesus, His love flows through you like a vine nourishing its branches. You'll find strength for every trial, joy in every season, and the power to love others the way He loves you.

Today, choose to remain in His love and let it guide your heart and actions.

Affirmation:
I abide in Christ's love, drawing strength and joy from His presence each day.

Action Step:
Take 10 minutes to sit quietly in God's presence. Reflect on His love for you and ask Him to help you remain rooted in Him.

Prayer:
Jesus, thank You for loving me as the Father loves You. Teach me to remain in Your love and to let it transform my heart. Amen.

July 12th, 2025: Love Your Enemies

Scripture:
"*But I tell you, love your enemies and pray for those who persecute you.*" (Matthew 5:44, NIV)

Reflection:
Loving your enemies is one of the most challenging commands Jesus gives. It goes against every human instinct, but it reflects the radical love of God.

When you choose to love those who have wronged you, you're not excusing their actions—you're choosing to overcome evil with good. Love has the power to break cycles of bitterness and hatred, bringing healing where there was once division.

Today, ask God for the strength to love even those who are hard to love.

Affirmation:
I choose to love my enemies, reflecting God's grace and forgiveness in my actions.

Action Step:
Think of someone who has hurt you or been difficult to love. Pray for them, asking God to bless them and help you see them through His eyes.

Prayer:
Father, thank You for loving me even when I fall short. Help me to love my enemies and to reflect Your forgiveness and grace. Amen.

July 13th, 2025: Love in Action

Scripture:
"*Dear children, let us not love with words or speech but with actions and in truth.*" (1 John 3:18, NIV)

Reflection:
Love isn't just something you say—it's something you do. True love is shown through acts of kindness, generosity, and service. It's about putting others' needs ahead of your own and reflecting God's heart through your actions.

When you love in action, you're living out your faith in a way that others can see and feel. It's a tangible expression of the gospel that points people to Jesus.

Today, look for an opportunity to put love into action and make a difference in someone's life.

Affirmation:
I show God's love through my actions, letting His truth guide my heart and hands.

Action Step:
Choose one specific act of love to do for someone today, whether it's meeting a need, offering encouragement, or serving them in a meaningful way.

Prayer:
Lord, thank You for showing me love through Your actions. Help me to reflect Your heart by loving others with my actions and in truth. Amen.

July 14th, 2025: Loving the Unlovable

Scripture:
"If you love those who love you, what credit is that to you? Even sinners love those who love them." (Luke 6:32, NIV)

Reflection:
Loving those who are easy to love is natural, but Jesus calls you to something greater—loving the unlovable. This might include people who frustrate you, those who have hurt you, or even strangers who seem difficult to approach.

When you choose to love beyond what's comfortable, you reflect the unconditional love of God. He loved you even when you were far from Him, and now He invites you to do the same for others.

Today, ask God for the grace to love those who feel unlovable.

Affirmation:
I love others as God loves me, extending grace and compassion to everyone.

Action Step:
Think of one person you find difficult to love. Ask God to soften your heart and show you one way to express love to them today.

Prayer:
Father, thank You for loving me even when I was unlovable. Help me to love others with Your grace and to see them as You see them. Amen.

July 15th, 2025: The Power of Forgiveness

Scripture:
"Bear with each other and forgive one another if any of you has a grievance against someone. Forgive as the Lord forgave you." (Colossians 3:13, NIV)

Reflection:
Forgiveness is a powerful act of love. It releases the weight of anger and bitterness, freeing both you and the person who wronged you.

Jesus forgave you completely, and He calls you to extend that same forgiveness to others. It's not about condoning wrongdoing—it's about choosing grace over resentment and trusting God to bring justice in His time.

Today, let go of any grudges and experience the freedom that comes from forgiveness.

Affirmation:
I forgive others as Christ has forgiven me, releasing anger and embracing peace.

Action Step:
Think of someone you need to forgive. Take a step toward releasing that hurt today, whether through prayer, a conversation, or an act of kindness.

Prayer:
Lord, thank You for forgiving me fully and unconditionally. Help me to extend that forgiveness to others, reflecting Your love and grace. Amen.

July 16th, 2025: Love and Humility

Scripture:
"*Do nothing out of selfish ambition or vain conceit. Rather, in humility value others above yourselves.*" (Philippians 2:3, NIV)

Reflection:
Love and humility go hand in hand. When you value others above yourself, you reflect the selfless love of Jesus. Humility isn't about thinking less of yourself—it's about thinking of yourself less and prioritizing the needs of others.

This kind of love is countercultural, but it's deeply transformational. It creates relationships built on trust, respect, and grace, mirroring the love of Christ.

Today, ask God to help you love with humility, putting others first in your thoughts and actions.

Affirmation:
I love with humility, valuing others above myself and reflecting Christ's selfless heart.

Action Step:
Look for one way to put someone else's needs ahead of your own today. Whether through a small gesture or a big decision, let humility guide your actions.

Prayer:
Jesus, thank You for showing me what humble love looks like. Teach me to love with humility, putting others before myself. Amen.

July 17th, 2025: Love Builds Up

Scripture:
"*But knowledge puffs up while love builds up.*" (1 Corinthians 8:1, NIV)

Reflection:
Knowledge without love can lead to pride, but love builds others up. It strengthens relationships, encourages hearts, and creates a foundation of trust and unity.

When you love others, you're building them up in ways that last far beyond the moment. Your words and actions become tools of God's grace, helping others see their worth and potential in Him.

Today, let love guide you in how you speak, act, and interact with those around you.

Affirmation:
My love builds others up, reflecting God's grace and strengthening their faith.

Action Step:
Think of someone who could use encouragement. Reach out with a kind word or action that lifts them up today.

Prayer:
Father, thank You for the way Your love builds me up. Help me to do the same for others, letting my words and actions reflect Your grace. Amen.

July 18th, 2025: Love is the Fulfillment of the Law

Scripture:
"Love does no harm to a neighbor. Therefore love is the fulfillment of the law." (Romans 13:10, NIV)

Reflection:
God's commandments are rooted in love. When you choose to love others, you naturally fulfill His law by treating them with kindness, respect, and grace.

Love doesn't seek harm or hold grudges—it seeks peace and builds bridges. It's the essence of who God is and how He calls you to live.

Today, let love guide your decisions and interactions, fulfilling God's law in every step.

Affirmation:
Love is my guide, fulfilling God's law and reflecting His heart in all I do.

Action Step:
Ask God to show you one way to express love to someone in your life today, fulfilling His law through your actions.

Prayer:
Lord, thank You for making love the fulfillment of Your law. Help me to live in love and to reflect Your heart to those around me. Amen.

July 19th, 2025: God Delights in You

Scripture:
"The Lord your God is with you, the Mighty Warrior who saves. He will take great delight in you; in His love He will no longer rebuke you but will rejoice over you with singing." (Zephaniah 3:17, NIV)

Reflection:
God doesn't just love you—He delights in you. His love is personal, joyful, and full of celebration. He rejoices over you, not because of what you've done, but because of who you are —His beloved child.

Today, rest in the truth that God's love isn't just dutiful; it's joyful. Let His delight in you renew your heart and inspire your worship.

Affirmation:
God delights in me. His love fills my heart with joy and peace.

Action Step:
Spend time in worship today, celebrating God's delight in you. Let His love fill your heart with joy and gratitude.

Prayer:
Father, thank You for delighting in me and rejoicing over me with singing. Help me to rest in Your love and to reflect it in my life. Amen.

July 20th, 2025: Love is Sacrificial

Scripture:
"*Greater love has no one than this: to lay down one's life for one's friends.*" (John 15:13, NIV)

Reflection:
Jesus demonstrated the ultimate act of love by laying down His life for you. His love is sacrificial, putting your needs above His own comfort and even His own life.

When you love sacrificially, you reflect the heart of Christ. It might mean giving your time, resources, or energy to serve others. It's not always easy, but it's always worth it.

Today, ask God to help you love with a sacrificial heart, putting others first.

Affirmation:
I love sacrificially, following the example of Jesus and reflecting His heart to the world.

Action Step:
Look for one opportunity to sacrifice something for someone else today, whether it's your time, energy, or resources.

Prayer:
Jesus, thank You for loving me sacrificially. Help me to follow Your example and to love others selflessly. Amen.

July 21st, 2025: God is Love

Scripture:
"*And so we know and rely on the love God has for us. God is love. Whoever lives in love lives in God, and God in them.*" (1 John 4:16, NIV)

Reflection:
Love isn't just something God does—it's who He is. Every act of kindness, mercy, and grace flows from His character. When you live in love, you're living in the presence of God Himself.

This love isn't something you have to strive for; it's something you receive and reflect. As you rest in God's love, it transforms your heart and spills over into your relationships.

Today, let the truth that "God is love" be the foundation of your faith and your actions.

Affirmation:
I live in God's love, letting His presence transform my heart and guide my life.

Action Step:
Spend time reflecting on God's love for you. Write down three ways you can share that love with others today.

Prayer:
Lord, thank You for being love itself. Help me to live in Your love and to reflect it in everything I do. Amen.

July 22nd, 2025: Love is the Mark of a Disciple

Scripture:
"By this everyone will know that you are My disciples, if you love one another." (John 13:35, NIV)

Reflection:
Love is the defining characteristic of a disciple of Jesus. It's not your knowledge, your talents, or even your good deeds that set you apart—it's the way you love others.

When you love as Jesus loves, you're showing the world what it means to follow Him. This love isn't conditional or selective; it's a selfless love that seeks the good of others, even when it's hard.

Today, let your love for others be a reflection of your commitment to Christ.

Affirmation:
Love is the mark of my discipleship. I reflect Jesus in the way I love others.

Action Step:
Think about how you interact with others daily. Choose one specific way to demonstrate Christ's love to someone today.

Prayer:
Jesus, thank You for teaching me how to love. Help me to reflect Your heart by loving others selflessly and faithfully. Amen.

July 23rd, 2025: Compassion Like Christ

Scripture:
"*When He saw the crowds, He had compassion on them, because they were harassed and helpless, like sheep without a shepherd.*" (Matthew 9:36, NIV)

Reflection:
Jesus' love was marked by compassion. He saw people's pain, understood their struggles, and responded with kindness and care. Compassion isn't just feeling sorry for someone—it's love in action, stepping into their need with a heart of mercy.

God calls you to show this same compassion to others. When you look at the world through Christ's eyes, you'll see opportunities to love and serve those who are hurting.

Today, ask God to give you a heart of compassion like Christ's.

Affirmation:
I show compassion like Christ, responding to others with love and mercy.

Action Step:
Look for someone in need today, whether emotionally, physically, or spiritually. Take a step to meet that need with Christ-like compassion.

Prayer:
Lord, thank You for Your compassion that meets me in my struggles. Help me to reflect Your heart by showing love and care to those in need. Amen.

July 24th, 2025: A Love That Never Quits

Scripture:
"*Because of the Lord's great love we are not consumed, for His compassions never fail. They are new every morning; great is Your faithfulness.*" (Lamentations 3:22-23, NIV)

Reflection:
God's love is steadfast and unchanging. No matter how many times you fall or how challenging life becomes, His love never gives up on you. Each morning is a fresh start, filled with His mercy and faithfulness.

This same love equips you to persevere in loving others. When relationships feel hard or forgiveness seems impossible, God's unending love strengthens you to keep going.

Today, let His faithful love inspire you to love others with the same perseverance.

Affirmation:
God's love never quits, and His faithfulness gives me strength to love others.

Action Step:
Think of someone you've struggled to love consistently. Pray for God's help to show them unwavering love today.

Prayer:
Father, thank You for Your love that never gives up on me. Teach me to love with faithfulness and perseverance, even when it's hard. Amen.

July 25th, 2025: Loving Through Service

Scripture:
"*Serve one another humbly in love.*" (Galatians 5:13, NIV)

Reflection:
Love often looks like service—putting others' needs ahead of your own and choosing to care for them in practical ways. When you serve with humility, you reflect the heart of Christ, who came not to be served but to serve.

Service doesn't have to be grand to be meaningful. Small acts of love, done with a willing heart, can make a lasting impact.

Today, look for opportunities to serve others as an expression of God's love.

Affirmation:
I serve others humbly in love, reflecting the heart of Christ in my actions.

Action Step:
Find a practical way to serve someone today, whether through a simple task, a kind gesture, or meeting a specific need.

Prayer:
Jesus, thank You for showing me what it means to serve in love. Help me to follow Your example and to care for others with humility and kindness. Amen.

July 26th, 2025: Love for the Lost

Scripture:
"For the Son of Man came to seek and to save the lost."
(Luke 19:10, NIV)

Reflection:
Jesus' mission was driven by love for the lost—those far from God, trapped in sin, and in need of a Savior. His love compelled Him to reach out, even to those society rejected.

As His follower, you're called to share that same love with those who don't yet know Him. Whether through prayer, conversation, or acts of kindness, you can be part of leading others to Christ.

Today, let God's love for the lost inspire you to share the hope of salvation.

Affirmation:
I share God's love with the lost, inviting them to experience His grace and salvation.

Action Step:
Pray for one person in your life who doesn't know Christ. Ask God to give you an opportunity to share His love with them.

Prayer:
Father, thank You for loving the lost and seeking me when I was far from You. Help me to share Your love and point others to Jesus. Amen.

July 27th, 2025: Sharing God's Love Boldly

Scripture:
"For the Spirit God gave us does not make us timid, but gives us power, love, and self-discipline." (2 Timothy 1:7, NIV)

Reflection:
Sharing God's love takes courage. It means stepping out of your comfort zone to tell others about the hope and joy you've found in Christ. But you're not alone—the Holy Spirit equips you with boldness, love, and wisdom.

When you rely on His strength, you'll find the courage to share your faith, knowing that God is working through you to touch hearts and change lives.

Today, ask God for boldness to share His love with confidence and joy.

Affirmation:
I am empowered by the Spirit to share God's love boldly and confidently.

Action Step:
Look for an opportunity to share your faith with someone today, whether through words, actions, or both.

Prayer:
Holy Spirit, thank You for giving me the courage to share God's love. Help me to speak boldly and act in love, trusting You to work through me. Amen.

July 28th, 2025: The Love of Christ Compels Us

Scripture:
"*For Christ's love compels us, because we are convinced that one died for all, and therefore all died.*" (2 Corinthians 5:14, NIV)

Reflection:
When you truly grasp the depth of Christ's love, it compels you to live differently. His sacrifice on the cross isn't just a story—it's a reality that changes everything.

This love motivates you to share the gospel, serve others, and live with purpose. It's not out of obligation, but out of gratitude for the love that has transformed your life.

Today, let Christ's love compel you to live for Him and to share His love with others.

Affirmation:
The love of Christ compels me to live with purpose and share His gospel with the world.

Action Step:
Write down one way you can live compelled by Christ's love today. Pray for courage to follow through.

Prayer:
Jesus, thank You for Your love that compels me to live for You. Help me to reflect Your love in all I do and to share it with those around me. Amen.

July 29th, 2025: Love Brings Unity

Scripture:
"And over all these virtues put on love, which binds them all together in perfect unity." (Colossians 3:14, NIV)

Reflection:
Love has the power to bring people together. It overcomes differences, heals divisions, and creates unity within the body of Christ.

When you choose love, you're contributing to the unity of God's kingdom. Your actions and attitudes can be a powerful testimony of His love to the world.

Today, let love guide your interactions, building unity in your relationships and community.

Affirmation:
Love binds us together in perfect unity. I am an instrument of God's peace and love.

Action Step:
Think about a relationship or group where unity is needed. Pray for God's love to bring healing and look for one way to contribute to unity today.

Prayer:
Lord, thank You for the love that unites us. Help me to reflect Your heart by building unity in my relationships and community. Amen.

July 30th, 2025: Love Never Gives Up

Scripture:
"*It always protects, always trusts, always hopes, always perseveres.*" (1 Corinthians 13:7, NIV)

Reflection:
God's love never gives up on you, and He calls you to love others with that same enduring commitment. This kind of love protects, trusts, hopes, and perseveres, even in the face of challenges.

When you love with perseverance, you reflect God's heart and invite His power into your relationships. It's not easy, but it's always worth it.

Today, ask God for the strength to love with perseverance, trusting Him to work through your efforts.

Affirmation:
Love never gives up. I trust God to strengthen my love and sustain my relationships.

Action Step:
Think about a relationship where perseverance is needed. Commit to one step of love and faithfulness in that situation today.

Prayer:
Father, thank You for loving me with a love that never gives up. Help me to reflect that love by persevering in my relationships and trusting You to work through them. Amen.

July 31st, 2025: Be Rooted in Love

Scripture:
"*And I pray that you, being rooted and established in love, may have power, together with all the Lord's holy people, to grasp how wide and long and high and deep is the love of Christ.*" (Ephesians 3:17-18, NIV)

Reflection:
God's love is the foundation of your faith. When you're rooted in His love, you have the strength to weather life's storms and the power to love others boldly.

Paul's prayer in Ephesians invites you to explore the limitless dimensions of Christ's love. The more you understand His love, the more your heart is transformed to reflect it.

Today, plant your roots deep in God's love and let it nourish your soul.

Affirmation:
I am rooted and established in God's love. His love gives me strength and power to live boldly.

Action Step:
Spend time meditating on the vastness of God's love. Write down one way you've experienced His love recently and thank Him for it.

Prayer:
Lord, thank You for rooting me in Your love. Help me to grasp the depth of Your love and to let it shape every part of my life. Amen.

AUGUST: ABUNDANT LIVING

Abundant living isn't about material wealth—it's about living a life full of God's blessings, peace, and purpose. Jesus promised a life overflowing with His goodness, but it's rooted in surrender, faith, and generosity. This month explores how to embrace the abundant life He offers, stewarding blessings well and finding joy in every season.

Day	Title	Scripture
August 1	Life to the Full	John 10:10
August 2	Blessed to Be a Blessing	Genesis 12:2
August 3	God Supplies All Your Needs	Philippians 4:19
August 4	The Joy of Generosity	2 Corinthians 9:7
August 5	Seeking First the Kingdom	Matthew 6:33
August 6	Contentment in Christ	1 Timothy 6:6-8

August 7	Overflowing with Thanksgiving	Colossians 2:6-7
August 8	Trusting God's Provision	Psalm 23:1
August 9	The Blessing of Obedience	Deuteronomy 28:1-2
August 10	Rejoice Always	1 Thessalonians 5:16-18
August 11	God's Grace is Sufficient	2 Corinthians 12:9
August 12	Living Generously	Acts 20:35
August 13	The Fruit of the Spirit: Joy	Galatians 5:22-23
August 14	The Power of Gratitude	Psalm 100:4
August 15	Abiding in the Vine	John 15:5
August 16	Strength in Every Season	Philippians 4:12-13
August 17	God Multiplies What You Surrender	Mark 6:41
August 18	Faith That Overflows	Romans 15:13
August 19	The Promise of Peace	Isaiah 26:3
August 20	An Eternal Perspective	2 Corinthians 4:17-18
August 21	The Beauty of Simplicity	Ecclesiastes 4:6
August 22	Delight in the Lord	Psalm 37:4

August 23	Walking in God's Favor	Proverbs 3:3-4
August 24	Purpose in Every Step	Jeremiah 29:11
August 25	The Reward of Faithfulness	Matthew 25:23
August 26	Overflowing Hope	Romans 15:13
August 27	Counting Your Blessings	Psalm 103:2
August 28	Rich in Good Works	1 Timothy 6:17-19
August 29	The Lord is My Shepherd	Psalm 23:1-2
August 30	Living with Open Hands	Proverbs 11:24-25
August 31	Abundant Life in Christ	John 15:11

August 1st, 2025: Life to the Full

Scripture:
"The thief comes only to steal and kill and destroy; I have come that they may have life, and have it to the full." (John 10:10, NIV)

Reflection:
Jesus didn't come just to give you eternal life—He came to give you abundant life here and now. This doesn't mean life without challenges, but it does mean a life overflowing with peace, purpose, and joy in Him.

The enemy wants to steal your joy, kill your hope, and destroy your peace. But Jesus offers a life that's rooted in His promises, filled with His Spirit, and guided by His love. When you walk with Him, you experience the fullness of life that nothing else can offer.

Today, choose to embrace the abundant life Jesus offers. Surrender your worries and trust Him to fill your heart with His peace and joy.

Affirmation:
Jesus came to give me life to the full. I walk in His joy, peace, and purpose.

Action Step:
Reflect on one area of your life where you feel "less than full." Surrender it to God in prayer, asking Him to fill it with His abundant life.

Prayer:
Jesus, thank You for offering me abundant life. Help me to trust in Your promises and to live in the fullness of Your joy and peace. Amen.

August 2nd, 2025: Blessed to Be a Blessing

Scripture:
"I will make you into a great nation, and I will bless you; I will make your name great, and you will be a blessing." (Genesis 12:2, NIV)

Reflection:
God's blessings are never meant to stop with you—they're meant to flow through you to others. Just as He promised Abraham, He blesses you so that you can be a blessing to those around you.

When you share your resources, time, or encouragement with others, you're reflecting God's heart and multiplying the impact of His blessings. The more you give, the more He fills you with His goodness.

Today, look for opportunities to bless someone else, knowing that you're carrying out God's purpose.

Affirmation:
I am blessed by God to be a blessing to others, reflecting His heart in my actions.

Action Step:
Find one way to be a blessing to someone today, whether through a kind gesture, a gift, or a word of encouragement.

Prayer:
Lord, thank You for blessing me so generously. Help me to share those blessings with others and to reflect Your love through my actions. Amen.

August 3rd, 2025: God Supplies All Your Needs

Scripture:
"*And my God will meet all your needs according to the riches of His glory in Christ Jesus.*" (Philippians 4:19, NIV)

Reflection:
God's provision isn't limited by your circumstances. He promises to supply all your needs—not according to your resources, but according to His limitless riches in Christ.

This doesn't mean He'll always give you what you want, but He'll always give you what you need. Whether it's peace, wisdom, or physical provision, you can trust that He sees your needs and will provide in His perfect timing.

Today, rest in the assurance that God is your provider. Trust Him to meet your needs as you walk in faith.

Affirmation:
God supplies all my needs according to His riches. I trust in His perfect provision.

Action Step:
Write down one need you have right now. Bring it to God in prayer, trusting Him to provide in His way and timing.

Prayer:
Father, thank You for being my provider. Help me to trust in Your promises and to rely on Your provision in every area of my life. Amen.

August 4th, 2025: The Joy of Generosity

Scripture:
"Each of you should give what you have decided in your heart to give, not reluctantly or under compulsion, for God loves a cheerful giver." (2 Corinthians 9:7, NIV)

Reflection:
Generosity is an expression of God's love working through you. It's not about the amount you give but the heart behind it. When you give cheerfully, you reflect God's character—He is the ultimate giver, lavishing you with grace and blessings.

Generosity isn't just about finances. It includes your time, talents, and encouragement. When you live with open hands, trusting God to supply all you need, you experience the joy of partnering with Him to bless others.

Today, ask God to help you give cheerfully and trust Him to multiply what you offer for His glory.

Affirmation:
I give generously and cheerfully, knowing that God supplies all I need.

Action Step:
Identify one way you can give today—whether it's your time, resources, or encouragement. Act on it with a cheerful heart.

Prayer:
Father, thank You for being so generous with me. Help me to give with joy, trusting You to use my offerings to bless others and glorify Your name. Amen.

August 5th, 2025: Seeking First the Kingdom

Scripture:
"*But seek first His kingdom and His righteousness, and all these things will be given to you as well.*" (Matthew 6:33, NIV)

Reflection:
Life is filled with competing priorities, but Jesus invites you to seek God's kingdom above all else. When you put God first—aligning your heart, time, and resources with His purposes—you discover that He faithfully provides for every other need.

Seeking the kingdom isn't about neglecting responsibilities; it's about letting God's priorities shape your decisions. It's choosing to trust His plan over your own and investing in what has eternal value.

Today, consider what it means to seek God's kingdom in your life. Let His purposes lead your heart and direct your steps.

Affirmation:
I seek God's kingdom first, trusting Him to provide for every need in my life.

Action Step:
Set aside time today to pray for God's guidance in aligning your priorities with His kingdom. Ask Him to reveal one way you can seek His purposes first.

Prayer:
Lord, help me to seek Your kingdom above all else. Align my heart with Your purposes, and teach me to trust Your provision for everything I need. Amen.

August 6th, 2025: Contentment in Christ

Scripture:
"*But godliness with contentment is great gain. For we brought nothing into the world, and we can take nothing out of it.*" (1 Timothy 6:6-7, NIV)

Reflection:
Contentment isn't about having everything you want; it's about trusting that God has already provided everything you need. When you find your satisfaction in Christ, you're free from the endless pursuit of more.

The world teaches that contentment comes from possessions, status, or achievements, but these things can't truly satisfy. Only Jesus can fill the deepest longings of your heart.

Today, rest in the truth that Christ is enough. Let His presence bring you peace and satisfaction in every circumstance.

Affirmation:
I am content in Christ. He is my satisfaction, and His presence is enough for me.

Action Step:
Take a moment to thank God for three things He has provided in your life. Reflect on how His blessings have met your needs.

Prayer:
Lord, thank You for being my source of contentment. Help me to trust in You fully and to rest in the peace of knowing that You are enough. Amen.

August 7th, 2025: Overflowing with Thanksgiving

Scripture:
"So then, just as you received Christ Jesus as Lord, continue to live your lives in Him, rooted and built up in Him, strengthened in the faith as you were taught, and overflowing with thankfulness." (Colossians 2:6-7, NIV)

Reflection:
A heart rooted in Christ naturally overflows with thanksgiving. Gratitude isn't just a response to blessings; it's a posture of the heart that recognizes God's faithfulness in every circumstance.

When you focus on His goodness, even in difficult seasons, thanksgiving becomes a wellspring of joy and strength. It shifts your perspective from what you lack to all that you've been given in Christ.

Today, let your heart overflow with gratitude, allowing it to deepen your faith and draw you closer to God.

Affirmation:
I am rooted in Christ, and my heart overflows with gratitude for His faithfulness.

Action Step:
Start a gratitude journal, listing three things you're thankful for each day. Let this practice become a daily reminder of God's goodness.

Prayer:
Father, thank You for Your faithfulness and the countless ways You've blessed me. Help me to live with a heart of gratitude that overflows in every season. Amen.

August 8th, 2025: Trusting God's Provision

Scripture:
"*The Lord is my shepherd; I lack nothing*." (Psalm 23:1, NIV)

Reflection:
God is your shepherd, faithfully providing for every need. Just as a shepherd guides and cares for His sheep, God watches over you, ensuring that you have everything required for this season.

Trusting His provision doesn't mean life will always be easy, but it does mean that you can rest in the assurance that He knows what's best for you. His provision is perfect, and His timing is always right.

Today, release any worry or fear about your needs and trust God to be your shepherd.

Affirmation:
The Lord is my shepherd, and I trust Him to provide for every need in my life.

Action Step:
Write down one area where you've been struggling to trust God's provision. Surrender it to Him in prayer, and choose to trust His care.

Prayer:
Lord, thank You for being my shepherd. Help me to trust Your provision and to rest in the knowledge that You are always caring for me. Amen.

August 9th, 2025: The Blessing of Obedience

Scripture:
"If you fully obey the Lord your God and carefully follow all His commands I give you today, the Lord your God will set you high above all the nations on earth. All these blessings will come on you and accompany you if you obey the Lord your God." (Deuteronomy 28:1-2, NIV)

Reflection:
Obedience to God isn't about following rules; it's about aligning your life with His perfect will. When you obey Him, you open the door to His blessings—peace, protection, provision, and purpose.

God's commands are given out of love, guiding you toward a life that reflects His goodness. Obedience doesn't mean life will always be easy, but it does mean you'll experience the fullness of His presence and favor.

Today, commit to walking in obedience, trusting God to bless and guide your steps.

Affirmation:
Obedience brings blessings. I trust God's commands and walk in alignment with His will.

Action Step:
Reflect on one area where you sense God calling you to greater obedience. Take a step today to align your actions with His Word.

Prayer:
Father, thank You for the blessings that come through obedience. Help me to trust Your commands and to walk faithfully in Your ways. Amen.

August 10th, 2025: Rejoice Always

Scripture:
"Rejoice always, pray continually, give thanks in all circumstances; for this is God's will for you in Christ Jesus." (1 Thessalonians 5:16-18, NIV)

Reflection:
Joy isn't dependent on circumstances—it's rooted in your relationship with Christ. Rejoicing always doesn't mean ignoring hardships; it means choosing to trust God and find joy in His faithfulness, no matter what.

When you cultivate a heart of prayer and gratitude, joy becomes a natural overflow of your faith. It's a declaration that God is good, even in the valleys, and that His promises are unshakable.

Today, choose joy in every moment, letting it be a reflection of your trust in God.

Affirmation:
I rejoice always, trusting in God's goodness and finding joy in His presence.

Action Step:
Take a moment to rejoice in God's goodness. Speak out loud three things you're thankful for, even in the midst of challenges.

Prayer:
Lord, thank You for the gift of joy. Help me to rejoice always, trusting in Your faithfulness and celebrating Your goodness in every circumstance. Amen.

August 11th, 2025: God's Grace is Sufficient

Scripture:
"*But He said to me, 'My grace is sufficient for you, for My power is made perfect in weakness.' Therefore I will boast all the more gladly about my weaknesses, so that Christ's power may rest on me*." (2 Corinthians 12:9, NIV)

Reflection:
Life's challenges can often leave you feeling inadequate or overwhelmed, but God's grace is your strength. His grace meets you exactly where you are, filling the gaps where your ability ends and His power begins.

Instead of hiding your weaknesses, you can bring them to God, knowing they become opportunities for His glory to shine. His grace isn't just enough—it's abundant, sustaining you through every trial and equipping you for every calling.

Today, embrace your weaknesses as a reminder of God's power working in and through you.

Affirmation:
God's grace is sufficient for me. His power is made perfect in my weakness.

Action Step:
Write down an area of your life where you feel weak or overwhelmed. Surrender it to God in prayer, asking for His grace to sustain and empower you.

Prayer:
Father, thank You for Your all-sufficient grace. Help me to trust in Your strength and to let Your power work through my weaknesses. Amen.

August 12th, 2025: Living Generously

Scripture:
"In everything I did, I showed you that by this kind of hard work we must help the weak, remembering the words the Lord Jesus Himself said: 'It is more blessed to give than to receive.'" (Acts 20:35, NIV)

Reflection:
Generosity reflects the heart of Jesus. He gave everything for you, and He calls you to live with open hands, ready to share His blessings with others.

Living generously isn't limited to financial giving—it's also about offering your time, attention, and encouragement. When you live this way, you not only bless others but also experience the joy and fulfillment that comes from being part of God's work in their lives.

Today, ask God to show you how you can live generously, trusting Him to supply all your needs.

Affirmation:
I live generously, reflecting the heart of Jesus and trusting in God's provision.

Action Step:
Identify someone who could use encouragement or support. Take an intentional step to bless them today, whether through your time, resources, or kindness.

Prayer:
Lord, thank You for blessing me so abundantly. Help me to live generously, trusting You to use my gifts to bless others and bring glory to Your name. Amen.

August 13th, 2025: The Fruit of the Spirit: Joy

Scripture:
"*But the fruit of the Spirit is love, joy, peace, forbearance, kindness, goodness, faithfulness, gentleness, and self-control.*" (Galatians 5:22-23, NIV)

Reflection:
Joy is more than a fleeting emotion—it's a fruit of the Spirit, rooted in your relationship with God. Unlike happiness, which depends on circumstances, joy comes from knowing that God is in control and that His promises are unshakable.

When the Holy Spirit dwells in you, He produces joy that overflows into your life, regardless of challenges. This joy strengthens you, uplifts others, and reminds you of the hope you have in Christ.

Today, let the Spirit cultivate His joy in your heart, drawing you closer to God's presence.

Affirmation:
The joy of the Lord is my strength. His Spirit fills me with joy that overflows.

Action Step:
Spend a few minutes worshipping God today. Let His presence fill your heart with joy, and reflect on how you can share that joy with others.

Prayer:
Holy Spirit, thank You for filling my heart with joy. Help me to live in the fullness of Your joy, sharing it with those around me. Amen.

August 14th, 2025: The Power of Gratitude

Scripture:
"*Enter His gates with thanksgiving and His courts with praise; give thanks to Him and praise His name.*" (Psalm 100:4, NIV)

Reflection:
Gratitude is a powerful spiritual practice that shifts your focus from what's wrong to what's right. It aligns your heart with God's goodness, reminding you of His faithfulness and provision.

When you choose gratitude, you open the door to God's presence. It transforms your perspective, lifting your spirit and renewing your faith. Even in challenging seasons, there's always something to thank Him for.

Today, let thanksgiving be the key that draws you closer to God and fills your heart with His peace.

Affirmation:
Gratitude fills my heart and opens the door to God's presence and peace.

Action Step:
Write a list of five things you're thankful for today, big or small. Spend time in prayer, thanking God for each one.

Prayer:
Father, thank You for Your goodness and faithfulness in my life. Help me to cultivate a heart of gratitude, seeing Your blessings in every season. Amen.

August 15th, 2025: Abiding in the Vine

Scripture:
"*I am the vine; you are the branches. If you remain in Me and I in you, you will bear much fruit; apart from Me you can do nothing.*" (John 15:5, NIV)

Reflection:
Abundant living starts with abiding in Jesus. Just as branches draw life and nourishment from the vine, you are sustained by your connection to Him.

When you remain in Christ—through prayer, His Word, and obedience—your life produces fruit that reflects His character. Apart from Him, even your best efforts fall short, but in Him, you find purpose, strength, and abundance.

Today, make abiding in Jesus your highest priority. Let Him be your source of life and fruitfulness.

Affirmation:
I abide in Christ, and His life flows through me, producing fruit for His glory.

Action Step:
Spend 15 minutes meditating on John 15:1-8. Reflect on what it means to remain in Jesus and how you can deepen your connection to Him.

Prayer:
Jesus, thank You for being my vine, my source of life and strength. Teach me to abide in You and to live a life that bears fruit for Your kingdom. Amen.

August 16th, 2025: Strength in Every Season

Scripture:
"*I know what it is to be in need, and I know what it is to have plenty. I have learned the secret of being content in any and every situation, whether well fed or hungry, whether living in plenty or in want. I can do all this through Him who gives me strength.*" (Philippians 4:12-13, NIV)

Reflection:
Life brings seasons of abundance and seasons of challenge, but God's strength is constant through them all. Paul learned to be content not because of his circumstances but because of Christ's sustaining power.

When you rely on God's strength, you find peace and resilience in every situation. He is your provider in times of need and your anchor in times of abundance.

Today, let His strength be your foundation, no matter what season you're in.

Affirmation:
I am content in every season, for Christ is my strength and sustains me always.

Action Step:
Reflect on the season you're currently in. Pray for God's strength to sustain you and for wisdom to embrace the lessons He's teaching you.

Prayer:
Father, thank You for Your strength that carries me through every season. Help me to trust in You and to find contentment in Your presence. Amen.

August 17th, 2025: God Multiplies What You Surrender

Scripture:
"Taking the five loaves and the two fish and looking up to heaven, He gave thanks and broke the loaves. Then He gave them to the disciples, and the disciples gave them to the people. They all ate and were satisfied, and the disciples picked up twelve basketfuls of broken pieces that were left over." (Mark 6:41-42, NIV)

Reflection:
God can do extraordinary things with what you offer to Him, no matter how small it seems. When the boy gave his simple meal to Jesus, it became enough to feed thousands.

In the same way, God multiplies your gifts, talents, and time when you surrender them to Him. What seems insignificant in your hands becomes abundant in His.

Today, consider what you can surrender to God. Trust Him to take it, bless it, and use it for His glory.

Affirmation:
What I surrender to God, He multiplies for His purpose and glory.

Action Step:
Identify one area of your life—time, talent, or resource—that you can surrender to God. Pray and ask Him to use it for His kingdom.

Prayer:
Father, thank You for taking what I surrender and using it in ways beyond my imagination. Help me to trust You with everything I have. Amen.

August 18th, 2025: Faith That Overflows

Scripture:
"*May the God of hope fill you with all joy and peace as you trust in Him, so that you may overflow with hope by the power of the Holy Spirit.*" (Romans 15:13, NIV)

Reflection:
Faith is the foundation of abundant living. When you trust in God, He fills your heart with joy and peace that overflow into every area of your life. This overflow doesn't just bless you—it impacts everyone around you.

Your faith doesn't need to be perfect; it simply needs to be rooted in the One who is faithful. As you rely on the Holy Spirit, He empowers you to live with confident hope, even in uncertain times.

Today, let your faith grow deeper and overflow with hope through the power of the Spirit.

Affirmation:
My faith overflows with joy, peace, and hope, by the power of the Holy Spirit.

Action Step:
Spend time in prayer, asking the Holy Spirit to deepen your trust in God and to fill your heart with overflowing hope.

Prayer:
Holy Spirit, thank You for filling my heart with joy and peace. Help me to trust in God's promises and to overflow with hope in every situation. Amen.

August 19th, 2025: The Promise of Peace

Scripture:
"*You will keep in perfect peace those whose minds are steadfast, because they trust in You.*" (Isaiah 26:3, NIV)

Reflection:
God's peace isn't fleeting—it's perfect and complete, guarding your heart and mind when you place your trust in Him. This peace isn't the absence of trouble but the presence of God, calming your soul in the midst of the storm.

When you fix your mind on God's promises instead of your problems, His peace anchors you. It strengthens your faith and quiets your fears.

Today, shift your focus to God and let His peace fill every corner of your heart.

Affirmation:
God's peace fills my heart and mind as I trust in Him.

Action Step:
Identify one worry or fear you're holding onto. Release it to God in prayer and ask Him to replace it with His peace.

Prayer:
Lord, thank You for Your perfect peace that sustains me. Help me to fix my mind on You and to trust in Your faithfulness. Amen.

August 20th, 2025: An Eternal Perspective

Scripture:
"For our light and momentary troubles are achieving for us an eternal glory that far outweighs them all. So we fix our eyes not on what is seen, but on what is unseen, since what is seen is temporary, but what is unseen is eternal." (2 Corinthians 4:17-18, NIV)

Reflection:
Abundant living comes from keeping an eternal perspective. When you view life through the lens of eternity, challenges lose their power, and God's glory becomes your focus.

Paul reminds us that every trial is temporary, but the eternal rewards of faithfulness are far greater. Fixing your eyes on the unseen—God's promises, His kingdom, and His presence—gives you strength to persevere and hope for what's to come.

Today, ask God to align your perspective with His eternal plan.

Affirmation:
I live with an eternal perspective, trusting in God's promises and purpose.

Action Step:
Spend time reflecting on one area where you need to shift your focus from the temporary to the eternal. Ask God for clarity and strength to align with His perspective.

Prayer:
Father, thank You for the promise of eternal glory. Help me to fix my eyes on what is unseen and to live with faith and hope in Your eternal plan. Amen.

August 21st, 2025: The Beauty of Simplicity

Scripture:
"*Better one handful with tranquility than two handfuls with toil and chasing after the wind.*" (Ecclesiastes 4:6, NIV)

Reflection:
Simplicity is a gift that frees you from the endless pursuit of "more." When you focus on what truly matters—God's presence, relationships, and purpose—you find tranquility and contentment.

The world often equates abundance with accumulation, but God invites you to embrace simplicity as a path to peace. Abundant living isn't about having everything; it's about treasuring what God has already given.

Today, let go of the unnecessary and embrace the beauty of simplicity in Christ.

Affirmation:
I find peace and contentment in the simplicity of God's presence and purpose.

Action Step:
Take inventory of your priorities. Identify one thing you can simplify or let go of to make more space for God and what truly matters.

Prayer:
Lord, thank You for the beauty of simplicity. Teach me to let go of what doesn't matter and to treasure the peace and joy found in You. Amen.

August 22nd, 2025: Delight in the Lord

Scripture:
"*Take delight in the Lord, and He will give you the desires of your heart.*" (Psalm 37:4, NIV)

Reflection:
When you delight in God, your heart aligns with His. His desires become your desires, and you find fulfillment not in what He gives but in who He is.

Delighting in the Lord means enjoying His presence, seeking Him above all else, and trusting Him with your dreams. This delight brings joy, peace, and purpose to your life, no matter your circumstances.

Today, let your delight in God guide your heart and refresh your spirit.

Affirmation:
I delight in the Lord, trusting Him to align my desires with His perfect will.

Action Step:
Spend time in worship today, focusing on God's character and goodness. Let your delight in Him deepen as you praise Him.

Prayer:
Father, thank You for the joy of delighting in You. Align my heart with Yours and help me to find fulfillment in Your presence. Amen.

August 23rd, 2025: Walking in God's Favor

Scripture:
"Let love and faithfulness never leave you; bind them around your neck, write them on the tablet of your heart. Then you will win favor and a good name in the sight of God and man." (Proverbs 3:3-4, NIV)

Reflection:
God's favor flows from a life marked by love and faithfulness. When your actions reflect His character, you bring glory to His name and draw others to His kingdom.

Walking in God's favor isn't about earning blessings—it's about living in alignment with His will. As you remain steadfast in love and faithfulness, His grace opens doors, strengthens relationships, and guides your steps.

Today, commit to living a life that reflects God's love and faithfulness.

Affirmation:
I walk in God's favor, living with love and faithfulness that glorify Him.

Action Step:
Reflect on how you can show love and faithfulness in your relationships today. Choose one action that reflects God's heart.

Prayer:
Lord, thank You for Your favor that flows from a life aligned with You. Help me to walk in love and faithfulness, bringing glory to Your name. Amen.

August 24th, 2025: Purpose in Every Step

Scripture:
"*'For I know the plans I have for you,' declares the Lord, 'plans to prosper you and not to harm you, plans to give you hope and a future.'*" (Jeremiah 29:11, NIV)

Reflection:
God's plans for you are not random or uncertain—they're purposeful, filled with hope and designed for your good. Even when life feels unclear, you can trust that He is working everything together for His glory and your ultimate fulfillment.

Abundant living means walking confidently in God's purpose, trusting that every step you take is part of His divine plan. When you align your desires with His will, you find peace, joy, and direction for the journey ahead.

Today, take a step of faith, trusting that God's purpose is unfolding in your life.

Affirmation:
I walk in God's purpose, trusting His plans to prosper me and give me hope.

Action Step:
Reflect on one area where you're seeking clarity. Pray and ask God to reveal His purpose for this season and to guide your next step.

Prayer:
Father, thank You for Your plans that are filled with hope and purpose. Help me to trust You with every step and to walk confidently in Your will. Amen.

August 25th, 2025: The Reward of Faithfulness

Scripture:
"His master replied, 'Well done, good and faithful servant! You have been faithful with a few things; I will put you in charge of many things. Come and share your master's happiness!'" (Matthew 25:23, NIV)

Reflection:
Faithfulness in the small things prepares you for greater opportunities in God's kingdom. Just as the servants in Jesus' parable were rewarded for their diligence, you too are called to steward what God has entrusted to you with care and commitment.

God sees your faithfulness, even in the unseen moments. When you serve with integrity and a heart of worship, you're not just fulfilling tasks—you're building His kingdom and bringing joy to His heart.

Today, choose faithfulness in everything you do, trusting that God is preparing you for greater things.

Affirmation:
I am faithful with what God has entrusted to me, and I find joy in serving Him.

Action Step:
Identify one responsibility you can approach with renewed faithfulness today, and commit to doing it wholeheartedly for God's glory.

Prayer:
Lord, thank You for calling me to faithfulness. Help me to serve You diligently, knowing that my work honors You and builds Your kingdom. Amen.

August 26th, 2025: Overflowing Hope

Scripture:
"May the God of hope fill you with all joy and peace as you trust in Him, so that you may overflow with hope by the power of the Holy Spirit." (Romans 15:13, NIV)

Reflection:
Hope in God isn't fragile—it's powerful and overflowing. When you trust in Him, He fills you with joy and peace that surpasses understanding, allowing hope to take root and flourish in your heart.

This hope isn't just for you; it's meant to be shared. As the Holy Spirit works within you, your hope becomes a light that encourages others, pointing them to the source of true life.

Today, let God's hope fill you and overflow to those around you.

Affirmation:
My heart overflows with hope, joy, and peace, by the power of the Holy Spirit.

Action Step:
Think of someone who could use encouragement today. Share a word of hope or a small act of kindness to lift their spirit.

Prayer:
Holy Spirit, thank You for filling my heart with hope. Help me to trust in God's promises and to share that hope with others. Amen.

August 27th, 2025: Counting Your Blessings

Scripture:
"Praise the Lord, my soul, and forget not all His benefits." (Psalm 103:2, NIV)

Reflection:
Gratitude unlocks the fullness of life. When you take time to count your blessings, you shift your focus from what's lacking to the abundant ways God has been faithful.

Every breath, every answered prayer, and every moment of joy is a reminder of His goodness. As you recount His blessings, your faith is strengthened, and your heart is drawn closer to Him.

Today, let gratitude guide your heart and open your eyes to the abundance of God's love.

Affirmation:
I count my blessings and praise God for His faithfulness in my life.

Action Step:
Make a list of 10 specific blessings you're grateful for today. Spend time in prayer, thanking God for each one.

Prayer:
Lord, thank You for the countless ways You've blessed me. Help me to live with a heart of gratitude, always remembering Your faithfulness. Amen.

August 28th, 2025: Rich in Good Works

Scripture:
"*Command them to do good, to be rich in good deeds, and to be generous and willing to share.*" (1 Timothy 6:18, NIV)

Reflection:
True abundance isn't measured by what you have but by how you use it. God calls you to be rich in good works, using your time, talents, and resources to bless others and advance His kingdom.

Generosity and service are acts of worship, reflecting God's heart to those around you. When you live this way, you experience the joy of partnering with Him to make an eternal impact.

Today, look for ways to be rich in good works, letting God's love flow through you.

Affirmation:
I am rich in good works, reflecting God's generosity and love in all I do.

Action Step:
Find one way to serve or give generously today, whether through your time, resources, or encouragement.

Prayer:
Lord, thank You for the opportunity to do good and to bless others. Help me to live generously, storing up treasures in heaven. Amen.

August 29th, 2025: The Lord is My Shepherd

Scripture:
"The Lord is my shepherd, I lack nothing. He makes me lie down in green pastures, He leads me beside quiet waters." (Psalm 23:1-2, NIV)

Reflection:
God, your Shepherd, cares for every detail of your life. He leads you to places of rest, refreshment, and restoration, meeting your needs with tender love.

Abundant living isn't about striving—it's about trusting the Shepherd to guide and provide. When you follow Him, you experience peace that calms your soul and joy that refreshes your spirit.

Today, rest in the care of your Shepherd and let Him lead you to quiet waters.

Affirmation:
The Lord is my Shepherd, and I trust Him to guide and provide for me.

Action Step:
Spend time in a quiet place today, reflecting on God's provision and thanking Him for His care in your life.

Prayer:
Lord, thank You for being my Shepherd. Help me to rest in Your care and to trust in Your perfect guidance. Amen.

August 30th, 2025: Living with Open Hands

Scripture:
"*One person gives freely, yet gains even more; another withholds unduly, but comes to poverty. A generous person will prosper; whoever refreshes others will be refreshed.*" (Proverbs 11:24-25, NIV)

Reflection:
Living with open hands means trusting God to provide as you give generously. When you refresh others, you're not only a blessing—you're blessed in return.

God's economy operates on generosity, not scarcity. The more you give, the more He fills you with His abundant grace, joy, and provision.

Today, ask God to help you live with open hands, ready to bless and be blessed.

Affirmation:
I live with open hands, trusting God to refresh me as I refresh others.

Action Step:
Give freely today—whether it's your time, resources, or encouragement—and trust God to provide.

Prayer:
Father, thank You for calling me to live with open hands. Help me to give generously and to trust You for all I need. Amen.

August 31st, 2025: Abundant Life in Christ

Scripture:
"*I have told you this so that My joy may be in you and that your joy may be complete.*" (John 15:11, NIV)

Reflection:
The abundant life Jesus offers is rooted in His joy, peace, and love. It's a life of fulfillment that comes from abiding in Him and living for His glory.

As you walk in Christ, His joy becomes your strength, His peace fills your heart, and His love overflows to those around you. This is the abundant life—complete and satisfying in Him alone.

Today, celebrate the fullness of life you have in Christ and let His joy be your strength.

Affirmation:
I live abundantly in Christ, filled with His joy, peace, and love.

Action Step:
Reflect on the journey of abundant living this month. Write down one way God has shown His abundance in your life and thank Him for it.

Prayer:
Jesus, thank You for offering me abundant life. Help me to remain in You, experiencing the fullness of Your joy and sharing it with the world. Amen.

SEPTEMBER: DISCIPLESHIP & EVANGELISM

Discipleship is about growing in your relationship with Christ and becoming more like Him, while evangelism is about sharing His love and truth with the world. This month explores both personal spiritual growth and practical ways to fulfill the Great Commission. It's a call to live intentionally as a disciple and to boldly share the hope of salvation.

Day	Title	Scripture
Sept 1	The Call to Follow	Matthew 4:19
Sept 2	Go and Make Disciples	Matthew 28:19-20
Sept 3	The Cost of Discipleship	Luke 14:27
Sept 4	Deny Yourself, Take Up Your Cross	Matthew 16:24
Sept 5	Abide in My Word	John 8:31-32
Sept 6	Becoming Fishers of Men	Mark 1:17
Sept 7	Equipped for Every Good Work	2 Timothy 3:16-17

Sept 8	The Heart of a Servant	Mark 10:45
Sept 9	Boldness in Sharing the Gospel	Acts 4:31
Sept 10	Being Salt and Light	Matthew 5:13-16
Sept 11	The Great Commission	Matthew 28:19-20
Sept 12	Bearing Much Fruit	John 15:8
Sept 13	The Power of Your Testimony	Revelation 12:11
Sept 14	Laborers for the Harvest	Luke 10:2
Sept 15	Sharing the Gospel in Love	1 Peter 3:15
Sept 16	The Ministry of Reconciliation	2 Corinthians 5:18-19
Sept 17	Go Into All the World	Mark 16:15
Sept 18	Walking as Jesus Walked	1 John 2:6
Sept 19	Counting the Cost	Luke 14:28
Sept 20	The Fields are White for Harvest	John 4:35
Sept 21	Leading by Example	1 Corinthians 11:1
Sept 22	Pray for Boldness	Ephesians 6:19-20
Sept 23	God Gives the Growth	1 Corinthians 3:6-7
Sept 24	The Lost Sheep	Luke 15:4-7

Sept 25	The Joy of Making Disciples	3 John 1:4
Sept 26	Do the Work of an Evangelist	2 Timothy 4:5
Sept 27	Living on Mission	Colossians 4:5-6
Sept 28	Be Ready in Season and Out	2 Timothy 4:2
Sept 29	God's Heart for the Nations	Psalm 67:2
Sept 30	Until the Whole World Hears	Revelation 7:9-10

September 1: The Call to Follow

Scripture:
"*'Come, follow Me,' Jesus said, 'and I will send you out to fish for people.'*" (Matthew 4:19, NIV)

Reflection:
Discipleship begins with a simple yet profound invitation: "Follow Me." Jesus didn't call His disciples because they were perfect or qualified; He called them because He saw their potential to grow, learn, and carry His mission forward.

When you say "yes" to following Jesus, you begin a journey of transformation. He doesn't just want you to know about Him—He wants you to walk with Him, learn from Him, and share His heart with the world.

Today, ask yourself: Are you fully following Jesus? Let His call renew your commitment to walk in His footsteps.

Affirmation:
I follow Jesus wholeheartedly, trusting Him to lead me and transform my life.

Action Step:
Take time to reflect on what it means to follow Jesus in your daily life. Identify one specific way you can grow closer to Him today.

Prayer:
Jesus, thank You for calling me to follow You. Help me to walk in Your footsteps, learning from Your example and trusting in Your plan. Amen.

September 2nd, 2025: Go and Make Disciples

Scripture:
"Therefore go and make disciples of all nations, baptizing them in the name of the Father and of the Son and of the Holy Spirit, and teaching them to obey everything I have commanded you. And surely I am with you always, to the very end of the age." (Matthew 28:19-20, NIV)

Reflection:
The Great Commission isn't a suggestion—it's a command to every believer. Jesus entrusted His mission to His disciples, calling them to spread the Gospel, teach His Word, and invite others into His kingdom.

Making disciples starts with building relationships and sharing the love of Christ. It requires intentionality, patience, and a willingness to invest in others. The promise of His presence gives you the confidence to step out in faith, knowing you're never alone.

Today, consider how you can live out the Great Commission in your own life.

Affirmation:
I am called to make disciples, sharing the Gospel and inviting others into God's kingdom.

Action Step:
Pray for one person in your life who doesn't know Christ. Ask God to open opportunities for you to share His love with them.

Prayer:
Lord, thank You for entrusting me with Your mission. Help me to make disciples and to share Your love with boldness and grace. Amen.

September 3rd, 2025: The Cost of Discipleship

Scripture:
"*And whoever does not carry their cross and follow Me cannot be My disciple*." (Luke 14:27, NIV)

Reflection:
Following Jesus comes with a cost. It means surrendering your plans, your comfort, and sometimes even your relationships to fully embrace His will. Discipleship isn't always easy, but the reward of walking closely with Christ far outweighs the sacrifices.

Carrying your cross is a daily decision to prioritize God's kingdom over your own desires. It's an act of love and trust, knowing that Jesus walked this path before you and promises to walk it with you.

Today, reflect on what carrying your cross looks like in your life.

Affirmation:
I embrace the cost of discipleship, trusting Jesus to lead me and strengthen me.

Action Step:
Identify one area where God is calling you to surrender or trust Him more deeply. Commit to taking that step today.

Prayer:
Jesus, thank You for leading me on the path of discipleship. Help me to carry my cross and to follow You with faith and courage. Amen.

September 4th, 2025: Deny Yourself, Take Up Your Cross

Scripture:
"Then Jesus said to His disciples, 'Whoever wants to be My disciple must deny themselves and take up their cross and follow Me.'" (Matthew 16:24, NIV)

Reflection:
Discipleship requires surrender. Denying yourself means choosing God's will over your own, trusting that His plans lead to greater fulfillment. Taking up your cross is a daily commitment to endure challenges for the sake of Christ, knowing He has overcome the world.

This calling isn't burdensome when you realize it's an invitation to walk closely with Jesus. The cross may be heavy at times, but He promises to carry the weight with you, strengthening you as you follow Him.

Today, renew your commitment to deny yourself and take up your cross, trusting Jesus every step of the way.

Affirmation:
I deny myself and take up my cross, following Jesus with faith and obedience.

Action Step:
Reflect on an area where you've been holding back from full surrender. Ask God for the strength to lay it down and trust Him completely.

Prayer:
Jesus, thank You for calling me to follow You. Help me to deny myself, take up my cross, and trust in Your plan for my life. Amen.

September 5th, 2025: Abide in My Word

Scripture:
"*To the Jews who had believed Him, Jesus said, 'If you hold to My teaching, you are really My disciples. Then you will know the truth, and the truth will set you free.'*" (John 8:31-32, NIV)

Reflection:
Discipleship is rooted in God's Word. Abiding in His teaching means more than hearing it—it means living it, letting it shape your decisions, and allowing His truth to transform your heart.

God's Word is a source of freedom, clarity, and strength. When you hold to His teachings, you're not only growing as a disciple but also experiencing the abundant life Jesus promised. His truth liberates you from fear, doubt, and sin, guiding you into His peace.

Today, commit to abiding in God's Word, letting it deepen your walk with Him.

Affirmation:
I abide in God's Word, knowing that His truth sets me free and guides my life.

Action Step:
Choose a Scripture to meditate on today. Reflect on how you can live out its teaching in a practical way.

Prayer:
Lord, thank You for the freedom found in Your Word. Help me to abide in Your truth and to let it shape my life as I follow You. Amen.

<u>September 6th, 2025: Becoming Fishers of Men</u>

Scripture:
"*'Come, follow Me,' Jesus said, 'and I will send you out to fish for people.'*" (Mark 1:17, NIV)

Reflection:
Jesus calls His disciples to become fishers of men—actively seeking to share the Gospel and draw others into His kingdom. This calling isn't reserved for pastors or missionaries; it's for everyone who follows Christ.

Being a fisher of men requires patience, intentionality, and reliance on the Holy Spirit. Just as fishermen use the right tools and timing, you are called to use love, prayer, and God's Word to share the hope of salvation.

Today, ask God to help you see opportunities to share His love with those around you.

Affirmation:
I am a fisher of men, sharing the Gospel and drawing others into God's kingdom.

Action Step:
Pray for someone in your life who doesn't know Christ. Ask God to open a door for you to share His love with them.

Prayer:
Jesus, thank You for calling me to be a fisher of men. Help me to share Your love with boldness and to trust You to work through me. Amen.

September 7th, 2025: Equipped for Every Good Work

Scripture:
"All Scripture is God-breathed and is useful for teaching, rebuking, correcting, and training in righteousness, so that the servant of God may be thoroughly equipped for every good work." (2 Timothy 3:16-17, NIV)

Reflection:
God doesn't just call you to be His disciple—He equips you for the journey. His Word is your guide, teaching you how to live, grow, and serve with righteousness and wisdom.

Through Scripture, God prepares you for every good work, whether it's serving in your community, sharing the Gospel, or encouraging others. As you spend time in His Word, He strengthens your faith and equips you to carry out His mission.

Today, let God's Word equip and empower you for the work He has prepared for you.

Affirmation:
God's Word equips me for every good work, strengthening me to fulfill His purpose.

Action Step:
Identify one area of your life where you feel unequipped. Spend time in Scripture, seeking God's guidance and encouragement for that area.

Prayer:
Lord, thank You for equipping me through Your Word. Help me to grow in righteousness and to use what You've taught me to serve and bless others. Amen.

September 8th, 2025: The Heart of a Servant

Scripture:
"For even the Son of Man did not come to be served, but to serve, and to give His life as a ransom for many." (Mark 10:45, NIV)

Reflection:
Jesus modeled the heart of a servant, willingly humbling Himself to meet the needs of others. As His disciple, you're called to reflect this same servant-hearted love, putting others before yourself and seeking ways to bless and uplift.

Serving isn't about recognition—it's about showing God's love in action. Every act of service, no matter how small, is a reflection of His heart and an opportunity to point others to Him.

Today, ask God to help you develop a heart of humility and a willingness to serve.

Affirmation:
I follow Jesus' example, serving others with humility and love.

Action Step:
Look for one specific way to serve someone today, whether through a kind gesture, encouragement, or meeting a need.

Prayer:
Jesus, thank You for showing me what it means to serve. Help me to love others with humility and to reflect Your heart in all I do. Amen.

September 9th, 2025: Boldness in Sharing the Gospel

Scripture:
"After they prayed, the place where they were meeting was shaken. And they were all filled with the Holy Spirit and spoke the word of God boldly." (Acts 4:31, NIV)

Reflection:
The early church was marked by boldness in sharing the Gospel, even in the face of opposition. This boldness didn't come from their own strength but from the Holy Spirit empowering them to speak and act with courage.

God calls you to share His Word boldly, trusting that He will give you the words and wisdom to speak. When you rely on the Spirit, you can step out in faith, knowing He is with you every step of the way.

Today, pray for boldness to share the Gospel with those God places in your path.

Affirmation:
I am filled with the Holy Spirit and speak God's Word boldly, trusting in His power.

Action Step:
Identify one person or situation where you can share the Gospel. Pray for boldness and take a step of faith to share God's love.

Prayer:
Holy Spirit, thank You for empowering me to share the Gospel. Fill me with boldness and confidence as I speak Your truth and reflect Your love. Amen.

September 10th, 2025: Being Salt and Light

Scripture:
"*You are the salt of the earth... You are the light of the world. A town built on a hill cannot be hidden.*" (Matthew 5:13-14, NIV)

Reflection:
As a disciple, you are called to be salt and light in the world. Salt preserves and enhances, reminding us to live lives that reflect God's purity and goodness. Light dispels darkness, shining hope and truth into every situation.

When you live as salt and light, your life becomes a testimony of God's love and grace. Even small acts of kindness and faithfulness can have a profound impact, drawing others closer to Him.

Today, ask God to help you live in a way that points others to His truth and love.

Affirmation:
I am salt and light, reflecting God's love and truth to the world around me.

Action Step:
Think of one way you can be salt and light today—whether through encouraging someone, sharing your testimony, or standing for truth.

Prayer:
Lord, thank You for calling me to be salt and light. Help me to live in a way that glorifies You and draws others to Your love. Amen.

September 11th, 2025: The Great Commission

Scripture:
"Therefore go and make disciples of all nations, baptizing them in the name of the Father and of the Son and of the Holy Spirit, and teaching them to obey everything I have commanded you. And surely I am with you always, to the very end of the age." (Matthew 28:19-20, NIV)

Reflection:
The Great Commission is a call to action, entrusted to every believer. It's not a task reserved for a select few—it's a mission for all who follow Christ. Making disciples means more than converting people; it involves walking alongside them, teaching, encouraging, and helping them grow in faith.

Jesus promises His presence as you go. You don't have to rely on your own strength or wisdom—He is with you, guiding every step and empowering every conversation.

Today, embrace the Great Commission as your personal mission, trusting Jesus to equip you for the journey.

Affirmation:
I am called to make disciples, knowing Jesus is with me always.

Action Step:
Pray for God to reveal someone in your life whom you can disciple or encourage in their faith. Take a step to reach out to them this week.

Prayer:
Jesus, thank You for entrusting me with the Great Commission. Help me to share Your love and truth with others, trusting in Your presence and guidance. Amen.

September 12th, 2025: Bearing Much Fruit

Scripture:
"This is to My Father's glory, that you bear much fruit, showing yourselves to be My disciples." (John 15:8, NIV)

Reflection:
A fruitful life is the evidence of true discipleship. As you abide in Christ, His Spirit works within you, producing fruit that glorifies God and blesses others. This fruit is seen in your character (the fruit of the Spirit) and in your impact (sharing the Gospel, serving others, and making disciples).

Bearing fruit requires staying connected to the Vine, trusting Jesus to provide the strength and nourishment you need. When you walk closely with Him, your life naturally reflects His love, joy, and purpose.

Today, ask God to help you bear fruit that glorifies Him and points others to His kingdom.

Affirmation:
I abide in Christ, and my life bears much fruit for God's glory.

Action Step:
Reflect on one area where you'd like to bear more fruit—whether in character, service, or evangelism. Pray for the Spirit's guidance to grow in that area.

Prayer:
Father, thank You for calling me to a life of fruitfulness. Help me to stay connected to Jesus, bearing fruit that glorifies You and blesses others. Amen.

September 13th, 2025: The Power of Your Testimony

Scripture:
"They triumphed over him by the blood of the Lamb and by the word of their testimony; they did not love their lives so much as to shrink from death." (Revelation 12:11, NIV)

Reflection:
Your testimony is a powerful tool for sharing the Gospel. It's the story of how Jesus has transformed your life, offering hope and encouragement to those who hear it.

You don't need a dramatic conversion story for your testimony to be impactful. What matters is your willingness to share how God has worked in your life, giving Him glory and pointing others to His grace.

Today, reflect on your testimony and ask God for opportunities to share it with someone in need of hope.

Affirmation:
My testimony is a powerful witness to God's grace and faithfulness.

Action Step:
Take a moment to write down your testimony. Practice sharing it in a clear and concise way, focusing on how God's love has changed your life.

Prayer:
Lord, thank You for the story You're writing in my life. Help me to share my testimony boldly, pointing others to Your love and grace. Amen.

September 14th, 2025: Laborers for the Harvest

Scripture:
"He told them, 'The harvest is plentiful, but the workers are few. Ask the Lord of the harvest, therefore, to send out workers into His harvest field.'" (Luke 10:2, NIV)

Reflection:
The world is full of people longing for hope, purpose, and salvation. The harvest is plentiful, but God is calling for laborers—those willing to step into the field, share the Gospel, and make disciples.

As a laborer in God's harvest field, your work matters. Every conversation, prayer, and act of kindness is part of His mission to bring people into His kingdom.

Today, ask God to use you as a laborer and to send others into the field alongside you.

Affirmation:
I am a laborer in God's harvest, sharing His love and bringing hope to the world.

Action Step:
Pray for God to send laborers into the harvest. Consider how you can be part of His mission, whether through prayer, giving, or direct involvement in ministry.

Prayer:
Lord, thank You for calling me to Your harvest. Use me to share Your love and truth, and send more laborers to bring people into Your kingdom. Amen.

September 15th, 2025: Sharing the Gospel in Love

Scripture:
"*But in your hearts revere Christ as Lord. Always be prepared to give an answer to everyone who asks you to give the reason for the hope that you have. But do this with gentleness and respect.*" (1 Peter 3:15, NIV)

Reflection:
Sharing the Gospel is most effective when it's done with love, gentleness, and respect. People are drawn to the hope within you when they see Christ reflected in your words and actions.

Being prepared to share your faith means knowing the reason for your hope and trusting the Holy Spirit to guide your conversations. It's not about winning arguments; it's about offering the love and truth of Jesus to those who need it.

Today, ask God to help you share the Gospel with wisdom and compassion.

Affirmation:
I share the Gospel with love, gentleness, and respect, reflecting Christ's heart.

Action Step:
Think of someone in your life who may be open to hearing about your faith. Pray for wisdom and an opportunity to share with them in love.

Prayer:
Holy Spirit, thank You for empowering me to share the Gospel. Help me to speak with love, gentleness, and respect, pointing others to Jesus. Amen.

September 16th, 2025: The Ministry of Reconciliation

Scripture:
"All this is from God, who reconciled us to Himself through Christ and gave us the ministry of reconciliation." (2 Corinthians 5:18, NIV)

Reflection:
Through Christ, you've been reconciled to God—brought into right relationship with Him. Now, He's entrusted you with the ministry of reconciliation, calling you to share His message of peace and restoration with others.

Reconciliation is at the heart of the Gospel. It's the invitation for broken people to be made whole in Christ. As you share this message, you're partnering with God to bring hope, healing, and salvation to the world.

Today, ask God to guide you in the ministry of reconciliation, pointing others to His love.

Affirmation:
I am entrusted with the ministry of reconciliation, sharing God's love and restoration.

Action Step:
Think of a relationship or situation that needs reconciliation. Pray for God's guidance to bring His peace and healing to that area.

Prayer:
Father, thank You for reconciling me to Yourself through Christ. Help me to share Your message of reconciliation with others, bringing hope and healing in Your name. Amen.

September 17: Go Into All the World

Scripture:
"He said to them, 'Go into all the world and preach the Gospel to all creation.'" (Mark 16:15, NIV)

Reflection:
Jesus' command to "go" extends beyond borders, cultures, and comfort zones. It's a call to take His message of salvation to every corner of the world, reaching those who have yet to hear the Good News.

You may not be called to travel the globe, but you are called to make an impact wherever you are. Whether through prayer, giving, or personal evangelism, your obedience to this command brings God's kingdom closer to those who need it most.

Today, consider how you can be part of taking the Gospel to the world.

Affirmation:
I am called to go into all the world, sharing the Gospel with boldness and love.

Action Step:
Pray for missionaries and ministries reaching unreached people groups. Ask God how you can support or participate in their work.

Prayer:
Jesus, thank You for calling me to share Your Gospel with the world. Use me to make an impact, whether near or far, for Your kingdom. Amen.

September 18th, 2025: Walking as Jesus Walked

Scripture:
"*Whoever claims to live in Him must live as Jesus did.*" (1 John 2:6, NIV)

Reflection:
Discipleship means modeling your life after Jesus. His love, humility, obedience, and compassion set the standard for how you're called to live.

Walking as Jesus walked isn't about perfection—it's about surrender. As you align your thoughts, words, and actions with His example, the Holy Spirit empowers you to reflect His character.

Today, invite Jesus to guide your steps. Let His example shape how you treat others, handle challenges, and pursue God's will.

Affirmation:
I walk as Jesus walked, reflecting His love, humility, and obedience.

Action Step:
Think of one situation where you can follow Jesus' example today. Commit to responding with His love and grace.

Prayer:
Jesus, thank You for showing me how to walk in love and obedience. Help me to live as You did, bringing glory to the Father in all I do. Amen.

September 19th, 2025: Counting the Cost

Scripture:
"*Suppose one of you wants to build a tower. Won't you first sit down and estimate the cost to see if you have enough money to complete it?*" (Luke 14:28, NIV)

Reflection:
Discipleship comes with a cost. It requires sacrifice, perseverance, and a willingness to prioritize God's kingdom above all else. Counting the cost isn't about hesitating—it's about understanding the commitment and trusting that God's rewards far outweigh the sacrifices.

When you follow Jesus, you may face challenges, but you also gain the eternal joy of walking in His purpose and presence. He gives you the strength to endure and the peace to press on.

Today, ask God to help you embrace the cost of discipleship with faith and courage.

Affirmation:
I count the cost of discipleship and trust in God's eternal rewards.

Action Step:
Reflect on an area where discipleship has required sacrifice in your life. Thank God for His strength and grace in those moments.

Prayer:
Father, thank You for the privilege of following You. Help me to embrace the cost of discipleship, knowing Your presence is my greatest reward. Amen.

September 20th, 2025: The Fields are White for Harvest

Scripture:
"*Don't you have a saying, 'It's still four months until harvest'? I tell you, open your eyes and look at the fields! They are ripe for harvest.*" (John 4:35, NIV)

Reflection:
The world is ready for the Gospel, and God invites you to be part of His harvest. People are searching for hope, love, and truth—things only Jesus can provide. Your role is to share His message and trust Him to do the rest.

The harvest may not always be visible, but it's there. God is at work in hearts and communities, preparing the soil for His kingdom. When you step out in faith, He uses your obedience to plant seeds and bring lives into His family.

Today, ask God to open your eyes to the harvest around you.

Affirmation:
The fields are ripe for harvest, and I am called to share the Gospel with boldness.

Action Step:
Pray for discernment to recognize opportunities to share God's love. Look for one person or situation where you can plant seeds of the Gospel today.

Prayer:
Lord, thank You for inviting me into Your harvest. Open my eyes to the opportunities around me, and use me to bring others into Your kingdom. Amen.

September 21st, 2025: Leading by Example

Scripture:
"Follow my example, as I follow the example of Christ." (1 Corinthians 11:1, NIV)

Reflection:
As a disciple of Christ, your actions speak louder than your words. Paul encouraged others to follow his example because he was modeling Christ. In the same way, your life can be a testimony that inspires others to grow in faith.

Leading by example doesn't mean being perfect—it means being authentic. When you reflect Jesus' love, humility, and faithfulness, you show others what it looks like to walk with Him.

Today, ask God to help you live in a way that points others to Christ.

Affirmation:
I lead by example, reflecting Jesus in my actions and inspiring others to follow Him.

Action Step:
Identify one area where you can model Christ-like behavior today. Act with intentionality, knowing your example can encourage others.

Prayer:
Jesus, thank You for being my perfect example. Help me to live in a way that reflects Your heart and inspires others to follow You. Amen.

September 22nd, 2025: Pray for Boldness

Scripture:
"Pray also for me, that whenever I speak, words may be given me so that I will fearlessly make known the mystery of the Gospel." (Ephesians 6:19, NIV)

Reflection:
Boldness in sharing the Gospel isn't something you muster up on your own—it's a gift from God, empowered by prayer and the Holy Spirit. Even Paul, one of the boldest evangelists, asked others to pray for his courage to proclaim the Gospel fearlessly.

When you pray for boldness, you're inviting God to work through your words and actions, giving you the confidence to share His truth with love and conviction.

Today, pray for boldness to speak God's truth in every opportunity He provides.

Affirmation:
I am filled with boldness by the Holy Spirit to fearlessly proclaim the Gospel.

Action Step:
Spend time in prayer, asking God for boldness and clarity to share His message with someone this week.

Prayer:
Lord, thank You for empowering me to share Your Gospel. Fill me with boldness and love, and give me the courage to proclaim Your truth fearlessly. Amen.

September 23rd, 2025: God Gives the Growth

Scripture:
"I planted the seed, Apollos watered it, but God has been making it grow." (1 Corinthians 3:6, NIV)

Reflection:
Sharing the Gospel is a team effort, but only God can bring the growth. Your role is to plant seeds of truth and water them with love and encouragement. Trust God to do the rest in His timing.

This truth reminds you that you don't have to carry the burden of results. God is the one who softens hearts, opens minds, and brings people into His kingdom. Your faithfulness in planting and watering is enough.

Today, trust God to bring growth as you faithfully share His message.

Affirmation:
I plant and water seeds of faith, trusting God to bring the growth.

Action Step:
Think of someone you've been praying for or sharing with. Commit to planting or watering a seed today through a kind word, act, or prayer.

Prayer:
Father, thank You for bringing the growth in Your perfect timing. Help me to faithfully plant and water seeds of faith, trusting in Your work. Amen.

September 24th, 2025: The Lost Sheep

Scripture:
"*Suppose one of you has a hundred sheep and loses one of them. Doesn't he leave the ninety-nine in the open country and go after the lost sheep until he finds it?*" (Luke 15:4, NIV)

Reflection:
God's heart is for the lost. Like a shepherd seeking a missing sheep, He goes to great lengths to bring people back into His fold. As His disciple, you're called to share this same love and pursue those who are far from Him.

Your role isn't to save the lost—that's God's work—but to show His love, grace, and truth in a way that draws them closer to Him. Every act of kindness and every word of truth can help lead someone back to the Shepherd.

Today, ask God to give you His heart for the lost and the courage to reach out.

Affirmation:
I share God's love for the lost, trusting Him to lead them back to His fold.

Action Step:
Pray for someone you know who may be far from God. Ask for wisdom and an opportunity to share His love with them.

Prayer:
Father, thank You for pursuing me when I was lost. Give me Your heart for the lost, and use me to reflect Your love and grace to those who need it. Amen.

September 25th, 2025: The Joy of Making Disciples

Scripture:
"*I have no greater joy than to hear that my children are walking in the truth.*" (3 John 1:4, NIV)

Reflection:
There's a unique and lasting joy in seeing others grow in their faith because of your encouragement and witness. As a disciple-maker, you're partnering with God to lead others toward truth, freedom, and purpose in Christ.

Discipleship isn't just a responsibility—it's a privilege. Each conversation, prayer, and act of encouragement contributes to someone's spiritual journey. This eternal impact brings joy that surpasses anything the world can offer.

Today, thank God for the joy of making disciples and pray for those you're helping grow in faith.

Affirmation:
I find joy in making disciples, knowing that their growth glorifies God.

Action Step:
Reach out to someone you've been discipling or encouraging in their faith. Share a word of encouragement or pray with them.

Prayer:
Father, thank You for the privilege of making disciples. Fill me with joy as I see others grow in their faith, and help me to continue pointing them to You. Amen.

September 26th, 2025: Do the Work of an Evangelist

Scripture:
"But you, keep your head in all situations, endure hardship, do the work of an evangelist, discharge all the duties of your ministry." (2 Timothy 4:5, NIV)

Reflection:
Evangelism isn't always easy, but it's an essential part of living out your faith. Paul encouraged Timothy to stay steady and committed, even in challenging circumstances, knowing the eternal significance of sharing the Gospel.

Doing the work of an evangelist means being ready to share the hope of Christ wherever God places you. Whether through conversations, acts of kindness, or personal testimony, your obedience can plant seeds of salvation.

Today, ask God to strengthen you for the work of evangelism and to give you a heart for the lost.

Affirmation:
I am called to do the work of an evangelist, sharing Christ's hope and love with others.

Action Step:
Identify one practical way you can engage in evangelism this week, such as initiating a spiritual conversation or inviting someone to church.

Prayer:
Lord, thank You for calling me to share Your Gospel. Give me the strength, wisdom, and love to do the work of an evangelist, pointing others to You. Amen.

September 27th, 2025: Living on Mission

Scripture:
"Be wise in the way you act toward outsiders; make the most of every opportunity. Let your conversation be always full of grace, seasoned with salt, so that you may know how to answer everyone." (Colossians 4:5-6, NIV)

Reflection:
Living on mission means approaching every day with purpose, knowing that every interaction is an opportunity to reflect Christ. Your words, actions, and attitude can open doors for the Gospel, even in ordinary moments.

Paul reminds you to be wise and gracious in your interactions, letting God's love and truth shine through you. Living on mission isn't about perfection—it's about being available and intentional in pointing others to Jesus.

Today, ask God to help you see the opportunities He's placed around you to live on mission.

Affirmation:
I live on mission, making the most of every opportunity to reflect Christ.

Action Step:
Choose one interaction today to approach with intentionality —whether at work, home, or in your community—and reflect Christ's love in that moment.

Prayer:
Father, thank You for calling me to live on mission. Help me to approach every interaction with grace and wisdom, making the most of every opportunity to reflect Your love. Amen.

September 28th, 2025: Be Ready in Season and Out

Scripture:
"*Preach the word; be prepared in season and out of season; correct, rebuke, and encourage—with great patience and careful instruction.*" (2 Timothy 4:2, NIV)

Reflection:
Evangelism requires readiness. Whether the moment feels convenient or unexpected, God calls you to be prepared to share His Word, offering correction, encouragement, and truth with patience and love.

Being ready means staying grounded in Scripture and sensitive to the Holy Spirit. As you prepare your heart daily, God equips you to seize every opportunity to share His message of hope, even when you least expect it.

Today, commit to being ready in season and out, trusting God to use you whenever He calls.

Affirmation:
I am prepared to share God's Word in every season, trusting His Spirit to guide me.

Action Step:
Spend time in prayer and Scripture today, asking God to prepare your heart and equip you to share His truth whenever opportunities arise.

Prayer:
Lord, thank You for calling me to share Your Word. Help me to stay ready, sensitive to Your Spirit, and faithful in proclaiming Your truth with love and patience. Amen.

September 29th, 2025: God's Heart for the Nations

Scripture:
"*May God be gracious to us and bless us and make His face shine on us—so that Your ways may be known on earth, Your salvation among all nations.*" (Psalm 67:1-2, NIV)

Reflection:
God's love isn't confined to one group of people—it's for every nation, tribe, and tongue. His heart is for the whole world to know His salvation and experience His grace.

As His disciple, you're invited to participate in this global mission, whether through prayer, giving, or going. Your obedience plays a part in making His name known among the nations, fulfilling His desire to see all people come to Him.

Today, align your heart with God's and ask Him how you can contribute to His mission for the nations.

Affirmation:
I share God's heart for the nations, participating in His mission to bring salvation to the world.

Action Step:
Spend time praying for a specific nation or people group. Ask God to send laborers to bring His salvation and consider how you can support global missions.

Prayer:
Father, thank You for Your heart for the nations. Use me to make Your salvation known and to bring Your love to those who have yet to hear. Amen.

September 30th, 2025: Until the Whole World Hears

Scripture:
"*After this I looked, and there before me was a great multitude that no one could count, from every nation, tribe, people, and language, standing before the throne and before the Lamb.*" (Revelation 7:9, NIV)

Reflection:
The mission of discipleship and evangelism points to a glorious future: a day when people from every nation will stand before God's throne in worship. This vision reminds you that your efforts to share the Gospel are part of a greater, eternal plan.

Until the whole world hears, God calls you to remain faithful, sharing His love and truth wherever He places you. Every seed planted, every word spoken, and every prayer lifted contributes to His kingdom.

Today, celebrate the hope of this eternal vision and commit to sharing God's love until the whole world hears.

Affirmation:
I am part of God's mission, sharing His love and truth until the whole world hears.

Action Step:
Reflect on how your life is contributing to God's mission. Write down one step you can take to continue sharing His love and truth with others.

Prayer:
Lord, thank You for the promise of a great multitude worshipping before Your throne. Help me to stay faithful to

Your mission, sharing Your love until the whole world hears. Amen.

OCTOBER: WALKING IN WISDOM

Wisdom is a priceless gift that comes from seeking God's guidance and aligning your life with His Word. This month's devotionals explore the richness of Biblical wisdom, practical steps to live wisely, and the power of discernment in navigating life's complexities.

Day	Title	Scripture
Oct 1	The Beginning of Wisdom	Proverbs 9:10
Oct 2	Ask for Wisdom	James 1:5
Oct 3	Wisdom from Above	James 3:17
Oct 4	The Fear of the Lord	Proverbs 1:7
Oct 5	Trust in the Lord	Proverbs 3:5-6
Oct 6	Wise Counsel	Proverbs 11:14
Oct 7	Guard Your Heart	Proverbs 4:23
Oct 8	The Word is a Lamp	Psalm 119:105
Oct 9	A Fool's Way vs. A Wise Path	Proverbs 12:15

Oct 10	Wise Speech	Proverbs 15:1
Oct 11	Avoiding Temptation	1 Corinthians 10:13
Oct 12	Wisdom in Relationships	Ephesians 5:15-16
Oct 13	Humility and Wisdom	Proverbs 22:4
Oct 14	God's Plan vs. My Plan	Jeremiah 29:11
Oct 15	Building Your House on the Rock	Matthew 7:24
Oct 16	Seeking Understanding	Proverbs 2:3-5
Oct 17	Wisdom Through Trials	Romans 5:3-4
Oct 18	The Company You Keep	1 Corinthians 15:33
Oct 19	Patience in Wisdom	Ecclesiastes 7:8-9
Oct 20	The Peace of God's Wisdom	Isaiah 26:3
Oct 21	Sowing in Peace	James 3:18
Oct 22	The Gift of Discernment	Philippians 1:9-10
Oct 23	Wisdom in Stewardship	Luke 16:10
Oct 24	Knowing the Times	Ecclesiastes 3:1
Oct 25	Trusting God's Timing	Habakkuk 2:3

Oct 26	Being Slow to Anger	Proverbs 14:29
Oct 27	Walking by Faith, Not by Sight	2 Corinthians 5:7
Oct 28	Wisdom in Trials	James 1:2-4
Oct 29	Light in the Darkness	John 8:12
Oct 30	Persevering in Wisdom	Galatians 6:9
Oct 31	Christ, the Wisdom of God	1 Corinthians 1:30

October 1st, 2025: The Beginning of Wisdom

Scripture:
"*The fear of the Lord is the beginning of wisdom, and knowledge of the Holy One is understanding.*" (Proverbs 9:10, NIV)

Reflection:
True wisdom begins with a reverent fear of the Lord—a deep respect and awe for His holiness, power, and authority. This isn't a fear that drives you away; it's one that draws you closer, inspiring trust and surrender.

When you acknowledge God as the source of all wisdom, you gain a foundation for making decisions, navigating challenges, and understanding life's purpose. The world offers countless paths, but only God's wisdom leads to lasting peace and fulfillment.

Today, choose to walk in the fear of the Lord, letting it guide your thoughts, decisions, and actions.

Affirmation:
The fear of the Lord is my foundation. I walk in wisdom, guided by His truth.

Action Step:
Spend a few moments in prayer, asking God to deepen your reverence for Him and to guide you with His wisdom in your decisions today.

Prayer:
Father, I stand in awe of Your greatness. Help me to walk in the fear of the Lord, seeking Your wisdom and trusting in Your guidance. Amen.

October 2nd, 2025: Ask for Wisdom

Scripture:
"*If any of you lacks wisdom, you should ask God, who gives generously to all without finding fault, and it will be given to you.*" (James 1:5, NIV)

Reflection:
God's wisdom isn't reserved for a select few—it's freely available to anyone who asks. When you approach Him in faith, He responds with generosity, equipping you to make decisions and navigate life with clarity and confidence.

Asking for wisdom requires humility, acknowledging that you can't rely on your own understanding. It's an act of surrender, trusting God to provide the insight you need at just the right time.

Today, boldly ask God for the wisdom you need, trusting Him to lead you with grace and truth.

Affirmation:
I ask for God's wisdom, trusting Him to guide me generously and faithfully.

Action Step:
Identify one area where you need wisdom—whether in a decision, relationship, or challenge. Bring it to God in prayer, asking for His guidance and clarity.

Prayer:
Lord, thank You for Your generous gift of wisdom. I ask for Your guidance in my life today, trusting You to lead me in truth and understanding. Amen.

October 3rd, 2025: Wisdom from Above

Scripture:
"But the wisdom that comes from heaven is first of all pure; then peace-loving, considerate, submissive, full of mercy and good fruit, impartial and sincere." (James 3:17, NIV)

Reflection:
God's wisdom is unlike the world's. It's pure and peaceable, producing good fruit and transforming the way you live and relate to others. Heavenly wisdom builds unity, fosters love, and reflects God's character in every interaction.

When you seek wisdom from above, you're inviting God to shape your thoughts and decisions. This wisdom equips you to respond to challenges with grace, to act with integrity, and to bring His peace into your relationships.

Today, let the wisdom from above guide your words, actions, and attitudes.

Affirmation:
I walk in wisdom from above, reflecting God's purity, peace, and love.

Action Step:
Reflect on how your decisions reflect God's wisdom. Choose one interaction today to approach with peace, mercy, and sincerity.

Prayer:
Lord, thank You for the gift of wisdom from above. Help me to live in a way that reflects Your character, bringing peace and good fruit into every situation. Amen.

October 4th, 2025: The Fear of the Lord

Scripture:
"The fear of the Lord is the beginning of knowledge, but fools despise wisdom and instruction." (Proverbs 1:7, NIV)

Reflection:
The fear of the Lord isn't about being afraid—it's about having a heart of reverence and humility before God. This kind of fear acknowledges His authority and invites His wisdom into every aspect of your life.

Without this foundation, knowledge becomes empty and misused. But when your life is built on a reverence for God, His wisdom leads you to live with purpose, integrity, and love.

Today, let the fear of the Lord be the starting point for your decisions, inviting His wisdom into every area of your life.

Affirmation:
I revere the Lord, letting His wisdom and instruction guide my path.

Action Step:
Spend time in prayer, reflecting on God's greatness. Ask Him to deepen your awe and respect for Him, letting it shape your decisions.

Prayer:
Father, I honor and revere You as the source of all wisdom. Teach me to walk in the fear of the Lord, letting Your wisdom guide my every step. Amen.

October 5th, 2025: Trust in the Lord

Scripture:
"*Trust in the Lord with all your heart and lean not on your own understanding; in all your ways submit to Him, and He will make your paths straight.*" (Proverbs 3:5-6, NIV)

Reflection:
Wisdom often begins where your understanding ends. Trusting in the Lord means surrendering your plans and relying on His infinite wisdom and perfect timing. When you lean on Him, rather than your own logic or emotions, He aligns your steps with His purpose.

Submitting to God doesn't mean passivity—it means choosing to actively trust Him in every area of your life, even when the path seems unclear. His guidance is steady, and His ways lead to peace.

Today, place your full trust in God, allowing Him to direct your steps and straighten your path.

Affirmation:
I trust in the Lord with all my heart, submitting my plans to His perfect wisdom.

Action Step:
Reflect on an area where you've been leaning on your own understanding. Surrender it to God in prayer, trusting Him to lead you.

Prayer:
Lord, thank You for Your faithful guidance. Help me to trust You with all my heart and to submit every part of my life to Your wisdom. Amen.

<u>October 6th, 2025: Wise Counsel</u>

Scripture:
"*For lack of guidance a nation falls, but victory is won through many advisers.*" (Proverbs 11:14, NIV)

Reflection:
Seeking wise counsel is an essential part of walking in wisdom. God often provides direction through others—trusted mentors, godly friends, and spiritual leaders. These voices can offer perspective, encouragement, and correction when needed.

Pride can sometimes keep you from asking for help, but humility recognizes the value of community. Surrounding yourself with wise counselors helps you avoid pitfalls and make decisions that honor God.

Today, seek out godly counsel in areas where you need clarity or encouragement, trusting God to guide you through their wisdom.

Affirmation:
I value wise counsel and seek godly guidance to walk in wisdom and victory.

Action Step:
Identify a decision or challenge where you need guidance. Reach out to a trusted, godly mentor or friend for their perspective.

Prayer:
Father, thank You for placing wise counselors in my life. Help me to seek their guidance with humility and to make decisions that align with Your will. Amen.

October 7th 2025: Guard Your Heart

Scripture:
"*Above all else, guard your heart, for everything you do flows from it.*" (Proverbs 4:23, NIV)

Reflection:
Your heart is the wellspring of your life—it's where your thoughts, desires, and actions originate. Guarding your heart means protecting it from influences that can lead you away from God's truth and purpose.

The world often bombards you with distractions, temptations, and negativity. But when you fill your heart with God's Word and align your desires with His, your life becomes a reflection of His wisdom and love.

Today, commit to guarding your heart, allowing God to shape your thoughts and desires.

Affirmation:
I guard my heart, filling it with God's truth and letting His love flow through me.

Action Step:
Evaluate what you're allowing into your heart—through media, relationships, or thoughts. Take one step to remove a negative influence and replace it with God's Word or prayer.

Prayer:
Lord, thank You for creating my heart to reflect Your love. Help me to guard it carefully, filling it with truth and wisdom that honors You. Amen.

October 8th, 2025: The Word is a Lamp

Scripture:
"*Your word is a lamp to my feet and a light for my path.*" (Psalm 119:105, NIV)

Reflection:
God's Word illuminates your path, providing clarity and direction in every season of life. Like a lamp in the darkness, Scripture guides your steps, helping you navigate challenges and make wise decisions.

When you immerse yourself in God's Word, you gain the wisdom to discern His will and the courage to follow it. His truth steadies your footing, ensuring you don't stumble as you walk in His light.

Today, let God's Word be your guide, lighting the way forward with His truth and promises.

Affirmation:
God's Word lights my path, giving me clarity and wisdom for every step.

Action Step:
Spend time reading and meditating on Psalm 119:105. Reflect on how God's Word has guided you and commit to seeking His direction daily.

Prayer:
Father, thank You for the light of Your Word. Help me to walk in its truth, letting it guide my decisions and bring clarity to my path. Amen.

October 9th, 2025: A Fool’s Way vs. A Wise Path

Scripture:
"The way of fools seems right to them, but the wise listen to advice." (Proverbs 12:15, NIV)

Reflection:
A fool is quick to trust their own judgment, refusing to listen to advice or consider alternate perspectives. In contrast, wisdom recognizes the value of humility and a teachable spirit.

Choosing the wise path means seeking God’s guidance, listening to wise counsel, and being open to correction. This approach leads to growth, peace, and alignment with God’s will, while the fool’s way often results in unnecessary struggle.

Today, examine whether you’re relying solely on your own understanding or allowing God and others to guide your decisions.

Affirmation:
I choose the path of wisdom, listening to God’s guidance and wise counsel.

Action Step:
Reflect on a recent decision. Did you seek advice or act independently? Commit to pursuing wisdom in your next decision by seeking God’s Word and counsel.

Prayer:
Lord, thank You for offering me the wise path. Teach me to listen to Your guidance and to seek advice from those who reflect Your truth. Amen.

October 10th, 2025: Wise Speech

Scripture:
"A gentle answer turns away wrath, but a harsh word stirs up anger." (Proverbs 15:1, NIV)

Reflection:
Your words have the power to build up or tear down, to bring peace or fuel conflict. Wisdom in speech comes from a heart aligned with God's truth, choosing words that reflect love, patience, and understanding.

A gentle answer doesn't mean compromising on truth—it means delivering it in a way that draws others closer, rather than pushing them away. This approach requires self-control and a commitment to honoring God in every conversation.

Today, ask God to guide your words, making them a source of peace and encouragement.

Affirmation:
My words reflect God's wisdom, bringing peace and encouragement to others.

Action Step:
Think of one conversation today where you can intentionally practice wise speech. Choose words that reflect gentleness and truth.

Prayer:
Father, thank You for the power of words. Help me to speak with wisdom and gentleness, bringing peace and encouragement in all I say. Amen.

October 11th, 2025: Avoiding Temptation

Scripture:
"No temptation has overtaken you except what is common to mankind. And God is faithful; He will not let you be tempted beyond what you can bear. But when you are tempted, He will also provide a way out so that you can endure it." (1 Corinthians 10:13, NIV)

Reflection:
Temptation is a reality for everyone, but God's faithfulness provides both strength to resist and a way out. Wisdom recognizes that giving in to temptation leads to regret, while choosing God's way leads to peace and freedom.

Avoiding temptation starts with awareness. By staying close to God through prayer and His Word, you gain the discernment and strength to overcome. He empowers you to walk away from what pulls you down and toward His higher calling.

Today, trust in God's faithfulness and seek His wisdom to avoid temptation and walk in victory.

Affirmation:
I trust in God's faithfulness, finding strength and wisdom to overcome temptation.

Action Step:
Identify one area where you face temptation. Commit it to God in prayer and ask Him to show you the way out.

Prayer:
Lord, thank You for Your faithfulness in every temptation. Help me to resist and to walk in the freedom and wisdom You provide. Amen.

October 12th, 2025: Wisdom in Relationships

Scripture:
"Be very careful, then, how you live—not as unwise but as wise, making the most of every opportunity." (Ephesians 5:15-16, NIV)

Reflection:
Wisdom in relationships means being intentional with your words, actions, and time. It's about investing in others with love, humility, and discernment, while also setting healthy boundaries that honor God.

Living wisely in relationships involves making the most of every opportunity to show kindness, offer forgiveness, and point others to Christ. When you treat others with wisdom, you reflect God's heart and build relationships that bring Him glory.

Today, ask God for wisdom in your interactions and the grace to build relationships that reflect His love.

Affirmation:
I live wisely in my relationships, making the most of every opportunity to show God's love.

Action Step:
Think of one relationship where you can act with greater wisdom. Take a step to strengthen that connection today.

Prayer:
Father, thank You for the gift of relationships. Teach me to live wisely in them, showing love and reflecting Your heart in all I do. Amen.

October 13th, 2025: Humility and Wisdom

Scripture:
"*Humility is the fear of the Lord; its wages are riches and honor and life.*" (Proverbs 22:4, NIV)

Reflection:
Humility is the foundation of true wisdom. It acknowledges God's authority, values others above self, and recognizes that every good thing comes from Him. A humble heart is teachable and open to God's direction, while pride leads to stagnation and missteps.

When you walk in humility, you align yourself with God's purposes, inviting His blessings and wisdom into your life. Humility is not weakness—it's strength under submission to the One who knows best.

Today, ask God to cultivate humility in your heart, allowing His wisdom to flow freely in your life.

Affirmation:
I walk in humility, allowing God's wisdom to shape my life and decisions.

Action Step:
Reflect on an area where pride may be holding you back. Pray for humility and take one step to surrender that area to God.

Prayer:
Lord, thank You for teaching me the power of humility. Help me to walk in it daily, seeking Your wisdom and trusting in Your ways. Amen.

October 14th, 2025: God's Plan vs. My Plan

Scripture:
"'*For I know the plans I have for you,' declares the Lord, 'plans to prosper you and not to harm you, plans to give you hope and a future.'*" (Jeremiah 29:11, NIV)

Reflection:
Your plans may seem good, but God's plans are perfect. While it can be challenging to trust when His timing or direction differs from your expectations, wisdom acknowledges that His ways are higher than yours.

Surrendering your plans to God requires faith and humility. It means trusting that He sees the bigger picture and is working all things for your good. His plans are filled with hope and purpose, leading to a future that glorifies Him.

Today, release your plans into God's hands, trusting Him to lead you in His perfect way.

Affirmation:
I trust in God's perfect plans, knowing they are filled with hope and purpose.

Action Step:
Write down one plan or goal you've been holding tightly. Surrender it to God in prayer, asking for His wisdom and guidance.

Prayer:
Father, thank You for Your perfect plans for my life. Help me to trust You fully, surrendering my desires to Your greater purpose. Amen.

October 15th, 2025: Building Your House on the Rock

Scripture:
"Therefore everyone who hears these words of Mine and puts them into practice is like a wise man who built his house on the rock." (Matthew 7:24, NIV)

Reflection:
A wise life is built on the solid foundation of God's Word. When you hear and apply His teachings, you're anchoring your life to truth that withstands any storm.

Building on the rock takes effort and intentionality. It means prioritizing time with God, obeying His instructions, and trusting Him to provide stability in every season. The storms of life will come, but a life built on Christ stands firm.

Today, commit to building your life on the unshakable foundation of God's Word.

Affirmation:
I build my life on the solid rock of God's Word, standing firm in every season.

Action Step:
Evaluate the foundation of your life. Are you relying on temporary things or on God's Word? Commit to one practical step to strengthen your spiritual foundation.

Prayer:
Lord, thank You for being my solid rock. Help me to build my life on Your Word, trusting in Your strength and wisdom through every storm. Amen.

October 16th, 2025: Seeking Understanding

Scripture:
"Indeed, if you call out for insight and cry aloud for understanding, and if you look for it as for silver and search for it as for hidden treasure, then you will understand the fear of the Lord and find the knowledge of God." (Proverbs 2:3-5, NIV)

Reflection:
Wisdom doesn't come passively—it requires seeking, asking, and pursuing God with diligence. Like searching for treasure, gaining understanding takes time, effort, and a heart devoted to knowing Him more deeply.

When you prioritize God's wisdom, you uncover truths that bring clarity, purpose, and joy. His insight enriches your life far more than earthly riches ever could.

Today, seek God's understanding with intentionality, trusting Him to reveal His truth as you pursue Him.

Affirmation:
I seek God's understanding, pursuing His wisdom like treasure.

Action Step:
Spend focused time in Scripture today, asking God to reveal new insights and understanding for your current season.

Prayer:
Father, thank You for the treasure of Your wisdom. Help me to seek Your understanding diligently, growing closer to You each day. Amen.

October 17th, 2025: Wisdom Through Trials

Scripture:
"*Not only so, but we also glory in our sufferings, because we know that suffering produces perseverance; perseverance, character; and character, hope.*" (Romans 5:3-4, NIV)

Reflection:
Trials often feel like roadblocks, but they're opportunities for growth. God uses challenges to refine your character, deepen your faith, and produce wisdom that strengthens you for what lies ahead.

While suffering is never easy, it's a tool in God's hands to shape you into the image of Christ. When you trust Him in the process, trials become pathways to perseverance, hope, and wisdom.

Today, embrace your trials as opportunities to grow in wisdom and faith.

Affirmation:
I trust God to use my trials to refine me and produce wisdom in my life.

Action Step:
Think of a current or past trial. Reflect on how God might be using it to develop your character and wisdom.

Prayer:
Lord, thank You for using trials to shape and strengthen me. Help me to trust Your purpose in every season of challenge. Amen.

October 18th, 2025: The Company You Keep

Scripture:
"Do not be misled: 'Bad company corrupts good character.'"
(1 Corinthians 15:33, NIV)

Reflection:
The people you surround yourself with influence your thoughts, actions, and decisions. Wise relationships encourage spiritual growth, while negative influences can lead you away from God's purpose.

Walking in wisdom means discerning the company you keep and investing in relationships that align with God's truth. While you're called to love everyone, it's important to choose your closest companions wisely.

Today, reflect on how your relationships are shaping your character and seek to surround yourself with those who encourage your walk with God.

Affirmation:
I choose relationships that encourage wisdom, truth, and spiritual growth.

Action Step:
Evaluate your closest relationships. Identify one that may need boundaries and one where you can invest more to encourage mutual growth in Christ.

Prayer:
Father, thank You for the gift of relationships. Help me to walk wisely, surrounding myself with people who inspire me to live for You. Amen.

October 19th, 2025: Patience in Wisdom

Scripture:
"The end of a matter is better than its beginning, and patience is better than pride." (Ecclesiastes 7:8, NIV)

Reflection:
Wisdom teaches you to value patience over haste. While the world often pushes for quick results, God calls you to trust His timing, allowing His work to unfold in your life.

Patience isn't passive—it's an active trust in God's plan. Waiting with wisdom refines your character, strengthens your faith, and prepares you for what's ahead.

Today, embrace patience as a key part of walking in wisdom, trusting God's perfect timing in all things.

Affirmation:
I walk in patience, trusting God's timing and wisdom in every season.

Action Step:
Identify an area where you've been impatient. Pray for God's peace and commit to waiting on His timing with faith.

Prayer:
Lord, thank You for teaching me patience. Help me to trust in Your timing and to walk in wisdom as I wait for Your plans to unfold. Amen.

October 20th, 2025: The Peace of God's Wisdom

Scripture:
"*You will keep in perfect peace those whose minds are steadfast, because they trust in You.*" (Isaiah 26:3, NIV)

Reflection:
God's wisdom brings peace that surpasses understanding. When your mind is steadfast—focused on Him—you experience calmness even in the midst of uncertainty. His wisdom reminds you that He is in control, guiding your steps and providing for your needs.

This peace is not the absence of challenges but the presence of God's assurance. Trusting His wisdom allows you to face life's complexities with confidence and serenity.

Today, let God's wisdom bring peace to your heart and mind, no matter what you're facing.

Affirmation:
I trust in God's wisdom, and His perfect peace steadies my heart and mind.

Action Step:
Spend 10 minutes in quiet reflection, focusing on God's faithfulness. Let His peace fill your heart as you trust in His wisdom.

Prayer:
Father, thank You for the peace that comes from trusting in Your wisdom. Help me to keep my mind steadfast and to rest in Your perfect assurance. Amen.

October 21st, 2025: Sowing in Peace

Scripture:
"*Peacemakers who sow in peace reap a harvest of righteousness.*" (James 3:18, NIV)

Reflection:
Walking in wisdom means being a peacemaker—someone who actively seeks to bring harmony, understanding, and resolution into relationships and situations. Peacemakers reflect God's character and create environments where His righteousness can flourish.

Sowing peace often requires humility, patience, and a willingness to listen. As you pursue peace, you're planting seeds that yield a harvest of righteousness, both in your life and in the lives of others.

Today, commit to being a peacemaker, sowing peace in your relationships and interactions.

Affirmation:
I sow peace in my relationships, reaping a harvest of righteousness for God's glory.

Action Step:
Identify a relationship or situation where you can sow peace today. Take one step—whether through a kind word, forgiveness, or prayer—to bring harmony.

Prayer:
Lord, thank You for calling me to be a peacemaker. Help me to sow peace in my relationships, reflecting Your love and wisdom. Amen.

October 22nd, 2025: The Gift of Discernment

Scripture:
"And this is my prayer: that your love may abound more and more in knowledge and depth of insight, so that you may be able to discern what is best." (Philippians 1:9-10, NIV)

Reflection:
Discernment is the ability to see beyond the surface, to understand what is true, right, and best in any situation. It's a gift from God, cultivated through prayer, Scripture, and a relationship with the Holy Spirit.

Walking in discernment helps you make wise decisions, avoid pitfalls, and align your life with God's will. It protects you from deception and empowers you to navigate life with clarity and confidence.

Today, ask God to sharpen your discernment, enabling you to see and choose what is best.

Affirmation:
I walk in discernment, guided by God's wisdom and insight in every decision.

Action Step:
Think of a decision you're facing. Pray for discernment and seek God's Word or godly counsel to guide you.

Prayer:
Lord, thank You for the gift of discernment. Help me to grow in knowledge and insight, making decisions that honor You. Amen.

October 23rd, 2025: Wisdom in Stewardship

Scripture:
"*Whoever can be trusted with very little can also be trusted with much.*" (Luke 16:10, NIV)

Reflection:
Wise stewardship means faithfully managing the resources, time, and opportunities God has entrusted to you. When you honor Him with what you have, He entrusts you with more—not just materially but spiritually and relationally.

Walking in wisdom requires viewing everything you have as a gift from God, to be used for His glory and the good of others. This perspective shifts your focus from ownership to responsibility.

Today, commit to being a wise steward, honoring God with all He has given you.

Affirmation:
I am a wise steward, honoring God with my resources, time, and opportunities.

Action Step:
Identify one resource—time, money, or talent—you can steward more faithfully. Take a practical step to use it for God's glory.

Prayer:
Father, thank You for entrusting me with Your gifts. Help me to be a wise steward, using all I have to honor You and bless others. Amen.

October 24th, 2025: Knowing the Times

Scripture:
"There is a time for everything, and a season for every activity under the heavens." (Ecclesiastes 3:1, NIV)

Reflection:
Wisdom recognizes the importance of timing. Just as there are seasons in nature, there are seasons in life. Knowing the times means discerning when to act, when to wait, and when to let go.

God's wisdom helps you align with His timing, ensuring that your efforts are fruitful and your steps are purposeful. Trusting His timing allows you to walk in peace, even when the season feels uncertain.

Today, ask God to help you discern the season you're in and to guide your steps accordingly.

Affirmation:
I walk in God's timing, trusting His wisdom for every season of life.

Action Step:
Reflect on your current season. Ask God to show you what He's teaching you and how you can align with His timing.

Prayer:
Lord, thank You for guiding my steps in every season. Help me to discern the times and to trust Your perfect plan for my life. Amen.

October 25th, 2025: Trusting God's Timing

Scripture:
"For the vision is yet for the appointed time; it hastens toward the goal and it will not fail. Though it tarries, wait for it; for it will certainly come, it will not delay." (Habakkuk 2:3, NASB)

Reflection:
God's promises never fail, but they often unfold in His perfect timing, not yours. Trusting His timing requires patience, faith, and a willingness to surrender control.

Waiting on God isn't idle—it's an active posture of expectation, knowing that His plans are always worth the wait. His timing refines your character and prepares you for the fullness of His blessing.

Today, trust that God's timing is perfect and that His vision for your life will come to pass.

Affirmation:
I trust in God's perfect timing, knowing His plans are worth the wait.

Action Step:
Think of a dream or promise you're waiting for. Surrender it to God in prayer, asking for patience and trust as you wait.

Prayer:
Father, thank You for Your perfect timing. Help me to wait with faith and to trust that Your plans will be fulfilled in due time. Amen.

October 26th, 2025: Being Slow to Anger

Scripture:
"*Whoever is patient has great understanding, but one who is quick-tempered displays folly.*" (Proverbs 14:29, NIV)

Reflection:
Patience is a hallmark of wisdom, especially when emotions run high. Being slow to anger allows you to respond thoughtfully rather than reacting impulsively. Quick tempers can damage relationships and cloud judgment, while patience fosters understanding and peace.

God's wisdom teaches you to pause, reflect, and choose responses that align with His truth. When you rely on the Holy Spirit, He equips you to act with restraint, even in challenging situations.

Today, ask God to help you be slow to anger, reflecting His wisdom in your words and actions.

Affirmation:
I am patient and slow to anger, allowing God's wisdom to guide my responses.

Action Step:
Identify a situation where you often feel impatient or frustrated. Commit to pausing and praying before responding next time.

Prayer:
Lord, thank You for Your patience with me. Help me to reflect Your wisdom by being slow to anger and quick to listen. Amen.

October 27th, 2025: Walking by Faith, Not by Sight

Scripture:
"*For we live by faith, not by sight.*" (2 Corinthians 5:7, NIV)

Reflection:
Walking in wisdom often means trusting God's unseen plan over what's visible. Faith invites you to rely on His promises, even when circumstances seem uncertain or challenging.

When you focus on what's seen, it's easy to feel overwhelmed or discouraged. But God's wisdom reminds you that He is always at work, leading you on a path of purpose and hope. Faith empowers you to move forward, trusting His guidance every step of the way.

Today, choose to walk by faith, trusting in God's wisdom over your own understanding.

Affirmation:
I walk by faith, trusting God's unseen plan and relying on His wisdom.

Action Step:
Identify an area of your life where you're struggling to see God's plan. Surrender it to Him, trusting His faithfulness.

Prayer:
Father, thank You for guiding me with Your wisdom. Help me to walk by faith, trusting in Your promises even when I don't see the full picture. Amen.

October 28th, 2025: Wisdom in Trials

Scripture:
"Consider it pure joy, my brothers and sisters, whenever you face trials of many kinds, because you know that the testing of your faith produces perseverance." (James 1:2-3, NIV)

Reflection:
Trials can feel overwhelming, but God uses them to grow your faith and develop wisdom. Each challenge is an opportunity to trust Him more deeply and to learn lessons that strengthen your character.

When you approach trials with joy, you're not denying their difficulty—you're choosing to focus on God's purpose in them. His wisdom helps you persevere, turning challenges into stepping stones for spiritual growth.

Today, ask God to help you see your trials through the lens of His wisdom and purpose.

Affirmation:
I find joy in trials, knowing they produce perseverance and deepen my faith.

Action Step:
Think of a current or past trial. Reflect on how it has shaped your character or brought you closer to God. Thank Him for the lessons learned.

Prayer:
Lord, thank You for using trials to grow my faith. Help me to persevere with joy, trusting in Your wisdom and purpose. Amen.

October 29th, 2025: Light in the Darkness

Scripture:
"*When Jesus spoke again to the people, He said, 'I am the light of the world. Whoever follows Me will never walk in darkness, but will have the light of life.'*" (John 8:12, NIV)

Reflection:
Jesus is the ultimate source of wisdom, illuminating the path before you and guiding you out of darkness. When you follow Him, you gain clarity, purpose, and peace, even in life's most uncertain moments.

Walking in the light means seeking His presence daily and aligning your decisions with His truth. His wisdom shines brightest in the dark, leading you toward life and hope.

Today, let Jesus' light guide your steps, dispelling fear and uncertainty.

Affirmation:
I follow Jesus, the light of the world, and walk in His wisdom and truth.

Action Step:
Spend time in prayer, asking Jesus to light your path and reveal areas where you need His wisdom and guidance.

Prayer:
Jesus, thank You for being my light in the darkness. Help me to follow You faithfully, walking in Your wisdom and truth each day. Amen.

October 30th, 2025: Persevering in Wisdom

Scripture:
"Let us not become weary in doing good, for at the proper time we will reap a harvest if we do not give up." (Galatians 6:9, NIV)

Reflection:
Walking in wisdom is a lifelong journey that requires perseverance. There will be moments of weariness, but God promises a harvest for those who remain faithful. Wisdom calls you to press on, trusting that your efforts are not in vain.

Perseverance is fueled by hope—hope in God's promises, His faithfulness, and His perfect timing. When you stay committed to living wisely, you sow seeds that yield eternal rewards.

Today, renew your commitment to persevere, trusting that God's harvest is worth the effort.

Affirmation:
I persevere in wisdom, trusting that God's harvest will come in His perfect time.

Action Step:
Identify one area where you feel weary in doing good. Pray for renewed strength and commit to pressing on with God's help.

Prayer:
Father, thank You for the promise of a harvest. Help me to persevere in wisdom, trusting in Your faithfulness and timing. Amen.

October 31st, 2025: Christ, the Wisdom of God

Scripture:
"*It is because of Him that you are in Christ Jesus, who has become for us wisdom from God—that is, our righteousness, holiness, and redemption.*" (1 Corinthians 1:30, NIV)

Reflection:
Jesus embodies the wisdom of God, offering you righteousness, holiness, and redemption through His life, death, and resurrection. True wisdom isn't just knowledge—it's knowing Christ and allowing His presence to transform your life.

When you follow Jesus, you walk in the fullness of God's wisdom. He gives you clarity in decision-making, strength in trials, and purpose in every season. Christ is the ultimate source of all you need to live wisely and abundantly.

Today, celebrate Jesus as the wisdom of God, and commit to walking closely with Him every day.

Affirmation:
Christ is my wisdom, my righteousness, and my redemption. I walk in His truth and grace.

Action Step:
Spend time in worship, thanking Jesus for being the wisdom of God in your life. Reflect on how His presence has shaped your journey.

Prayer:
Jesus, thank You for being the wisdom of God, leading me in righteousness and redemption. Help me to follow You faithfully and to walk in Your truth always. Amen.

NOVEMBER: GRATITUDE & THANKSGIVING

Gratitude is more than a fleeting feeling—it's a lifestyle rooted in God's goodness and faithfulness. This month's devotionals will guide readers to reflect on His blessings, give thanks in all circumstances, and share that gratitude with others.

Day	Title	Scripture
Nov 1	Give Thanks in All Circumstances	1 Thessalonians 5:18
Nov 2	A Grateful Heart Pleases God	Psalm 69:30
Nov 3	Gratitude Unlocks Peace	Philippians 4:6-7
Nov 4	Counting Your Blessings	Psalm 103:2
Nov 5	Rejoice Always	1 Thessalonians 5:16-17
Nov 6	The Power of Thanksgiving	Colossians 3:15
Nov 7	Gratitude in Trials	James 1:2-3
Nov 8	Thanksgiving and Generosity	2 Corinthians 9:11

Nov 9	Giving Thanks for God's Creation	Psalm 95:3-5
Nov 10	The Sacrifice of Praise	Hebrews 13:15
Nov 11	Gratitude Fuels Faith	Psalm 107:8-9
Nov 12	Giving Thanks for God's Mercy	Lamentations 3:22-23
Nov 13	Gratitude for Spiritual Gifts	Ephesians 1:3
Nov 14	Thanksgiving and Worship	Psalm 100:4
Nov 15	Remembering God's Faithfulness	Deuteronomy 7:9
Nov 16	Sharing Your Gratitude	1 Chronicles 16:8
Nov 17	Thankfulness in Community	Romans 12:5
Nov 18	Gratitude for God's Provision	Matthew 6:26
Nov 19	The Joy of Giving Thanks	Psalm 118:24
Nov 20	Gratitude for Redemption	Colossians 1:13-14
Nov 21	The Overflow of Thanksgiving	2 Corinthians 4:15
Nov 22	Grateful for God's Guidance	Psalm 32:8
Nov 23	Thanking God for His Promises	Joshua 21:45
Nov 24	Gratitude for Eternal Life	John 3:16

Nov 25	A Heart of Thanksgiving	Psalm 136:1
Nov 26	The Fruit of Gratitude	Galatians 5:22-23
Nov 27	Thankful for God's Patience	2 Peter 3:9
Nov 28	Gratitude Changes Perspective	Psalm 118:1
Nov 29	Grateful in Every Season	Ecclesiastes 3:11
Nov 30	Thanksgiving as a Lifestyle	Colossians 3:17

<u>November 1st, 2025: Give Thanks in All Circumstances</u>

Scripture:
"*Give thanks in all circumstances; for this is God's will for you in Christ Jesus.*" (1 Thessalonians 5:18, NIV)

Reflection:
Gratitude isn't just for the good times—it's a discipline that invites you to thank God in every situation. When life feels overwhelming, giving thanks shifts your perspective from problems to God's presence, reminding you of His faithfulness and provision.

Gratitude in difficult circumstances isn't about denying reality—it's about declaring trust in God's sovereignty. When you give thanks, you're aligning your heart with His will and inviting His peace to guard your mind.

Today, practice gratitude in every circumstance, trusting that God is working all things for your good.

Affirmation:
I give thanks in all circumstances, trusting God's goodness and faithfulness.

Action Step:
Write down three things you're grateful for today, including one challenge where you see God's hand at work.

Prayer:
Father, thank You for Your goodness in every season of life. Help me to give thanks in all circumstances, trusting Your plan and resting in Your peace. Amen.

November 2nd, 2025: A Grateful Heart Pleases God

Scripture:
"*I will praise God's name in song and glorify Him with thanksgiving. This will please the Lord more than an ox, more than a bull with its horns and hooves.*" (Psalm 69:30-31, NIV)

Reflection:
God delights in a heart of gratitude. While sacrifices were part of worship in ancient Israel, David reminds us that thanksgiving is even more pleasing to the Lord. Gratitude flows from a heart that recognizes His goodness and responds in praise.

When you glorify God with thanksgiving, you deepen your connection with Him and reflect His love to the world. A grateful heart turns ordinary moments into acts of worship, bringing joy to the Father.

Today, let your gratitude glorify God, offering it as a pleasing sacrifice of praise.

Affirmation:
My gratitude pleases God and glorifies His name.

Action Step:
Pause during your day to thank God for something ordinary —a sunrise, a kind word, or a moment of rest.

Prayer:
Lord, thank You for delighting in my gratitude. Help me to glorify Your name through thanksgiving in every moment. Amen.

November 3rd, 2025: Gratitude Unlocks Peace

Scripture:
"Do not be anxious about anything, but in every situation, by prayer and petition, with thanksgiving, present your requests to God. And the peace of God, which transcends all understanding, will guard your hearts and your minds in Christ Jesus." (Philippians 4:6-7, NIV)

Reflection:
Anxiety fades in the presence of gratitude. When you approach God with thanksgiving, you acknowledge His control over every situation, inviting His peace to guard your heart and mind.

Gratitude isn't ignoring challenges—it's trusting God in the midst of them. As you thank Him, you shift your focus from worry to worship, experiencing the supernatural peace that only He can provide.

Today, let gratitude unlock God's peace in your heart, replacing anxiety with trust.

Affirmation:
Gratitude fills my heart, unlocking God's peace and guarding my mind.

Action Step:
The next time you feel anxious, pause and list five things you're thankful for. Present your concerns to God with thanksgiving.

Prayer:
Father, thank You for the peace that comes through gratitude. Help me to trust You in every situation and to rest in Your unfailing love. Amen.

November 4th 2025: Counting Your Blessings

Scripture:
"*Praise the Lord, my soul, and forget not all His benefits*." (Psalm 103:2, NIV)

Reflection:
Gratitude grows when you take time to reflect on God's blessings. From the gift of salvation to daily provisions, every benefit is a reminder of His faithfulness.

Counting your blessings shifts your perspective, filling your heart with joy and your spirit with praise. As you recall God's goodness, you're reminded of His love and care, strengthening your trust in Him.

Today, take time to count your blessings, letting gratitude fill your heart and overflow into praise.

Affirmation:
I remember God's benefits, counting His blessings with gratitude and praise.

Action Step:
Create a gratitude journal and write down 10 blessings you're thankful for today. Reflect on how each one reveals God's goodness.

Prayer:
Lord, thank You for Your countless blessings in my life. Help me to remember Your goodness and to live with a heart of gratitude each day. Amen.

November 5th, 2025: Rejoice Always

Scripture:
"Rejoice always, pray continually, give thanks in all circumstances; for this is God's will for you in Christ Jesus." (1 Thessalonians 5:16-18, NIV)

Reflection:
Gratitude and joy are interconnected. When you choose to rejoice, even in challenging times, you're aligning your heart with God's will and declaring His goodness over your circumstances.

Rejoicing always doesn't mean ignoring hardships; it means trusting that God is working all things for your good. Prayer and thanksgiving keep your focus on Him, allowing His joy to sustain you in every season.

Today, embrace joy as an act of gratitude, rejoicing in God's presence and promises.

Affirmation:
I rejoice always, trusting in God's faithfulness and finding joy in His presence.

Action Step:
Pause three times today to rejoice in God's goodness. Thank Him for something specific, even if it's small.

Prayer:
Lord, thank You for the joy that comes from Your presence. Help me to rejoice always, trusting in Your plans and praising You in every season. Amen.

November 6th, 2025: The Power of Thanksgiving

Scripture:
"Let the peace of Christ rule in your hearts, since as members of one body you were called to peace. And be thankful." (Colossians 3:15, NIV)

Reflection:
Thanksgiving isn't just a response to blessings—it's a practice that unleashes God's peace and unity in your heart and relationships. Gratitude shifts your focus from what you lack to what God has provided, filling you with His peace.

As members of Christ's body, thanksgiving also strengthens community. When you express gratitude, you foster an atmosphere of love and encouragement, building stronger connections with those around you.

Today, let thanksgiving shape your thoughts and interactions, inviting God's peace to rule your heart.

Affirmation:
Thanksgiving fills my heart, unleashing God's peace and building unity in my relationships.

Action Step:
Take a moment to express gratitude to someone in your life today. Let them know how much they mean to you.

Prayer:
Lord, thank You for the power of thanksgiving. Help me to live with a grateful heart, bringing Your peace and love into every relationship. Amen.

November 7th, 2025: Gratitude in Trials

Scripture:
"Consider it pure joy, my brothers and sisters, whenever you face trials of many kinds, because you know that the testing of your faith produces perseverance." (James 1:2-3, NIV)

Reflection:
Gratitude in trials may seem counterintuitive, but it's a pathway to growth. When you thank God in the midst of challenges, you're acknowledging His sovereignty and trusting His purpose.

Trials test your faith, producing perseverance and refining your character. Gratitude shifts your perspective, helping you see difficulties as opportunities for God to work in your life.

Today, thank God for the lessons and growth He's bringing through your trials, trusting that His plans are for your good.

Affirmation:
I thank God in trials, trusting that He is producing perseverance and refining my character.

Action Step:
Reflect on a current or past trial. Identify one way God has used it for your growth and thank Him for His faithfulness.

Prayer:
Father, thank You for using trials to strengthen my faith and shape my character. Help me to trust You in every challenge and to give thanks for Your refining work in my life. Amen.

November 8th, 2025: Thanksgiving and Generosity

Scripture:
"*You will be enriched in every way so that you can be generous on every occasion, and through us your generosity will result in thanksgiving to God.*" (2 Corinthians 9:11, NIV)

Reflection:
God blesses you so that you can bless others. Gratitude fuels generosity, and generosity leads to thanksgiving, creating a cycle of blessing that glorifies God.

When you share what you've been given—time, resources, or encouragement—you're reflecting God's heart and inspiring others to praise Him. Generosity isn't just about giving; it's about living with open hands and a grateful heart.

Today, let gratitude overflow into generosity, pointing others to God's goodness.

Affirmation:
Gratitude fuels my generosity, and my generosity inspires thanksgiving to God.

Action Step:
Look for an opportunity to be generous today, whether through your time, resources, or encouragement.

Prayer:
Lord, thank You for enriching my life in so many ways. Help me to share Your blessings generously, bringing glory to Your name and inspiring others to give thanks. Amen.

November 9th, 2025: Giving Thanks for God's Creation

Scripture:
"For the Lord is the great God, the great King above all gods. In His hand are the depths of the earth, and the mountain peaks belong to Him. The sea is His, for He made it, and His hands formed the dry land." (Psalm 95:3-5, NIV)

Reflection:
The beauty of creation reflects God's greatness and invites you to worship. From the vastness of the oceans to the intricate details of a flower, every part of nature testifies to His power, creativity, and love.

Gratitude for creation deepens your appreciation for God's provision and care. It reminds you that He holds the world in His hands and is intimately involved in every detail of your life.

Today, thank God for the gift of creation, letting its beauty draw you closer to Him.

Affirmation:
I give thanks for God's creation, marveling at His power, creativity, and love.

Action Step:
Spend time outdoors today, even if just for a moment. Reflect on one aspect of creation that inspires gratitude and praise God for it.

Prayer:
Father, thank You for the beauty of creation that reflects Your greatness. Help me to see Your hand in the world around me and to worship You with a grateful heart. Amen.

November 10th 2025: The Sacrifice of Praise

Scripture:
"Through Jesus, therefore, let us continually offer to God a sacrifice of praise—the fruit of lips that openly profess His name." (Hebrews 13:15, NIV)

Reflection:
Praise is a sacrifice that honors God, especially when it comes from a place of difficulty. When you choose to praise Him despite challenges, you're declaring your trust in His goodness and faithfulness.

The fruit of your lips—your spoken or sung praise—is a powerful testimony that glorifies God and strengthens your faith. Gratitude expressed through praise draws you closer to Him and brings joy to His heart.

Today, offer a sacrifice of praise, lifting your voice to thank Him for who He is and all He's done.

Affirmation:
I offer God a sacrifice of praise, trusting His goodness in every circumstance.

Action Step:
Sing a worship song or speak a prayer of thanksgiving aloud, even if you don't feel like it. Let your praise be an offering to God.

Prayer:
Lord, thank You for being worthy of all my praise. Help me to continually offer You a sacrifice of thanksgiving, trusting in Your faithfulness and love. Amen.

November 11th, 2025: Gratitude Fuels Faith

Scripture:
"Let them give thanks to the Lord for His unfailing love and His wonderful deeds for mankind, for He satisfies the thirsty and fills the hungry with good things." (Psalm 107:8-9, NIV)

Reflection:
Gratitude strengthens your faith by reminding you of God's faithfulness. When you recall His wonderful deeds and unfailing love, you're encouraged to trust Him for the future. Gratitude keeps your focus on what God has done and what He promises to do.

Thankfulness satisfies your soul, like water for the thirsty or food for the hungry. It nourishes your spirit and draws you closer to the One who fills your life with good things.

Today, let gratitude deepen your faith, trusting God to continue His good work in your life.

Affirmation:
Gratitude fuels my faith, reminding me of God's faithfulness and love.

Action Step:
Write down one specific way God has met your needs recently. Thank Him for His provision and trust Him for the future.

Prayer:
Father, thank You for Your unfailing love and faithfulness. Help me to live with gratitude, trusting You to satisfy every need. Amen.

November 12th, 2025: Giving Thanks for God's Mercy

Scripture:
"*Because of the Lord's great love we are not consumed, for His compassions never fail. They are new every morning; great is Your faithfulness.*" (Lamentations 3:22-23, NIV)

Reflection:
God's mercy is unending, renewed each day by His great love. Gratitude for His mercy transforms your perspective, reminding you that no matter what mistakes you've made, His faithfulness never wavers.

When you give thanks for God's mercy, you're acknowledging His grace and the hope it brings. His compassion sustains you, giving you the strength to move forward with confidence in His promises.

Today, thank God for His mercy, letting it inspire a heart of humility and gratitude.

Affirmation:
I thank God for His mercy, renewed every morning by His great love.

Action Step:
Reflect on a time when God's mercy sustained you. Thank Him for His compassion and faithfulness in that moment.

Prayer:
Lord, thank You for Your mercy that never fails. Help me to live with a grateful heart, trusting in Your faithfulness each day. Amen.

November 13th, 2025: Gratitude for Spiritual Blessings

Scripture:
"Praise be to the God and Father of our Lord Jesus Christ, who has blessed us in the heavenly realms with every spiritual blessing in Christ." (Ephesians 1:3, NIV)

Reflection:
Beyond material blessings, God has poured out every spiritual blessing in Christ. These include salvation, forgiveness, the Holy Spirit, and an eternal inheritance. Gratitude for these gifts deepens your awareness of God's love and grace.

When you focus on spiritual blessings, you're reminded of your identity in Christ and the hope you have in Him. Gratitude for these eternal treasures strengthens your faith and inspires joy, regardless of life's circumstances.

Today, thank God for the spiritual blessings you've received in Christ, letting them fill your heart with joy.

Affirmation:
I am blessed with every spiritual blessing in Christ, and I thank God for His abundant grace.

Action Step:
Write down three spiritual blessings you're thankful for today. Reflect on how they've impacted your life and strengthened your faith.

Prayer:
Father, thank You for the spiritual blessings You've given me in Christ. Help me to live with gratitude and to share these blessings with others. Amen.

November 14th, 2025: Thanksgiving and Worship

Scripture:
"*Enter His gates with thanksgiving and His courts with praise; give thanks to Him and praise His name.*" (Psalm 100:4, NIV)

Reflection:
Thanksgiving opens the door to God's presence. When you approach Him with gratitude, you're drawn into a deeper connection with Him, where praise flows naturally from your heart.

Worship is more than a song—it's a lifestyle of thankfulness that honors God for who He is and all He's done. Gratitude shifts your focus from yourself to Him, filling you with joy and inspiring reverence.

Today, let thanksgiving lead you into worship, celebrating God's goodness and faithfulness.

Affirmation:
Gratitude draws me into God's presence, inspiring worship and praise.

Action Step:
Spend time in worship today, focusing on thanking God for who He is. Let your praise flow from a heart of gratitude.

Prayer:
Lord, thank You for the privilege of worshiping You. Help me to approach You with thanksgiving and to honor You with my praise. Amen.

November 15th, 2025: Remembering God's Faithfulness

Scripture:
"*Know therefore that the Lord your God is God; He is the faithful God, keeping His covenant of love to a thousand generations of those who love Him and keep His commandments.*" (Deuteronomy 7:9, NIV)

Reflection:
God's faithfulness spans generations, demonstrating His unchanging love and commitment to His promises. Remembering His faithfulness strengthens your trust and inspires gratitude for all He's done.

When you reflect on God's past faithfulness, you're reminded that He will continue to fulfill His promises. Gratitude for His consistency builds confidence to face the future with hope and peace.

Today, take time to remember God's faithfulness and thank Him for His unchanging love.

Affirmation:
I remember God's faithfulness and trust in His unchanging love and promises.

Action Step:
Think back on a time when God answered a prayer or fulfilled a promise in your life. Write it down and thank Him for His faithfulness.

Prayer:
Father, thank You for being faithful through every season. Help me to remember Your promises and to live with gratitude for Your unchanging love. Amen.

November 16th, 2025: Sharing Your Gratitude

Scripture:
"*Give praise to the Lord, proclaim His name; make known among the nations what He has done.*" (1 Chronicles 16:8, NIV)

Reflection:
Gratitude isn't meant to be kept to yourself—it's meant to be shared, proclaiming God's goodness to those around you. When you share what God has done in your life, you inspire others to see His hand at work and to give thanks as well.

Sharing your gratitude glorifies God and encourages others, spreading His light and hope. It's a powerful way to witness to His love and faithfulness.

Today, let your gratitude overflow into testimony, proclaiming His name with joy.

Affirmation:
I share my gratitude, proclaiming God's goodness and inspiring others to give thanks.

Action Step:
Take time to share with someone what God has done for you recently. Encourage them to reflect on His goodness in their own life.

Prayer:
Lord, thank You for all You've done in my life. Help me to share my gratitude with others, bringing glory to Your name and encouragement to those around me. Amen.

November 17th, 2025: Thankfulness in Community

Scripture:
"*So in Christ we, though many, form one body, and each member belongs to all the others.*" (Romans 12:5, NIV)

Reflection:
Gratitude strengthens the bonds of community by fostering love, unity, and appreciation among believers. When you thank God for the people He has placed in your life, you're reminded of the value of relationships and the beauty of belonging to His body.

Thankfulness in community goes beyond words—it's expressed through acts of kindness, encouragement, and mutual support. A grateful heart creates an atmosphere where others feel loved and valued, reflecting God's love in tangible ways.

Today, thank God for your community and commit to being a source of encouragement to those around you.

Affirmation:
I thank God for my community and seek to strengthen it with love and gratitude.

Action Step:
Take a moment to thank someone in your church, family, or circle of friends for their impact on your life.

Prayer:
Father, thank You for the gift of community. Help me to show gratitude through my words and actions, strengthening the bonds of love among Your people. Amen.

November 18th, 2025: Gratitude for God's Provision

Scripture:
"Look at the birds of the air; they do not sow or reap or store away in barns, and yet your heavenly Father feeds them. Are you not much more valuable than they?" (Matthew 6:26, NIV)

Reflection:
God's provision is constant, faithful, and abundant. Just as He cares for the birds of the air, He provides for your every need, demonstrating His love and value for you. Gratitude for His provision helps you trust in His care, even when life feels uncertain.

When you focus on what God has provided rather than what you lack, your perspective shifts from worry to worship. Gratitude reminds you that He is your ultimate source of sustenance and security.

Today, thank God for His provision, trusting Him to meet every need with His abundant grace.

Affirmation:
I thank God for His faithful provision, trusting Him to meet all my needs.

Action Step:
Write down one way God has provided for you recently—materially, emotionally, or spiritually—and thank Him for His faithfulness.

Prayer:
Father, thank You for being my provider. Help me to trust in Your care and to live with gratitude for all You have given me. Amen.

November 19th, 2025: The Joy of Giving Thanks

Scripture:
"This is the day the Lord has made; let us rejoice and be glad in it." (Psalm 118:24, NIV)

Reflection:
Gratitude brings joy that transforms ordinary moments into opportunities for celebration. Each day is a gift from God, filled with His presence, purpose, and blessings. When you choose to give thanks, you're inviting joy into your heart and declaring God's goodness.

Rejoicing in the Lord doesn't depend on your circumstances —it flows from a heart that recognizes His faithfulness. Gratitude shifts your focus from challenges to blessings, filling your day with hope and praise.

Today, rejoice in the Lord and let the joy of giving thanks fill your heart and mind.

Affirmation:
I rejoice in the Lord, finding joy in giving thanks for His goodness and faithfulness.

Action Step:
Start your day by thanking God for three specific blessings. Let that gratitude set the tone for the rest of your day.

Prayer:
Lord, thank You for the joy that comes from giving thanks. Help me to rejoice in each day You've made, celebrating Your goodness and grace. Amen.

November 20th, 2025: Gratitude for Redemption

Scripture:
"For He has rescued us from the dominion of darkness and brought us into the kingdom of the Son He loves, in whom we have redemption, the forgiveness of sins." (Colossians 1:13-14, NIV)

Reflection:
The greatest reason for gratitude is your redemption in Christ. Through His sacrifice, He rescued you from darkness, forgave your sins, and welcomed you into His kingdom. This gift is eternal, transforming your identity and destiny.

Gratitude for redemption deepens your love for God and inspires a life of worship. It reminds you that you are forgiven, free, and dearly loved—a testimony of His grace and mercy.

Today, thank God for the gift of redemption, letting His love inspire your gratitude and joy.

Affirmation:
I thank God for redeeming me through Christ, celebrating His grace and forgiveness.

Action Step:
Spend time reflecting on what redemption means to you. Write a prayer or song of thanksgiving, expressing your gratitude for His love.

Prayer:
Jesus, thank You for rescuing me from darkness and redeeming me through Your sacrifice. Help me to live with gratitude for Your grace and to share Your love with others. Amen.

November 21st, 2025: The Overflow of Thanksgiving

Scripture:
"All this is for your benefit, so that the grace that is reaching more and more people may cause thanksgiving to overflow to the glory of God." (2 Corinthians 4:15, NIV)

Reflection:
Gratitude is contagious. When you live with a heart full of thanksgiving, it inspires others to see God's grace and respond with praise. Your gratitude becomes a testimony that draws people closer to Him.

As you reflect on God's blessings, let your thanksgiving overflow into your words, actions, and relationships. This overflow glorifies God and brings His joy and hope into the lives of others.

Today, ask God to help your gratitude spill over, pointing others to His goodness and grace.

Affirmation:
Gratitude overflows from my heart, bringing glory to God and blessing to others.

Action Step:
Share a testimony of God's grace with someone today, letting your gratitude encourage their faith.

Prayer:
Father, thank You for the overflow of Your grace in my life. Help my gratitude to inspire others and to bring glory to Your name. Amen.

November 22nd, 2025: Grateful for God's Guidance

Scripture:
"I will instruct you and teach you in the way you should go; I will counsel you with My loving eye on you." (Psalm 32:8, NIV)

Reflection:
God's guidance is a priceless gift. He lovingly directs your steps, teaching and counseling you with wisdom and care. Gratitude for His guidance acknowledges your trust in His plan and your reliance on His wisdom.

When you thank God for His direction, you're reminded that you're never alone. His loving eye is always on you, providing clarity and peace in every decision.

Today, thank God for His guidance, trusting Him to lead you in the way you should go.

Affirmation:
I thank God for His loving guidance, trusting Him to direct my steps.

Action Step:
Think of a time when God guided you through a challenging decision. Reflect on His faithfulness and thank Him for His counsel.

Prayer:
Lord, thank You for being my guide. Help me to trust Your wisdom and to follow Your direction with gratitude and faith. Amen.

November 23rd, 2025: Thanking God for His Promises

Scripture:
"*Not one of all the Lord's good promises to Israel failed; every one was fulfilled.*" (Joshua 21:45, NIV)

Reflection:
God's promises are unshakable. From the beginning of time, He has faithfully fulfilled every word He has spoken, demonstrating His trustworthiness and power. Gratitude for His promises builds your faith and strengthens your hope.

When you thank God for His promises, you're declaring your trust in His Word and aligning your heart with His truth. His promises are your anchor, giving you confidence in every season.

Today, thank God for the promises He has fulfilled and trust Him for those yet to come.

Affirmation:
I trust in God's unfailing promises, thanking Him for His faithfulness and truth.

Action Step:
Choose a promise from Scripture that resonates with your current season. Write it down and thank God for it throughout the day.

Prayer:
Father, thank You for Your unfailing promises. Help me to trust in Your Word and to live with gratitude for all You have done and will do. Amen.

November 24th, 2025: Gratitude for Eternal Life

Scripture:
"For God so loved the world that He gave His one and only Son, that whoever believes in Him shall not perish but have eternal life." (John 3:16, NIV)

Reflection:
The gift of eternal life is the ultimate reason for gratitude. Through Jesus' sacrifice, you are offered forgiveness, redemption, and the promise of life with Him forever. This gift is undeserved yet freely given, a testament to God's overwhelming love.

Gratitude for eternal life fuels your worship and gives you hope beyond this world. It reminds you that no matter what you face, your future is secure in Christ.

Today, thank God for the gift of eternal life and let His love inspire your gratitude and joy.

Affirmation:
I thank God for the gift of eternal life, celebrating His love and grace in Christ.

Action Step:
Spend time reflecting on the meaning of eternal life and how it impacts your daily walk with God. Thank Him for this precious gift.

Prayer:
Jesus, thank You for giving Your life so I could have eternal life. Help me to live with gratitude and to share Your love with those who need it. Amen.

November 25th, 2025: A Heart of Thanksgiving

Scripture:
"Give thanks to the Lord, for He is good. His love endures forever." (Psalm 136:1, NIV)

Reflection:
A heart of thanksgiving is rooted in the goodness and enduring love of God. His faithfulness is unchanging, His mercy is everlasting, and His love knows no bounds. When you focus on these truths, gratitude overflows naturally.

Thanksgiving isn't limited to a single day or season—it's a way of life that honors God and strengthens your relationship with Him. Gratitude transforms your perspective, reminding you of His constant presence and care.

Today, cultivate a heart of thanksgiving, letting it flow from your awareness of God's goodness and love.

Affirmation:
My heart overflows with thanksgiving for God's goodness and enduring love.

Action Step:
Read all of Psalm 136 aloud, reflecting on each statement of God's enduring love. Let it inspire your gratitude.

Prayer:
Father, thank You for Your goodness and love that never ends. Help me to live with a heart of thanksgiving, honoring You in all I do. Amen.

November 26th, 2025: The Fruit of Gratitude

Scripture:
"But the fruit of the Spirit is love, joy, peace, forbearance, kindness, goodness, faithfulness, gentleness, and self-control. Against such things there is no law." (Galatians 5:22-23, NIV)

Reflection:
Gratitude nurtures the fruit of the Spirit in your life. When you live with thankfulness, you're more likely to experience love, joy, peace, and other fruits that reflect God's character. Gratitude softens your heart, allowing His Spirit to work more freely.

A grateful heart creates a fertile ground for spiritual growth, impacting not only your relationship with God but also your interactions with others. Gratitude invites the Holy Spirit to cultivate these fruits in abundance.

Today, let gratitude be the foundation for the fruit of the Spirit in your life.

Affirmation:
Gratitude nurtures the fruit of the Spirit, shaping my heart and character.

Action Step:
Identify one fruit of the Spirit you'd like to grow in. Reflect on how gratitude can help cultivate it, and pray for the Holy Spirit's guidance.

Prayer:
Holy Spirit, thank You for producing good fruit in my life. Help me to live with gratitude, allowing Your character to shine through me. Amen.

November 27th, 2025: Thankful for God's Patience

Scripture:
"The Lord is not slow in keeping His promise, as some understand slowness. Instead, He is patient with you, not wanting anyone to perish, but everyone to come to repentance." (2 Peter 3:9, NIV)

Reflection:
God's patience is a gift of grace. He is slow to anger and abundant in mercy, giving you time to grow, repent, and draw closer to Him. His patience reflects His deep love and desire for all to experience His salvation.

Thankfulness for God's patience reminds you to extend that same grace to others. As you experience His love and forgiveness, you're empowered to be more patient and compassionate in your relationships.

Today, thank God for His patience with you, and ask Him to help you show the same patience to others.

Affirmation:
I am thankful for God's patience, and I reflect His grace in my relationships.

Action Step:
Think of an area in your life where you've experienced God's patience. Thank Him for His mercy and commit to being patient with someone in your life.

Prayer:
Father, thank You for Your patience with me. Help me to reflect Your grace and love to others, growing in patience and compassion. Amen.

November 28th, 2025: Gratitude Changes Perspective

Scripture:
"*Give thanks to the Lord, for He is good; His love endures forever.*" (Psalm 118:1, NIV)

Reflection:
Gratitude shifts your focus from problems to promises, from lack to abundance. When you give thanks, you're choosing to see life through the lens of God's goodness and faithfulness. This perspective brings joy and hope, even in the midst of challenges.

Gratitude doesn't deny hardships—it declares that God is greater than them. It aligns your heart with His truth, opening your eyes to the blessings that might otherwise go unnoticed.

Today, let gratitude transform your perspective, filling your heart with hope and joy.

Affirmation:
Gratitude changes my perspective, helping me to see life through God's goodness.

Action Step:
Take a moment to reflect on a current challenge. Write down three ways God's goodness is still evident in your situation.

Prayer:
Lord, thank You for the power of gratitude to change my perspective. Help me to focus on Your goodness and to trust in Your faithfulness, no matter what I face. Amen.

November 29th, 2025: Grateful in Every Season

Scripture:
"He has made everything beautiful in its time. He has also set eternity in the human heart; yet no one can fathom what God has done from beginning to end." (Ecclesiastes 3:11, NIV)

Reflection:
Each season of life holds its own beauty and purpose, even when it's hard to see in the moment. Gratitude helps you appreciate the unique lessons and blessings of every stage, trusting that God is working all things for good.

When you thank God in every season, you're embracing His timing and sovereignty. Gratitude transforms waiting into worship and challenges into opportunities to grow in faith.

Today, choose to be grateful for the season you're in, trusting that God is making all things beautiful in His time.

Affirmation:
I am grateful in every season, trusting God to make all things beautiful in His time.

Action Step:
Reflect on the current season of your life. Write down one lesson or blessing you're experiencing and thank God for it.

Prayer:
Father, thank You for the beauty in every season. Help me to trust Your timing and to find gratitude in every part of the journey. Amen.

November 30th, 2025: Thanksgiving as a Lifestyle

Scripture:
"And whatever you do, whether in word or deed, do it all in the name of the Lord Jesus, giving thanks to God the Father through Him." (Colossians 3:17, NIV)

Reflection:
Gratitude isn't just an occasional act—it's a lifestyle that flows from a heart aligned with God's love. When you live with thanksgiving, every word and action becomes an offering of praise, glorifying God in all you do.

A lifestyle of thanksgiving transforms ordinary moments into sacred opportunities to honor God. It shifts your focus from temporary concerns to eternal truths, allowing His joy and peace to fill your life.

Today, commit to making gratitude a daily habit, letting it guide your words, actions, and worship.

Affirmation:
Gratitude is my lifestyle, glorifying God in all I do and say.

Action Step:
Start a gratitude journal if you haven't already. Write down three things you're thankful for each day, and reflect on how God is working in your life.

Prayer:
Lord, thank You for the gift of gratitude. Help me to live a life of thanksgiving, glorifying You in every word and deed. Amen.

DECEMBER: CHRIST OUR KING

December is a time to reflect on the birth of Christ, the fulfillment of God's promises, and His role as King over all creation. This month's devotionals will explore the humility of His first coming, the hope of His return, and the joy of worshiping Him as our eternal King.

Day	Title	Scripture
Dec 1	The King of Kings	Revelation 19:16
Dec 2	The Word Became Flesh	John 1:14
Dec 3	His Kingdom Will Never End	Luke 1:33
Dec 4	The Promise of a Savior	Isaiah 9:6
Dec 5	The Humble King	Philippians 2:6-7
Dec 6	The Light of the World	John 8:12
Dec 7	The Good Shepherd	John 10:11
Dec 8	The Prince of Peace	Isaiah 9:6
Dec 9	Worshiping Christ Our King	Matthew 2:11

Dec 10	Born to Redeem	Galatians 4:4-5
Dec 11	The King's Victory	1 Corinthians 15:57
Dec 12	The Hope of His Coming	Titus 2:13
Dec 13	Christ's Eternal Reign	Hebrews 1:8
Dec 14	God With Us	Matthew 1:23
Dec 15	The Gift of His Presence	Zephaniah 3:17
Dec 16	A Kingdom of Righteousness	Isaiah 32:1
Dec 17	The Lamb and the Lion	Revelation 5:5-6
Dec 18	The Joy of His Birth	Luke 2:10-11
Dec 19	Preparing the Way	Isaiah 40:3-5
Dec 20	The King's Return	Revelation 22:12
Dec 21	The Power of His Name	Philippians 2:9-10
Dec 22	Christ, the Cornerstone	Psalm 118:22
Dec 23	The Glory of the Incarnation	Colossians 1:15-16
Dec 24	O Come, Let Us Adore Him	Luke 2:15-16
Dec 25	Christ Is Born!	Luke 2:11

Dec 26	The Radiance of God's Glory	Hebrews 1:3
Dec 27	The Kingdom of Heaven Is Near	Matthew 4:17
Dec 28	The First and the Last	Revelation 22:13
Dec 29	The King's Commission	Matthew 28:19-20
Dec 30	Living as Kingdom Citizens	Philippians 3:20
Dec 31	Crown Him with Many Crowns	Revelation 5:13

December 1st, 2025: The King of Kings

Scripture:
"On His robe and on His thigh He has this name written: King of Kings and Lord of Lords." (Revelation 19:16, NIV)

Reflection:
Jesus is not just a king—He is the King of Kings, ruling over all creation with power and authority. His reign is eternal, unshaken by earthly events or kingdoms. As King, He deserves your worship, allegiance, and trust.

When you acknowledge Jesus as King of Kings, you're placing Him at the center of your life, surrendering to His rule and trusting in His sovereignty. No matter what challenges you face, His authority brings peace and assurance.

Today, honor Jesus as your King, letting His reign guide your thoughts and actions.

Affirmation:
Jesus is the King of Kings, and I surrender to His reign with faith and trust.

Action Step:
Spend a moment in quiet reflection, acknowledging Jesus as King over every area of your life.

Prayer:
Jesus, thank You for being the King of Kings. I surrender to Your authority and trust in Your perfect reign over my life. Amen.

December 2nd, 2025: The Word Became Flesh

Scripture:
"The Word became flesh and made His dwelling among us. We have seen His glory, the glory of the one and only Son, who came from the Father, full of grace and truth." (John 1:14, NIV)

Reflection:
The incarnation of Christ is a profound mystery and a beautiful truth. Jesus, the eternal Word, became fully human to dwell among us, revealing the Father's glory and bringing grace and truth to a broken world.

When you reflect on the Word becoming flesh, you're reminded of God's incredible love and His desire to be close to you. Jesus didn't come to judge but to save, to bridge the gap between heaven and earth.

Today, thank God for sending His Son and let the wonder of the incarnation fill your heart with awe and gratitude.

Affirmation:
Jesus, the Word made flesh, reveals God's glory and fills my life with grace and truth.

Action Step:
Take a few moments to meditate on John 1:14. Write down what the incarnation means to you personally.

Prayer:
Father, thank You for sending Jesus to dwell among us. Help me to live in awe of His glory and to share His grace and truth with others. Amen.

December 3rd, 2025: His Kingdom Will Never End

Scripture:
"He will reign over Jacob's descendants forever; His kingdom will never end." (Luke 1:33, NIV)

Reflection:
The kingdom of Jesus is eternal, unlike earthly kingdoms that rise and fall. His reign is marked by justice, righteousness, and peace, and it extends over every heart that surrenders to Him as King.

When you live with the understanding that His kingdom will never end, it brings hope and purpose to your life. No matter what happens in the world, you are part of an unshakable kingdom, ruled by a loving and faithful King.

Today, reflect on the eternal nature of Christ's kingdom and find hope in His unending reign.

Affirmation:
Jesus' kingdom is eternal, and I live with hope and purpose under His reign.

Action Step:
Consider one way you can reflect the values of Christ's eternal kingdom in your daily life. Act on it today.

Prayer:
Jesus, thank You for Your eternal kingdom. Help me to live as a faithful citizen of Your reign, reflecting Your love and righteousness in all I do. Amen.

December 4th, 2025: The Promise of a Savior

Scripture:
"For to us a child is born, to us a son is given, and the government will be on His shoulders. And He will be called Wonderful Counselor, Mighty God, Everlasting Father, Prince of Peace." (Isaiah 9:6, NIV)

Reflection:
Centuries before Jesus' birth, the prophet Isaiah foretold His coming, describing the Savior's roles and attributes. Each title reveals a facet of His character: He guides with wisdom, rules with power, loves with eternity in view, and brings peace that surpasses understanding.

This promise of a Savior reminds you that God always fulfills His Word. In Christ, every prophecy is realized, and every hope finds its answer.

Today, rejoice in the fulfillment of God's promise and the gift of Jesus, our Wonderful Counselor and Prince of Peace.

Affirmation:
Jesus is my Wonderful Counselor, Mighty God, Everlasting Father, and Prince of Peace.

Action Step:
Write down one way each title of Jesus—Counselor, Mighty God, Father, and Prince of Peace—applies to your life today.

Prayer:
Father, thank You for fulfilling Your promise through Jesus. Help me to trust in Him as my Counselor, Savior, and source of peace. Amen.

December 5th, 2025: The Humble King

Scripture:
"*Who, being in very nature God, did not consider equality with God something to be used to His own advantage; rather, He made Himself nothing by taking the very nature of a servant, being made in human likeness.*" (Philippians 2:6-7, NIV)

Reflection:
Jesus, the King of Kings, chose to humble Himself, leaving His heavenly throne to become a servant. His birth in a manger and His life of sacrifice demonstrate the depth of His love and the humility that marks His kingdom.

The humility of Jesus invites you to live with the same attitude—valuing others above yourself, serving with love, and walking in obedience to God. True greatness is found in surrender and selflessness, just as Jesus modeled.

Today, let the humility of Christ inspire you to serve others and live with a heart surrendered to Him.

Affirmation:
I follow the example of my humble King, serving others with love and obedience.

Action Step:
Perform an act of service today, following Christ's example of humility.

Prayer:
Jesus, thank You for humbling Yourself to save me. Help me to reflect Your heart by serving others with love and humility. Amen.

December 6th, 2025: The Light of the World

Scripture:
"*When Jesus spoke again to the people, He said, 'I am the light of the world. Whoever follows Me will never walk in darkness, but will have the light of life.'*" (John 8:12, NIV)

Reflection:
In a world darkened by sin and fear, Jesus shines as the Light of the World. His light dispels darkness, revealing truth, guiding your path, and bringing hope to every corner of your life.

When you follow Jesus, His light illuminates your heart, enabling you to reflect His love to others. You become a beacon of His grace, pointing the way to His salvation.

Today, let the light of Christ shine in you and through you, bringing hope to those around you.

Affirmation:
Jesus is the Light of the World, and His light shines in my heart, guiding me each day.

Action Step:
Spend a moment in prayer, asking Jesus to reveal any areas of your life where His light needs to shine.

Prayer:
Jesus, thank You for being my light in the darkness. Shine brightly in my heart and help me to reflect Your love to others. Amen.

December 7th, 2025: The Good Shepherd

Scripture:
"I am the good shepherd. The good shepherd lays down His life for the sheep." (John 10:11, NIV)

Reflection:
As the Good Shepherd, Jesus knows you intimately and cares for you deeply. He leads you to green pastures, protects you from harm, and ultimately laid down His life to rescue you from sin.

In Christ, you find safety, provision, and guidance. His love is sacrificial and personal, reminding you that you are cherished and never alone. Following the Good Shepherd leads to abundant life, filled with His peace and purpose.

Today, thank Jesus for being your Good Shepherd, and trust Him to lead you on paths of righteousness.

Affirmation:
Jesus is my Good Shepherd, and I trust Him to lead, protect, and provide for me.

Action Step:
Reflect on an area of your life where you need Jesus' guidance. Surrender it to Him, trusting in His care.

Prayer:
Jesus, thank You for being my Good Shepherd. Help me to follow Your voice, trusting in Your love and care each day. Amen.

December 8th, 2025: The Prince of Peace

Scripture:
"For to us a child is born, to us a son is given, and the government will be on His shoulders. And He will be called...Prince of Peace." (Isaiah 9:6, NIV)

Reflection:
Jesus, the Prince of Peace, offers a peace that surpasses all understanding. This peace isn't the absence of conflict but the presence of His assurance, even in life's storms. It is rooted in His victory over sin and death, giving you confidence in His reign.

When you embrace Jesus as the Prince of Peace, you experience harmony with God, yourself, and others. His peace guards your heart and mind, empowering you to face challenges with calmness and trust.

Today, let the Prince of Peace reign in your heart, bringing calm to your spirit and hope to your soul.

Affirmation:
Jesus is my Prince of Peace, and His presence fills my heart with calm and assurance.

Action Step:
Take a moment to reflect on a situation where you need God's peace. Pray and ask Jesus to reign over it with His perfect calm.

Prayer:
Jesus, thank You for being my Prince of Peace. Help me to trust in Your presence and to rest in the peace that only You can provide. Amen.

December 9th, 2025: Worshiping Christ Our King

Scripture:

"*On coming to the house, they saw the child with His mother Mary, and they bowed down and worshiped Him. Then they opened their treasures and presented Him with gifts of gold, frankincense, and myrrh.*" (Matthew 2:11, NIV)

Reflection:

The Magi traveled great distances to worship Jesus, recognizing Him as the promised King. Their gifts symbolized His royalty, divinity, and sacrifice. Worshiping Christ is a response to His greatness and a declaration of His worth.

True worship goes beyond words—it involves offering your time, talents, and treasures to honor Him. When you bow before Christ, you acknowledge His reign and invite His presence into your life.

Today, worship Jesus as your King, offering Him the gift of your heart and devotion.

Affirmation:

I worship Christ my King, offering Him my heart, my gifts, and my praise.

Action Step:

Spend time in worship today, expressing your love and devotion to Jesus through prayer, song, or an act of service.

Prayer:

Jesus, thank You for being my King. I bow before You in worship, offering all that I am to glorify Your name. Amen.

December 10th, 2025: Born to Redeem

Scripture:
"But when the set time had fully come, God sent His Son, born of a woman, born under the law, to redeem those under the law, that we might receive adoption to sonship." (Galatians 4:4-5, NIV)

Reflection:
Jesus' birth was not an accident—it was a divine plan to redeem humanity. Born under the law, He fulfilled it perfectly, offering His life to pay the price for your sins. Through His sacrifice, you are adopted into God's family, loved and accepted as His child.

Gratitude for redemption fuels a life of worship and obedience. Knowing that Jesus was born to save you gives your life purpose and hope, anchoring your identity in His love.

Today, thank Jesus for being born to redeem you and embrace your identity as a child of God.

Affirmation:
Jesus was born to redeem me, and I am a beloved child of God.

Action Step:
Write down one way your life has been transformed by Jesus' redemption. Reflect on His love and grace.

Prayer:
Jesus, thank You for being born to redeem me. Help me to live as Your child, confident in Your love and filled with gratitude for Your sacrifice. Amen.

December 11th, 2025: The King's Victory

Scripture:
"But thanks be to God! He gives us the victory through our Lord Jesus Christ." (1 Corinthians 15:57, NIV)

Reflection:
Jesus, our victorious King, conquered sin, death, and the powers of darkness through His death and resurrection. His victory is your victory, granting you freedom, forgiveness, and eternal life.

When you live in light of Christ's victory, you can face life's challenges with confidence, knowing that the battle is already won. His triumph assures you that nothing can separate you from His love and purpose.

Today, celebrate the victory of your King and walk boldly in the freedom He has won for you.

Affirmation:
I share in Christ's victory and walk confidently in the freedom He has secured.

Action Step:
Identify one area where you need to trust in Christ's victory. Surrender it to Him in prayer, declaring His triumph over it.

Prayer:
Jesus, thank You for the victory You won on the cross. Help me to live in the freedom and confidence of Your triumph each day. Amen.

December 12th, 2025: The Hope of His Coming

Scripture:
"While we wait for the blessed hope—the appearing of the glory of our great God and Savior, Jesus Christ." (Titus 2:13, NIV)

Reflection:
The return of Christ is the blessed hope that fuels your faith and perseverance. As you wait for His glorious appearing, you're reminded that His promises are sure, and His reign will be fully realized.

Hope in His coming isn't passive—it inspires you to live with purpose, sharing His love and preparing your heart for His return. This hope brings peace in the present and joy for the future.

Today, let the hope of Christ's coming fill you with anticipation and purpose.

Affirmation:
I live with hope and purpose, eagerly awaiting the glorious return of Christ.

Action Step:
Spend time reflecting on the promise of Christ's return. Pray for a renewed sense of hope and readiness to meet Him.

Prayer:
Jesus, thank You for the promise of Your return. Fill my heart with hope and help me to live each day with anticipation and purpose. Amen.

December 13th, 2025: Christ's Eternal Reign

Scripture:
"But about the Son He says, 'Your throne, O God, will last forever and ever; a scepter of justice will be the scepter of Your kingdom.'" (Hebrews 1:8, NIV)

Reflection:
Jesus reigns eternally, ruling with justice and righteousness. His throne is unshakable, and His kingdom is marked by peace, truth, and love. While earthly rulers may falter, Christ's reign is forever, offering hope and security to all who follow Him.

When you acknowledge His eternal reign, you're reminded that He is in control, and His plans are unchanging. Living under His rule brings stability and peace, even in uncertain times.

Today, rejoice in Christ's eternal reign and surrender every part of your life to His authority.

Affirmation:
Christ reigns eternally, and I trust in His justice, righteousness, and unfailing rule.

Action Step:
Write down one area of your life where you need to surrender to Christ's reign. Pray for His guidance and authority over it.

Prayer:
Jesus, thank You for reigning eternally with justice and love. Help me to trust in Your rule and to live fully surrendered to Your authority. Amen.

December 14th, 2025: God With Us

Scripture:
"The virgin will conceive and give birth to a son, and they will call Him Immanuel" (which means "God with us"). (Matthew 1:23, NIV)

Reflection:
The birth of Jesus fulfilled the promise of Immanuel—God with us. In Christ, God stepped into humanity, bringing His presence, love, and salvation to a broken world. His presence reminds you that you are never alone.

Immanuel is not just a name; it's a reality. Jesus is with you in every season, offering comfort, guidance, and peace. His presence is the greatest gift, drawing you closer to the heart of the Father.

Today, thank God for the gift of Immanuel and embrace His presence in your daily life.

Affirmation:
Jesus is Immanuel, God with me, bringing His presence, love, and peace into my life.

Action Step:
Take a moment to sit in silence, reflecting on the reality of God's presence with you. Thank Him for being near.

Prayer:
Father, thank You for sending Jesus, my Immanuel. Help me to live in the awareness of Your presence and to trust in Your love each day. Amen.

December 15th, 2025: The Gift of His Presence

Scripture:
"The Lord your God is with you, the Mighty Warrior who saves. He will take great delight in you; in His love He will no longer rebuke you, but will rejoice over you with singing." (Zephaniah 3:17, NIV)

Reflection:
God's presence is a gift that transforms your life. He is not distant or detached—He is with you, delighting in you and rejoicing over you with love. His presence brings strength, joy, and peace in every circumstance.

When you recognize the gift of His presence, you're reminded that you are loved and cherished by the Creator of the universe. This awareness invites you to walk confidently, knowing that He is always by your side.

Today, rejoice in the gift of God's presence and let it fill your heart with peace and joy.

Affirmation:
God's presence is with me, bringing strength, joy, and peace in every moment.

Action Step:
Spend time in prayer, thanking God for His presence and reflecting on how it has sustained you in a specific situation.

Prayer:
Lord, thank You for the gift of Your presence. Help me to live with the confidence that You are always with me, rejoicing over me in love. Amen.

December 16th, 2025: A Kingdom of Righteousness

Scripture:
"*See, a king will reign in righteousness and rulers will rule with justice.*" (Isaiah 32:1, NIV)

Reflection:
Jesus' kingdom is one of righteousness and justice, a stark contrast to the brokenness of the world. His reign brings restoration, fairness, and peace, reflecting the perfect will of God.

As a citizen of His kingdom, you are called to reflect His righteousness in your own life, standing for truth and living with integrity. Your actions and attitudes should mirror the justice and love of your King.

Today, align your life with the values of Christ's kingdom, living as a reflection of His righteousness.

Affirmation:
I live as a citizen of Christ's kingdom, reflecting His righteousness and justice.

Action Step:
Think of one way you can demonstrate righteousness or justice in your interactions today. Act on it with intention.

Prayer:
Jesus, thank You for reigning in righteousness and justice. Help me to reflect Your kingdom values in my life and to stand for truth and love. Amen.

December 17th, 2025: The Lamb and the Lion

Scripture:
"Do not weep! See, the Lion of the tribe of Judah, the Root of David, has triumphed. He is able to open the scroll and its seven seals." (Revelation 5:5, NIV)

Reflection:
Jesus is both the Lamb of God, who takes away the sin of the world, and the Lion of Judah, who reigns with power and authority. These dual roles reveal His humility and majesty, His sacrifice and strength.

As the Lamb, He gave His life for your redemption. As the Lion, He rules victoriously over all creation. Worshiping Jesus means embracing Him as both Savior and King, honoring His grace and His power.

Today, reflect on the wonder of Christ as both Lamb and Lion, and let it deepen your worship.

Affirmation:
Jesus is the Lamb who redeems and the Lion who reigns, worthy of all my worship.

Action Step:
Spend time in worship, focusing on Jesus as both the Lamb of God and the Lion of Judah.

Prayer:
Jesus, thank You for being my Redeemer and King. Help me to honor You in every area of my life, worshiping You for both Your sacrifice and Your victory. Amen.

December 18th, 2025: The Joy of His Birth

Scripture:
"*But the angel said to them, 'Do not be afraid. I bring you good news that will cause great joy for all the people. Today in the town of David a Savior has been born to you; He is the Messiah, the Lord.'*" (Luke 2:10-11, NIV)

Reflection:
The birth of Jesus is the greatest news in history—a Savior born for all people, bringing hope, peace, and joy. His arrival fulfilled centuries of prophecy, marking the beginning of God's redemptive plan.

This joy is not temporary; it is eternal, rooted in the truth that Christ came to save and restore. When you reflect on His birth, you are reminded of God's overwhelming love and faithfulness.

Today, rejoice in the joy of Christ's birth and share this good news with others.

Affirmation:
The birth of Jesus fills my heart with great joy and hope.

Action Step:
Take time today to reflect on the joy of Jesus' birth. Share this good news with someone who may need encouragement.

Prayer:
Lord, thank You for the joy of Jesus' birth. Help me to celebrate this good news and to share it with others in love and gratitude. Amen.

December 19th, 2025: Preparing the Way

Scripture:
"*A voice of one calling: 'In the wilderness prepare the way for the Lord; make straight in the desert a highway for our God.'*" (Isaiah 40:3, NIV)

Reflection:
John the Baptist fulfilled this prophecy by preparing hearts for Jesus' arrival. His message of repentance and hope was a call to turn back to God and make room for the Savior.

Today, you are called to prepare the way for Christ in your own heart and in the lives of others. This means removing distractions, turning from sin, and focusing on His presence. It's also a call to share His love, pointing others to the One who transforms lives.

Today, ask God to prepare your heart for His presence and use you to point others to Him.

Affirmation:
I prepare the way for the Lord, making room for His presence and pointing others to His love.

Action Step:
Reflect on one thing that may be distracting you from fully experiencing Christ this season. Surrender it to Him in prayer.

Prayer:
Father, thank You for calling me to prepare the way for Christ. Help me to make room for Him in my heart and to share His love with others. Amen.

December 20th, 2025: The King's Return

Scripture:
"Look, I am coming soon! My reward is with Me, and I will give to each person according to what they have done." (Revelation 22:12, NIV)

Reflection:
The return of Christ is a promise that fills believers with hope and anticipation. As the King of Kings, He will come again to establish His eternal kingdom, bringing justice, restoration, and glory.

This promise inspires you to live with purpose, aligning your life with His will and eagerly awaiting His coming. It's not a time of fear but of joyful expectation, knowing that the King will set all things right.

Today, reflect on the hope of Christ's return and live with readiness and purpose.

Affirmation:
I live with hope and anticipation, preparing my heart for the return of my King.

Action Step:
Spend time reading Revelation 22. Reflect on the hope of Christ's return and how it inspires you to live for Him today.

Prayer:
Jesus, thank You for the promise of Your return. Help me to live with joyful anticipation and to honor You in all I do. Amen.

December 21st, 2025: The Power of His Name

Scripture:
"Therefore God exalted Him to the highest place and gave Him the name that is above every name, that at the name of Jesus every knee should bow, in heaven and on earth and under the earth." (Philippians 2:9-10, NIV)

Reflection:
The name of Jesus carries unparalleled power and authority. It is a name that commands worship, brings healing, and offers salvation to all who call upon it.

When you bow before the name of Jesus, you're acknowledging His lordship and aligning your life with His purpose. His name is your refuge, your strength, and your hope in every situation.

Today, exalt the name of Jesus in your life, declaring His power and authority over every circumstance.

Affirmation:
The name of Jesus is my strength and hope, and I bow in worship before Him.

Action Step:
Speak the name of Jesus over a specific area in your life where you need His power or peace.

Prayer:
Jesus, thank You for the power of Your name. I exalt You as my Lord and trust in Your authority over my life. Amen.

December 22nd, 2025: Christ, the Cornerstone

Scripture:
"The stone the builders rejected has become the cornerstone; the Lord has done this, and it is marvelous in our eyes." (Psalm 118:22, NIV)

Reflection:
Jesus is the cornerstone of your faith—the foundation upon which everything else is built. Though He was rejected by the world, He is the solid rock that brings stability, strength, and salvation to those who trust in Him.

Building your life on Christ ensures that you are rooted in truth, able to withstand life's challenges. His unchanging character provides a firm foundation for your faith, hope, and purpose.

Today, reaffirm Jesus as the cornerstone of your life, trusting Him to sustain and guide you.

Affirmation:
Jesus is my cornerstone, the foundation of my faith and the strength of my life.

Action Step:
Examine your priorities. Ensure that Christ is at the center of your decisions and actions.

Prayer:
Jesus, thank You for being my cornerstone. Help me to build my life on Your unshakable truth and to trust in Your guidance every day. Amen.

December 23rd, 2025: The Glory of the Incarnation

Scripture:
"The Son is the image of the invisible God, the firstborn over all creation." (Colossians 1:15, NIV)

Reflection:
In Jesus, the invisible God is made visible. The incarnation reveals the glory of God's character—His love, grace, and power—through the life and work of Christ.

The glory of the incarnation is not just in what Jesus did but in who He is. He is fully God and fully man, bridging the gap between heaven and earth and inviting you into an intimate relationship with Him.

Today, marvel at the glory of the incarnation and worship Jesus as the image of the invisible God.

Affirmation:
Jesus is the image of the invisible God, revealing His glory and inviting me into His presence.

Action Step:
Spend time meditating on the significance of Jesus as the image of God. Reflect on how this truth impacts your relationship with Him.

Prayer:
Father, thank You for revealing Yourself through Jesus. Help me to live in awe of His glory and to draw closer to You each day. Amen.

December 24th, 2025: O Come, Let Us Adore Him

Scripture:
"*When the shepherds had seen Him, they spread the word concerning what had been told them about this child, and all who heard it were amazed at what the shepherds said to them.*" (Luke 2:17-18, NIV)

Reflection:
The shepherds were among the first to witness the wonder of Jesus' birth. Overwhelmed with awe, they couldn't keep the news to themselves. Their joy and adoration overflowed into testimony, inspiring others to marvel at the Savior.

Adoring Christ is a natural response to encountering His presence. Worship draws you closer to Him, deepening your gratitude and spreading His light to the world around you.

Today, come and adore Him, letting your worship and joy proclaim the good news of His birth.

Affirmation:
I adore Christ my King and joyfully share the good news of His birth.

Action Step:
Take a moment to sing or reflect on the words of a favorite Christmas hymn, like "O Come, All Ye Faithful." Let its message deepen your worship.

Prayer:
Jesus, I come to adore You as my Savior and King. Fill my heart with joy and awe, and help me to share the good news of Your birth with others. Amen.

December 25th, 2025: Christ Is Born!

Scripture:
"Today in the town of David a Savior has been born to you; He is the Messiah, the Lord." (Luke 2:11, NIV)

Reflection:
Christmas is a celebration of God's greatest gift—Jesus Christ, born to save. His birth is a fulfillment of God's promise, a demonstration of His love, and the beginning of a plan to redeem the world.

On this day, reflect on the significance of His coming. The Savior has arrived, bringing light to darkness and hope to all. Rejoice in the miracle of His birth and the salvation it brings.

Today, celebrate Jesus with a heart full of joy, gratitude, and worship.

Affirmation:
Christ is born, and I rejoice in the hope, love, and salvation He brings.

Action Step:
Spend time in prayer and thanksgiving, focusing on the meaning of Jesus' birth and what it means for your life.

Prayer:
Jesus, thank You for being born to save me. Today I celebrate Your love and the hope You bring to the world. Amen.

December 26th, 2025: The Radiance of God's Glory

Scripture:
"*The Son is the radiance of God's glory and the exact representation of His being, sustaining all things by His powerful word.*" (Hebrews 1:3, NIV)

Reflection:
Jesus reveals the full glory of God, radiating His character, power, and love. He is not a reflection but the exact representation of God, making Him the perfect Savior and King.

As you reflect on Jesus' glory, you're reminded of His power to sustain all things—including your life. His presence fills you with hope and peace, knowing that He is in control and His Word is unshakable.

Today, worship Jesus as the radiance of God's glory, letting His light fill your heart and mind.

Affirmation:
Jesus is the radiance of God's glory, sustaining me with His power and love.

Action Step:
Spend time meditating on Hebrews 1:3. Reflect on what it means for Jesus to sustain all things by His powerful Word.

Prayer:
Lord, thank You for revealing Your glory through Jesus. Help me to trust in His power to sustain and guide me in every season. Amen.

December 27th, 2025: The Kingdom of Heaven Is Near

Scripture:
"From that time on Jesus began to preach, 'Repent, for the kingdom of heaven has come near.'" (Matthew 4:17, NIV)

Reflection:
Jesus proclaimed the arrival of God's kingdom—a kingdom not of this world but one that transforms hearts and lives. Through Him, the kingdom is near, inviting you to turn from sin and live in alignment with His will.

Living as a citizen of heaven means embracing Jesus as King and letting His values shape your decisions, relationships, and purpose. His kingdom is marked by love, humility, and righteousness, reflecting His heart.

Today, live with the awareness that the kingdom of heaven is near, letting its reality shape your daily life.

Affirmation:
I live as a citizen of heaven, aligning my life with the values of God's kingdom.

Action Step:
Reflect on one area of your life where you can better align with God's kingdom values. Take a step to bring it under His reign.

Prayer:
Jesus, thank You for bringing Your kingdom near. Help me to live as a faithful citizen, reflecting Your love and righteousness in all I do. Amen.

December 28th, 2025: The First and the Last

Scripture:
"I am the Alpha and the Omega, the First and the Last, the Beginning and the End." (Revelation 22:13, NIV)

Reflection:
Jesus is eternal, encompassing the beginning and the end of all things. His sovereignty reminds you that He holds all of time and creation in His hands, working everything according to His purpose.

Trusting in the Alpha and Omega gives you peace, knowing that He is unchanging and faithful. No matter what happens in life, He remains your constant source of hope and strength.

Today, rest in the assurance that Jesus is the First and the Last, and let His eternal presence bring you peace.

Affirmation:
Jesus is the Alpha and Omega, and I trust in His eternal power and purpose.

Action Step:
Spend time reflecting on how Jesus has been faithful in the past and how you can trust Him for the future.

Prayer:
Jesus, thank You for being the Alpha and Omega, holding all things in Your hands. Help me to trust in Your eternal plan and to find peace in Your presence. Amen.

December 29th, 2025: The King's Commission

Scripture:
"Therefore go and make disciples of all nations, baptizing them in the name of the Father and of the Son and of the Holy Spirit." (Matthew 28:19, NIV)

Reflection:
As followers of Christ, you are called to share the good news and make disciples. This commission is a command from your King, empowering you to be His ambassador in a world that needs His love and truth.

The King's commission reminds you that your life has a purpose beyond yourself. You are part of God's mission to bring His kingdom to the world, sharing His hope and salvation with others.

Today, embrace the call to make disciples, letting your life reflect the love and authority of Christ.

Affirmation:
I am commissioned by Christ my King to share His love and truth with the world.

Action Step:
Think of one person you can share the love of Christ with today. Take a step to encourage or pray for them.

Prayer:
Jesus, thank You for commissioning me to make disciples. Help me to share Your love boldly and to live as a reflection of Your truth. Amen.

December 30th, 2025: Living as Kingdom Citizens

Scripture:
"*But our citizenship is in heaven. And we eagerly await a Savior from there, the Lord Jesus Christ.*" (Philippians 3:20, NIV)

Reflection:
As a follower of Christ, your true citizenship is in heaven. This identity shapes how you live, guiding you to reflect the values of His kingdom while eagerly awaiting His return.

Living as a kingdom citizen means prioritizing eternal treasures over earthly pursuits. It calls you to walk in love, humility, and faithfulness, knowing that your ultimate home is with Christ.

Today, embrace your heavenly citizenship, letting it shape your decisions and perspective.

Affirmation:
I live as a citizen of heaven, reflecting the values of Christ's kingdom in all I do.

Action Step:
Reflect on one way you can focus more on eternal treasures this week. Make a plan to act on it.

Prayer:
Jesus, thank You for making me a citizen of heaven. Help me to live with an eternal perspective, reflecting Your kingdom in every part of my life. Amen.

December 31st, 2025: Crown Him with Many Crowns

Scripture:
"Then I heard every creature in heaven and on earth and under the earth and on the sea, and all that is in them, saying: 'To Him who sits on the throne and to the Lamb be praise and honor and glory and power, for ever and ever!'" (Revelation 5:13, NIV)

Reflection:
As the year ends, join the eternal chorus of praise to Jesus, the Lamb of God and King of Kings. He is worthy of all honor, glory, and power, reigning over heaven and earth forever.

Crowning Jesus with many crowns is a declaration of His authority and an act of worship. It is a reminder that all creation bows before Him, and one day every knee will acknowledge His reign.

Today, end the year in worship, crowning Christ as King over every part of your life.

Affirmation:
Jesus is my King, and I crown Him with praise, honor, and glory forever.

Action Step:
Spend time in worship, reflecting on the majesty of Christ and offering Him the crown of your praise.

Prayer:
Jesus, You are worthy of all honor and praise. I crown You as my King and rejoice in Your eternal reign. Amen.

Made in the USA
Middletown, DE
31 March 2025

73466749R00223